Real Convergence in Central, Eastern and South-Eastern Europe

Also By Reiner Martin

THE REGIONAL DIMENSION IN EUROPEAN PUBLIC POLICY

Also By Adalbert Winkler

BANKING AND MONETARY POLICY IN EASTERN EUROPE – THE FIRST TEN YEARS

Real Convergence in Central, Eastern and South-Eastern Europe

Edited by

Reiner Martin

and

Adalbert Winkler

First published 2009 by
PALGRAVE MACMILLAN

Palgrave Macmillan in the UK is an imprint of Macmillan Publishers Limited,
registered in England, company number 785998, of Houndmills, Basingstoke,
Hampshire RG21 6XS.

Palgrave Macmillan in the US is a division of St Martin's Press LLC,
175 Fifth Avenue, New York, NY 10010.

Palgrave Macmillan is the global academic imprint of the above companies
and has companies and representatives throughout the world.

Palgrave® and Macmillan® are registered trademarks in the United States,
the United Kingdom, Europe and other countries.

ISBN-13: 978–0–230–22018–8 hardback

A catalogue record for this book is available from the British Library.

A catalog record for this book is available from the Library of Congress.

10 9 8 7 6 5 4 3 2 1
18 17 16 15 14 13 12 11 10 09

Contents

Illustrations

Tables

Figures

Boxes

Acknowledgements

We would like to take this opportunity to thank all the people involved in the production of this collected volume. In addition to the authors and discussants, we wish to thank the participants of the ECB Economic Conference on Central, Eastern and South-Eastern Europe, which was held in Frankfurt am Main on 1 and 2 October 2007, as well as the large number of people who helped in organising and managing this event. In particular we would like to thank Frank Moss and Hans-Joachim Klöckers for supporting this project throughout and Éva Katalin Polgár and Carolin Nerlich for playing a very important role in the process. Finally, and perhaps most importantly, we would like to thank in particular Stefanie Peuckmann as well as Gudrun Becker, whose hard work and attention to detail were invaluable for the success of the conference and for the completion of the collected volume.

Contributors

Angana Banerji, born in 1964, holds economics degrees from Calcutta University and Jawaharlal Nehru University (Masters) (India) and Columbia University (PhD) (US). In the IMF, Ms Banerji has worked in the Policy Development and Review department on a broad range of countries – low-income countries in Africa and Asia, transition economies in Europe, and emerging markets during the Asian crisis (Malaysia, Indonesia and Brazil). In addition, she has been involved in the policy work within the Fund to change the international financial architecture. Subsequently, in the European department, she has been the desk for Russia and Greece, and the mission chief to San Marino, and has been involved in various projects assessing vulnerabilities in Eastern Europe. She is currently heading the IMF's mission to the Netherlands Antilles.

Lorenzo Bini Smaghi, born in 1956, graduated from the Université Catholique de Louvain (Belgium) and holds an MA in Economics from the University of Southern California and a PhD in Economics from the University of Chicago (US). He is Member of the Executive Board of the ECB and was previously Director General for International Financial Relations at the Italian Ministry of the Economy and Finance from 1998 to 2005. Previously, he was Deputy Director General for Research at the European Central Bank in 1998, Head of Policy Division at the European Monetary Institute in Frankfurt from 1994 to 1998, Head of Exchange Rate and International Trade Division at the Research Department of Banca d'Italia from 1988 to 1994 and Economist in the International Section of the Research Department of Banca d'Italia from 1983 to 1988.

Herbert Brücker, born in 1960, studied sociology, political science and economics at the University of Frankfurt a.M. (Germany). He received his doctoral degree in economics from the same university in 1994 and his habilitation degree from the Technical University of Berlin (Germany) in 2005. Herbert Brücker is Professor of Economics at the University of Bamberg since 2008, and head of the Department for International Comparisons and European Integration at the Institute for Employment Research (IAB) in Nuremberg since 2005. His research interests cover international migration, European integration and labour economics. He has published on these topics in journals such as Economic Policy, Journal of Comparative Economics, Journal of European Integration, Empirical Economics and World Economics.

Juha Kähkönen, born in 1955, holds economics degrees from the Helsinki School of Economics in Finland (Masters) and the University of Michigan in the US (PhD). Prior to joining the IMF in 1986, he held positions at New York University (Assistant Professor), the Helsinki School of Economics (Professor), and the Bank of Finland (Research Advisor). In the IMF, Mr Kähkönen has held various positions in area departments, including resident representative to India in 1991–92 and mission chief for Albania, Bulgaria, and Turkey during 1997–2003. In 2003–06, while in the Policy Development and Review Department, he reviewed IMF work on some thirty countries from various regions. He is presently Senior Advisor in the European Department, heading IMF missions to Germany and supervising the department's work on some ten emerging European countries.

Sarah Lein, born in 1979, holds a master degree in economics from the University of Konstanz (Germany). She currently works as a research and teaching assistant at the chair of Applied Macroeconomics at the ETH Zurich (Switzerland). Since 2005 she is a PhD student at the University of Zurich and took part in the Swiss Program for Beginning Doctoral Students in Economics in Gerzensee. She works mostly on monetary economics and empirical macroeconomics.

Miguel Leon-Ledesma, born in 1972, holds a degree and PhD in Economics from the University of La Laguna. He has been a Lecturer at La Laguna from 1995 to 1999, when he joined the Department of Economics at the University of Kent, where he is now a Reader in Economics. His research and publications have focused mainly on macro-economics and applied econometrics with special focus on growth and technical progress, international macroeconomics and nonlinear time series models. He has also been consultant for the ECB and Asian Development Bank and visiting researcher at several universities.

Reiner Martin, born in 1966, holds master's degrees in economics and political science and a PhD in economics from the University of Hamburg (Germany). He was Research Fellow at the Centre for European Policy Studies (CEPS) in Brussels and Deputy Head of Division at the German Federal Ministry of Economics in Bonn. Since 1999 he is with the European Central Bank in Frankfurt. In 2001 he became Head of the Convergence and Structural Analysis Section in the Directorate

General Economics of the ECB. In 2008/2009 he is working at the Foreign Research Division of the Oesterreichische Nationalbank. He focuses mostly on economic developments in the EU Member States outside the euro area and on issues related to euro area enlargement. In addition, he worked on structural reforms in product and labour markets including labour mobility.

Magdalena Morgese Borys, born in 1978, holds master's degrees in economics and public administration from Gdansk University (Poland) and Grand Valley State University (US). She is a PhD candidate in Economics at the Center for Economic Research and Graduate Education (CERGE-EI) in Prague (Czech Republic). Her research interests include monetary policy and empirical finance. Since September 2007 she has worked as a Junior Researcher at the CERGE-EI. In summer 2007 she spent three months working in the European Central Bank on a study of real convergence in the EU candidate and potential candidate countries. Since September 2008, she has also served as an Adjunct Professor at the American University of Rome (Italy) where she teaches a course in Macroeconomics.

Carolin Nerlich holds a master's degree in economics from the University of Kiel and a PhD in economics from the University of Cologne (Germany). She was Research Fellow at the Institute for Economic Policy, Cologne, and a Visiting Research Fellow at the Institute for International Economics, Washington (US). Before joining the European Central Bank she worked at Deutsche Bank Research and Deutsche Bundesbank. Since 2004, she is Senior Economist in the Directorate General Economics of the ECB, focusing mainly on macroeconomic developments in the EU Member States outside the euro area and on issues related to euro area enlargement.

Éva Katalin Polgár, born in 1974, holds a master's degree and a PhD in economics from the Corvinus University of Budapest (Hungary). Holding different scholarships she studied at the University of Maastricht (the Netherlands) and the Freie Universität Berlin (Germany) and was a Marie Curie research fellow at the University of Southampton (UK). She became an assistant lecturer at the Corvinus University of Budapest and a visiting lecturer at the Budapest University of Technology and Economics in 2003. She works mostly on international economics, monetary policy and theory as well as finance. In May 2005 she joined the Directorate General Economics of the European Central Bank and since May 2006 she has been working in the

Directorate General International and European Relations of the ECB, focusing on EU neighbouring regions.

Jürgen Stark, born in 1948, studied economics at the universities of Hohenheim and Tübingen (Germany). He gained a Doctorate in economics in 1975 and was appointed honorary professor by the University of Tübingen in 2005. He is a member of the Executive Board of the ECB. Before joining the ECB, he was Vice-President of the Deutsche Bundesbank. Prior to this position he served as State Secretary at the German Federal Ministry of Finance and Personal Representative of the Federal Chancellor in the preparation of G7/G8 Economic Summits for four years. Before that he held various positions at the Ministry of Finance, the Federal Chancellery and the Federal Ministry of Economics, dealing with national and international monetary and financial issues. His publications include many articles and papers in professional journals on public finances, European monetary integration, institution building and the global financial system.

István P. Székely holds degrees from Corvinus University, Budapest, and the University of Cambridge, UK. He is director for economic studies and research in the Directorate General for Economic and Financial Affairs of the European Commission. Before joining the European Commission, he worked in the European Department of the International Monetary Fund (1999–2007), and was a general manager and advisor to the governor of the National Bank of Hungary (1996–1999). His research focuses on financial market issues and Central and Eastern European economies.

Max Watson, born in 1946, holds degrees from Cambridge University (UK) and the INSEAD business school (France). He is a Fellow of Wolfson College, Oxford, and an Associate Fellow of Chatham House (the Royal Institute of International Affairs). Until December 2007, he was a senior economic adviser at the European Commission, where he worked on financial stability in Eastern Europe and on the euro area economy. Previously he was a Deputy Director of the IMF. During some 20 years at the Fund, he held the positions of Personal Assistant to the Managing Director, Head of the Debt Issues Unit, and Chief of the International Capital Markets Division. He was also mission IMF chief for many countries in Eastern and Western Europe. Mr Watson's early career was spent at the Bank of England as an international economist and bank supervisor; as secretary of the EU bank supervisors' Groupe de Contact; and as a manager at the London merchant bank S. G. Warburg and Co., Ltd.

Adalbert Winkler, born in 1962, studied economics at the University of Trier (Germany) and at Clark University, Worcester, Mass. (US). From 1994 to 2001, he headed the Economics Department at Internationale Projekt Consult (IPC), a consulting company which specialises in development finance and carries out financial institution building projects worldwide. After joining the European Central Bank, he worked in the Directorate General International and European Relations of the European Central Bank, focusing on EU neighbouring regions and the international role of the euro. Since September 2008 Mr Winkler is Professor for Development Finance at Frankfurt School of Finance & Management, where monetary policy and financial sector issues and the economics of transition are his main fields of teaching.

Andrei Zlate, born in 1978, holds master's degrees in economics from Boston College (US) and Copenhagen Business School (Denmark). He is currently a PhD candidate in economics at Boston College. His main fields of research are international macroeconomics, trade and applied econometrics. In his dissertation work, he investigates the roles of trade, offshore production and foreign direct investment as transmission channels of business cycle fluctuations across countries. He has worked as a consultant for the EU Neighbouring Regions Division in the Directorate General International and European Relations of the European Central Bank and has recently been a visiting scholar in the Research Departments of the Federal Reserve Banks of Atlanta and Boston.

Introduction

On 1 and 2 October 2007 the European Central Bank organised at its Headquarters in Frankfurt am Main the second economic conference on Central, Eastern and South-Eastern Europe. The conference's main objectives were to foster cooperation among the central banks of the region and to provide a platform for multilateral discussion between the Eurosystem/ESCB, the South-Eastern European central banks, international institutions and academics.

The central theme of the 2007 conference was the real convergence process in the region, defined as the catching up of countries with a comparatively low per capita income with the level of economic development in relatively richer economies, and the interaction of this process with monetary and exchange rate policies including the euro adoption prospects of the Central, Eastern and South-Eastern European countries.

The starting point for academic debates on real convergence is normally neoclassical growth theory, which predicts a gradual process of real convergence between different economies. However, the empirical evidence on real convergence is rather mixed. On the one hand, a review of the global growth process between 1870 and 1990 suggests that the dominant feature of modern economic history has been not convergence, but divergence (Pritchett, 1997). Indeed, Abramovitz (1986), Baumol (1986) and the World Bank (1993), among others, have argued that convergence processes have been rare observations and limited to specific convergence clubs, mainly today's advanced western economies, or – as in the case of East Asia – have to be interpreted as the result of 'miracles'. On the other hand, Barro and Sala-i-Martin (1991, 1995) found that the per capita income across many economies tends to converge at a rate of 2 per cent per year, if properly accounting for

1

a robust set of macroeconomic, financial sector and institutional variables supporting the real convergence process. The insight that real convergence is not solely driven by the level of the initial per capita income and the marginal returns to factors of production – as the most simple version of neoclassic convergence theory would suggest – is of particular importance for policy makers, given that it puts the 'right' policies at the core of the real convergence process.

In recent years real convergence has been facilitated by an overall very benign global economic environment. In fact, since the early 2000s global growth has been much more rapid than at any time since the early 1970s (Sommer and Spatafora, 2007). In particular, emerging markets and developing countries, which in the second half of the 1990s still experienced a series of financial and currency crises, have seen strong advances in output, even though heterogeneity among countries and regions has remained significant. Countries of emerging Asia have been recording particularly rapid progress in income convergence, notably China and India (Bussiére and Mehl, 2008). Moreover, benefiting from high and rising raw material prices, resource-rich countries have seen high rates of growth.

Central, Eastern and South-Eastern Europe has been the third region showing a rapid pace of convergence since the turn of the century. Indeed, Central, Eastern and South-Eastern European countries rank prominently among the top 30 countries with regard to the speed of convergence relative to average euro area GDP per capita (in PPP terms).

There are several dimensions of the convergence process in Central, Eastern and South-Eastern Europe that distinguish it from convergence processes in other regions of the world.

First, with the exception of Turkey, all countries in the region have been transition economies. Thus, the catching-up process has taken place at the same time as the economies of the countries concerned have undergone a deep and historically unprecedented transformation from a planned to a market economy.

Second, all countries in the region have been participating in the European integration process. Thus, their economies have become (fully or at least to some extent) part of the single European market, a highly integrated economic area. In line with neoclassic economic reasoning, this integration process should have helped to foster real convergence by lowering or removing barriers to the mobility of factors of production. This in turn is expected to have helped to equalise factor returns across countries. As part of the European integration process, the new EU member states have also been adopting European standards in terms of economic policies, institutions and governance and the EU candidate and potential candidate countries are preparing to do so. Adopting the so-called *acquis communautaire* is the most visible and known institutional aspect of the EU integration process, but not by far the only one. For example, upon EU accession economic policies become subject to a number of multilateral surveillance procedures within the EU framework, like the Stability and Growth Pact which sets certain rules in the field of fiscal policy. In a nutshell, the countries in the region have been facing the challenge of managing two interrelated convergence processes in parallel: a process of real income and a process of real structural convergence towards the level and standards of the EU-15 (Padoa-Schioppa, 2003), with the latter expected to support the former.

Third, by participating in the process of European integration, all countries in the region are sooner or later also set to participate in European monetary integration. All EU member states that have not yet adopted the euro, most of which have joined the EU in 2004 or 2007, are according to the EU Treaty committed to striving towards the eventual adoption of the euro upon fulfilment of the convergence criteria laid down in the Treaty (ECB, 2003). This implies that in addition to managing the process of real convergence, those countries in the region that have already become EU member states also face the challenge of ensuring nominal convergence.[1]

Despite these common features, countries in the region are still characterised by a significant degree of heterogeneity, as also shown in Table 0.1. Indeed, the need for a case-by-case analysis, taking into account cross-country differences with regard to progress in transition, EU integration and nominal convergence, is one of the central themes running through the contributions in this volume. At the same time, and apart from the far-reaching institutional process of European integration mentioned above, there have been several economic features in the convergence process of the countries in the region that have been markedly different from those seen in other parts of the world. They include, among others, strong growth of total factor productivity (TFP), reflecting efficiency gains due to the transition process from plan to market as well as rapid real and financial integration with the EU-15 countries via FDI, including the widespread presence of foreign banks and cross-border financial transactions as well as migration.

The contributions compiled in this volume focus on four specific aspects of the convergence process in Central, Eastern and South-Eastern Europe: inflation, potential growth and the 'speed limits' of convergence, migration and labour market developments and the

Table 0.1   The global convergence process: Increase in GDP-PPP per capita (Relative to the euro area average)

Rank	2006 vs 1998		Rank	2002 vs 1998		Rank	2006 vs 2002	
1	Equatorial Guinea	34.04	1	Equatorial Guinea	21.96	1	China, PR Hong Kong	20.20
2	China, PR Hong Kong	25.28	2	Korea	10.33	2	Qatar	17.04
3	Estonia	24.99	3	Estonia	8.03	3	Estonia	16.97
4	Trinidad and Tobago	22.65	4	Turkmenistan	7.51	4	Trinidad and Tobago	16.16
5	Latvia	20.91	5	Trinidad and Tobago	6.48	5	Singapore	14.75
6	Korea	17.89	6	Latvia	6.42	6	Latvia	14.49
7	Singapore	17.77	7	Botswana	5.31	7	Lithuania	13.09
8	Lithuania	16.47	8	Hungary	5.22	8	Equatorial Guinea	12.08
9	Turkmenistan	15.65	9	Russia	5.15	9	Argentina	11.47
10	Qatar	13.52	10	Kazakhstan	5.11	10	Bahrain	11.05
11	Russia	13.27	11	China, PR Hong Kong	5.08	11	Czech Rep	10.19
12	Kazakhstan	13.24	12	Slovenia	4.35	12	United Arab Emirates	9.48
13	Hungary	12.88	13	Armenia	3.62	13	Slovakia	9.40
14	Slovenia	12.58	14	Lithuania	3.38	14	Azerbaijan, Rep of	9.35
15	Botswana	12.05	15	China, PR Mainland	3.29	15	Uruguay	8.87
16	Bahrain	11.91	16	Singapore	3.01	16	Slovenia	8.23
17	Azerbaijan, Rep of	11.26	17	Ukraine	2.64	17	Belarus	8.20

Rank	Country	Value	Rank	Country	Value	Rank	Country	Value
18	**Czech Rep**	**11.03**	18	Belize	2.50	18	Turkmenistan	8.14
19	Belarus	10.47	19	St. Kitts and Nevis	2.47	19	Kazakhstan	8.13
20	China, PR Mainland	10.10	20	**Albania**	**2.45**	20	Russia	8.12
21	**Slovakia**	**9.03**	21	**Bulgaria**	**2.43**	21	**Hungary**	**7.65**
22	Armenia	8.86	22	Cape Verde	2.41	22	Korea	7.56
23	Ukraine	8.74	23	Dominican Rep	2.39	23	Antigua and Barbuda	7.22
24	Iceland	8.70	24	**Bosnia and Herzegovina**	**2.29**	24	China, PR Mainland	6.81
25	**Bulgaria**	**8.47**	25	Belarus	2.28	25	Botswana	6.74
26	**Poland**	**7.76**	26	Cyprus	2.19	26	Kuwait	6.42
27	**Croatia**	**7.52**	27	Azerbaijan, Rep of	1.92	27	**Poland**	**6.25**
28	St. Kitts and Nevis	7.45	28	Mauritius	1.73	28	**Romania**	**6.16**
29	**Romania**	**7.32**	29	**Croatia**	**1.72**	29	Ukraine	6.10
30	Antigua and Barbuda	5.86	30	**Poland**	**1.51**	30	**Bulgaria**	**6.04**

Other Central, Eastern and South-Eastern European countries

Rank	Country	Value	Rank	Country	Value	Rank	Country	Value
31	*Bosnia and Herzegovina*	*5.63*	34	*Romania*	*1.17*	31	*Croatia*	*5.81*
32	*Albania*	*4.91*	39	*Czech Rep*	*0.84*	37	*Turkey*	*4.45*
85	*Serbia*	*0.66*	88	*Slovakia*	*-0.38*	47	*Serbia*	*3.42*
86	*FYR Macedonia*	*0.65*	116	*FYR Macedonia*	*-1.21*	49	*Bosnia and Herzegovina*	*3.33*
103	*Turkey*	*0.12*	131	*Serbia*	*-2.76*	57	*Albania*	*2.47*
			142	*Turkey*	*-4.33*	74	*FYR Macedonia*	*1.86*

balance of payments. In turn, all these variables are related to nominal convergence, which is at the heart of the Maastricht criteria on the adoption of the euro (ECB, 2003).

Against this background, the volume starts with two speeches held by members of the Executive Board of the European Central Bank, *Lorenzo Bini Smaghi* and *Jürgen Stark*. *Lorenzo Bini Smaghi's* speech, opening the conference on which this volume is based, sets the stage by outlining those elements of the real convergence process that are of key interest from a central banker's view. In particular, he defines the policy issues that derive from a comparison of the convergence process in the region with the predictions of economic theory and the experience of convergence processes in other emerging markets. Does the dominance of TFP growth as a driver of growth suggest that potential growth will slow down when the impact of transition is phasing out? Are high and rising current account deficits, driven by domestic demand reflecting large capital inflows and rapid credit growth, a cause for concern? Or do they indicate a textbook-like convergence process with capital flowing from rich to poor countries, exploiting return differentials and allowing for consumption smoothing? *Lorenzo Bini Smaghi* ends by noting that the recent acceleration of the real convergence process constitutes a major challenge for economic policies, including monetary policy, in keeping nominal convergence on track. In countries with a pegged exchange rate the question arises whether the de facto adoption of euro area monetary policy is consistent with sustainable growth and financial stability in an environment of rapid convergence. While tight budgetary policies and structural policies can mitigate overheating pressures, they might prove to be insufficient in counteracting the demand effects of a pro-cyclical monetary policy.

Jürgen Stark develops this issue further by asking whether the fast catching-up process in the Central and Eastern European countries that acceded to the EU in 2004 and 2007 is sustainable. Despite remarkable progress with real convergence, these countries still have a substantial income per capita gap relative to the euro area. At the same time – as emphasised in the speech of *Lorenzo Bini Smaghi* – they experienced in recent years substantial domestic and external imbalances, notably high inflation and high current account deficits. Against this background, *Jürgen Stark* discusses the available policy options for these countries. After briefly reviewing the catching-up experience of the former so-called cohesion countries (Greece, Ireland, Portugal and Spain), he identifies four areas for possible policy intervention for the Central and Eastern European countries: fiscal policy, structural policy, supervisory and prudential policy and monetary and exchange rate policy. On the latter, he emphasises that the ultimate question for a country is which monetary policy and exchange rate regime is best suited to ensuring a fast and stable convergence process. In addition – and irrespective of the chosen exchange rate regime – he stresses the need for reforms in the areas of fiscal, structural and prudential policies, which should be seen as complementary to monetary and exchange rate policy. *Jürgen Stark* concludes by emphasising that the Central and Eastern European countries cannot solve their challenges related to the catching-up process by joining the euro area before a fully sustainable level of convergence has been achieved.

The chapter by *Magdalena Morgese Borys (CERGE-EI), Éva Katalin Polgár (ECB)* and *Andrei Zlate (Boston College)* provides an overview of key facts and figures on real convergence in the Central, Eastern and South-Eastern European countries under review, using a production function approach. The analysis shows that real convergence has gained momentum, even though gaps in terms of income per capita relative to the euro area as well as cross-country differences remain large. TFP growth has been the main driver of convergence, whereas labour has contributed only marginally to economic growth, as employment and participation rates have been falling until recently. Thus, on average employment rates are at significantly lower levels than in the euro area, while – in particular in candidate and potential candidate countries – unemployment rates are much higher on average than in the euro area. Investment rates, while still comparatively low compared with rates seen in emerging economies in other parts of the world, in particular in East Asia, have been rising rapidly in recent years, strengthening the contribution of capital for growth. Moreover, FDI flows continue to provide a good basis for further investment growth, leading to improvements in capital accumulation and its efficiency. Overall, the analysis suggests that the prospects for a sustained convergence process depend on improvements in terms of labour productivity and utilisation, as well as in terms of capital accumulation. To this end further reforms and economic restructuring aiming at improving labour markets, as well as facilitating strong investment, are crucial.

Sarah Lein (ETH Zürich), Miguel Leon-Ledesma (University of Kent) and *Carolin Nerlich (ECB)* discuss several channels through which real convergence can affect inflation and how the impact of these channels is likely to develop in the coming years. More specifically, they examine the Balassa-Samuelson effect, changes in the consumption pattern, the declining energy intensity of production, lower macroeconomic volatility, higher credit growth and increased trade openness. On the basis of this analysis they conclude that the current level of real convergence in the Central and Eastern European EU member states has at present an upward effect on inflation in these countries. Its overall magnitude, however, is uncertain, given that not all channels point in the same direction. Moreover, the relative importance of the convergence-related variables for inflation seems to differ significantly across countries, reflecting different starting positions and different macroeconomic policies including the underlying monetary and exchange rate regimes as well as differences in their structural rigidities. Finally, the authors argue that the inflationary impact of real convergence is expected to decline over time. Whether the inflationary impact of real convergence triggers any second-round effects hinges, however, to a large extent on the conduct of stability-oriented macroeconomic policy and structural reforms to further improve the supply side conditions, enhance competition and reduce existing bottlenecks. With respect to euro adoption, the authors argue that the Central and Eastern European EU countries should join the euro area only if the inflationary impact of real convergence is sufficiently limited, so that those policy instruments that remain available for euro area members are sufficient to prevent unsustainable price developments. Thus, the findings on the inflationary impact of real convergence underline the importance of focusing on sustainable real convergence.

Against the background of accelerating growth in many Central, Eastern and South-Eastern European countries in recent years *István P. Székely (European Commission)* and *Max Watson (Wolfson College, Oxford, and Chatham House)* tackle the question of whether there are speed limits to real convergence. In answering the question they distinguish between two different interpretations of the speed limit concept. First, there are limits set by the potential rate of growth. However, these limits can be stretched by appropriate macroeconomic and structural policies, as well as by exploiting the above-mentioned unique opportunities provided by European integration. Domestically, policies enhancing the efficiency of government consumption and social transfers may raise the speed limits of growth by reducing resource waste in the public sector, increasing incentives for labour participation and promoting labour mobility to more productive sectors of the economy. The second interpretation of the speed limit concept focuses on the management of vulnerabilities that may arise when bringing actual growth close to potential growth. In Central, Eastern and South-Eastern Europe these vulnerabilities are mainly linked to the process of rapid financial integration and financial development. This process and the associated substantial easing of household borrowing constraints might raise adjustment risks, in particular, but not only under a fixed exchange rate regime. In addition, policy makers face the challenge of distinguishing between the nature of shocks, that is, shocks having an impact on the rate of potential growth and shocks raising the vulnerability of the growth process. Against this background, *István P. Székely* and *Max Watson* call for a comprehensive policy approach for fostering potential growth, containing vulnerability risks and enhancing adjustment capacities.

Herbert Brücker (IAB Nürnberg) looks at the role of labour mobility in the real convergence process between the 'new' and the 'old' member states of the EU. Labour mobility is part and parcel of the overall EU integration process, which, as mentioned above, foresees the free movement of goods, services, capital and labour and – as *Herbert Brücker* illustrates – it can have a significant impact on the real convergence process.

More specifically he raises two questions. First, does real convergence of GDP mitigate migration pressures? Second, what is the impact of migration on convergence and labour markets? With regard to the first question he finds that, under reasonable assumptions regarding the speed of real convergence, the catching-up process in per capita GDP can reduce migration levels only to a limited extent. On the second question, he finds that migration supports the convergence of per capita GDP levels, wages and unemployment rates between 'old' and 'new' EU member states. The main winners are the migrants themselves, while the aggregate impact on the income of natives in the receiving countries is neutral or even slightly negative. Moreover, in the long run, the GDP of the enlarged EU will increase by some 0.6 per cent if 4 per cent of the population of the 'new' member states emigrate to the 'old' member states. These gains dwarf those of a further integration of goods and capital markets.

Large and widening current account deficits financed by massive capital inflows have been one of the peculiar characteristics of real convergence in Central, Eastern and South-Eastern Europe. *Angana Banerji* and *Juha Kähkönen (IMF)* analyse whether this constitutes a major vulnerability, indicating that the region is heading for a crisis, or whether the convergence process will continue to be smooth due to the special environment created by European integration. While they stop short of drawing definitive conclusions, *Angana Banerji* and *Juha Kähkönen* provide a list of policy priorities that reflect the experience of countries

facing similar situations in the past and – in the spirit of the comprehensive approach advocated by *István P. Székely* and *Max Watson* – aim
at reducing vulnerabilities without impeding the convergence process
as such. These policy priorities include sound macroeconomic policies, in particular fiscal tightening, as counter-cyclical fiscal policy
has proven to be associated with a smaller adjustment of output in the
period of lower or even reversing capital flows. In addition, they call for
strong financial sector regulation and supervision as well as continued
productivity-enhancing structural reforms. Finally, policy makers have
to ensure timely information in order to be able to assess risks and take
pre-emptive measures when needed.

Note

1. In this context it should be noted that the years before EU membership are
   characterised by a comprehensive dialogue between the Eurosystem and the
   central banks of candidate countries on monetary integration issues. For the
   member states that joined in 2004 and 2007 this process started as early as
   1999; see ECB (1999).

Bibliography

M. Abramovitz (1986) 'Catching Up, Forging Ahead, and Falling Behind', *The
Journal of Economic History*, 46(2), 385–406.
R.J. Barro and X. Sala-i-Martin (1991) 'Convergence across States and Regions',
Brookings Papers on Economic Activity, 1, 107–82.
R.J. Barro and X. Sala-i-Martin (1995) Economic Growth, New York: McGraw-Hill.
W. Baumol (1986) 'Productivity Growth, Convergence, and Welfare: What the
Long-Run Data Show', *American Economic Review*, 76(5), 1072–85.
M. Bussiére and A. Mehl (2008) China's and India's Roles in Global Trade and
Finance; Twin Titans for the New Millennium? ECB Occasional paper No. 80,
Frankfurt am Main.
ECB (1999) Helsinki Seminar on the Accession Process, Press Release, http://
www.ecb.int/press/pr/date/1999/html/pr991112.en.html
ECB (2003) Policy Position of the Governing Council of the European Central
Bank on Exchange Rate Issues Relating to the Acceding Countries, http://
www.ecb.int/pub/pdf/other/policyaccexchangerateen.pdf
T. Padoa-Schioppa (2003) 'Trajectories towards the Euro and the Role of ERM II',
International Finance, 6(1), 129–44.
L. Pritchett (1997) 'Divergence, Big Time', *Journal of Economic Perspectives*, 11(3),
Summer 1997, 3–17.
M. Sommer and N. Spatafora (2007) 'The Changing Dynamics of the Global
Business Cycle', World Economic Outlook, September 2007, International
Monetary Fund, Washington DC, 67–94.
World Bank (1993) *The East Asian Miracle: Economic Growth and Public Policy*,
Washington DC: World Bank Policy Research Report.

1
Real Convergence in Central, Eastern and South-Eastern Europe: A Central Banker's View

Lorenzo Bini Smaghi

1.1 Introduction

Central bankers are used to discussing nominal convergence. It is at the heart of their main task, maintaining price stability. It is also at the heart of the Maastricht criteria on the adoption of the euro. This chapter, however, focuses on the other side of the coin, namely real convergence. There are three reasons for this. First, catching-up is the main goal of all the countries in Central, Eastern and South-Eastern Europe. Second, real convergence has gained momentum in recent years, also in countries where progress had been slower in the 1990s. Third, real convergence has important implications for nominal convergence.

Against this background, the chapter is structured as follows. After this introduction, Section 1.2 briefly reviews some stylised facts of real convergence in Central, Eastern and South-Eastern Europe. Section 1.3 aims at drawing the attention to some unresolved issues and to identify key policy challenges authorities in the region are currently facing. To this end it contains an analysis of the convergence process in the region, contrasting it with theoretical predictions as well as empirical evidence in other emerging market economies experiencing a rapid catching-up. Four aspects that are of key interest from a central banker's view are examined in some more detail: (1) growth and convergence (2) financial globalisation and the current account (3) financial development and (4) implications for monetary policy. Section 1.4 summarises and concludes.

1.2   Real convergence in Central, Eastern and South-Eastern Europe – where do we stand?

Following notable output losses during the early 1990s, all countries in the region have seen a strong recovery. With a few exceptions, most of them have passed their pre-transition levels of real per capita income. Moreover, the recovery resulted in convergence towards the real income per capita level in the euro area. In the EU member states of the region, real per capita income reached 40 per cent of the euro area level in 2005, an increase of about nine percentage points since 1993. In candidate and potential candidate countries – excluding Turkey – a rise of seven percentage points was recorded in the same period, so that at end-2005 their average real per capita income stood at about 23 per cent of the euro area level.

The timing and speed of convergence has varied substantially, reflecting differences in political stability and progress in structural reforms. Strong growth, fostered by structural reforms, investment and FDI, has been a key feature of economic developments in almost all new member states since the mid-1990s. In most candidate and potential candidate countries, instead, the catching-up process has gained speed only in this decade.

Total factor productivity has been the main driver of growth and convergence across the region. Labour productivity has increased in all countries, closing the gap relative to the euro area. At the same time, in many countries labour utilisation is substantially below the euro area level, reflecting the large size of the informal sector as well as labour market frictions and mismatches.

To sum up: substantial progress has been made, but gaps in terms of income per capita relative to the euro area remain large. This suggests that the challenges of real convergence will remain relevant for several years.

1.3   Convergence in Central, Eastern and South-Eastern Europe – theory and evidence

1.3.1   Growth and convergence

In the last few years, the economic profession has been engaged in a controversial discussion on the origins of growth.[1] To a large extent, the debate was triggered by the empirical observation of increasing divergence of per capita income across countries.[2] Indeed, the evidence seemed to contradict a key prediction of standard growth theory: countries with relatively low per capita income should catch up with richer ones. In theory, since capital is generally scarce in low-income countries its rate of return should be higher than in richer economies, investment should be stronger, resulting in an increasing capital stock, production and finally income. Thus, per capita income differences should fall over time. Clearly, the global evidence on divergence of per capita income is inconsistent with this reasoning.

Two avenues have been followed to address this contradiction. The first one tries to take into account factors that actually prevent the marginal product of capital from falling – or at least prevent it from falling to zero – even if the capital intensity of production is rising over time, as theory would predict. Literally millions of cross-country regressions[3] have been run to identify factors conditioning convergence, from the investment rate itself to macroeconomic, financial sector and institutional variables. And while absolute convergence has not been supported by the data, conditional convergence has been found to hold, even if not in all samples and periods.

Evidence of convergence in Central, Eastern and South-Eastern Europe lends strong support to the conditional convergence hypothesis of standard growth theory. To be sure the *acquis communautaire* is a structural factor which has provided a common framework for the countries in the region to engage in rapid convergence.[4] To sustain the catching-up with living standards in the euro area, continued structural convergence along the lines of the *acquis communautaire* is crucial, in particular in candidate and potential candidate countries.

However, there are also features in the current catching-up process that are at odds with established growth empirics. In particular, several empirical studies suggest that convergence in the region seems to have been driven by the growth of total factor productivity.[5] This contrasts with the evidence found for other rapidly converging economies, for example in Asia, where capital accumulation has been identified as the main driver of real convergence with advanced economies.[6]

Transition is the prime candidate to account for this anomaly. The heritage of central planning left many economies with large inefficiencies in production, which offered a vast potential for efficiency gains in the course of the regime shift. Economies in the region have made extensive use of this potential. This nevertheless raises an important question on the sustainability of the convergence process in the future. If strong TFP growth has been mainly the result of transition, it is not a renewable source of convergence for the future (i.e., when transition is over). Other sources must be found. One factor is efficient financial intermediation.[7] The empirical literature on finance and growth suggests that financial development is significantly correlated with total factor productivity and less so with private savings rates or capital accumulation.[8] Clearly, financial development in the region has advanced rapidly. Nonetheless, capital accumulation should be expected to make a larger contribution to growth and real convergence in the future. However, while investment rates have been rising in Central, Eastern and South-Eastern Europe, they are not particularly high by emerging market standards. Compared with emerging Asia they can even be considered as rather low. Why have investment rates been relatively subdued and what are the policies to be pursued fostering capital formation?

1.3.2 Financial globalisation and the current account

Conceptually, the policy question may be easy to answer: continued structural reforms, enhancing flexibility in labour and product markets, improving the business climate and governance. These are the standard responses. However, a rise in investment might contribute to a further widening of current account deficits. Indeed, in recent years investment in the region has been increasingly financed by tapping foreign savings. As a result, current account deficits have reached levels of more than 10 per cent of GDP in several countries.

From a theoretical perspective, current account deficits may actually be interpreted as in line with the predictions of standard theory.[9] However, other emerging market economies have seen just the opposite pattern, namely convergence accompanied by improving current account balances, most visible in the high and widening current account surpluses in emerging Asia. It is even more striking that current account surpluses have been observed in parallel with increasing financial globalisation. Financial globalisation should facilitate capital flowing from rich to poor countries, the opposite of what we observe. This is known as the 'Lucas paradox', from the seminal article where Lucas pointed out that capital is flowing from emerging to advanced economies, contradicting predictions of standard models of trade and growth.[10] This paradox can still be observed in many parts of the world, resulting in what are commonly known as global imbalances.[11]

Various explanations have been suggested to account for this at least seemingly paradoxical development. On the one hand, rate of return differentials might be smaller than suggested by the relative scarcity and abundance of capital, reflecting larger risks related to a higher level of uncertainty due to less developed legal and financial systems.

Vice versa, the lower level of institutional quality in many emerging market economies might result in an outflow of capital because of lesser opportunities for financial investment.[12]

Countries in Central, Eastern and South-Eastern Europe seem once again to be special among emerging markets. Their process of real convergence has been accompanied by current account developments very different from those in other emerging markets. This raises the question why countries in the region, while accumulating sizeable foreign exchange reserves, have used so much foreign savings to finance current spending. Have financial factors that explain the current account surpluses in emerging Asia had a different impact in emerging Europe?[13]

Finding an answer to these questions is important not only to square empirical evidence with theory, but also from a policy perspective. Policy makers may, however, get little comfort from the fact that the imbalances in Central, Eastern and South-Eastern Europe are in line with standard economic theory.[14]

1.3.3 Financial development

Financial markets in the region have seen a very peculiar form of structural convergence and financial integration. In most countries the banking sector is dominated by subsidiaries or branches of banks headquartered in the euro area.[15] While similar developments have been observed in other emerging market economies as well,[16] the process is unique in emerging Europe,[17] where banks have expanded their presence in what has been perceived to become a single, large European financial market in the future.

Financial deepening in the region has been extremely rapid. Credit growth rates have been particularly high for consumer and mortgage lending, reaching in some countries and in some years more than 100 per cent per annum. This has been a reason for concern, as research suggests that rapid credit growth – while not necessarily leading to financial turbulence – is one of its main predictors.[18] Moreover, the structure of credit has been characterised by a significant share of loans denominated in foreign currency. Thus, debt burdens may become unsustainable in the case of an economic downturn or significant exchange rate depreciation.

1.3.4 The main policy challenge: Overheating

Until recently, demand pressures arising from strong credit growth and capital inflows have not been reflected in rising inflation in the region due to three reasons. First, there has been a strong increase in productivity growth. Second, the current account, financed largely by FDI, has served as a convenient outlet for buoyant demand. Third, nearly all economies have been characterised by substantial slack in the labour market, even though it has been rapidly absorbed recently.

Over the last years, however, domestic demand pressures have started to increase and have been increasingly reflected in domestic price developments. This may indicate that countries have reached or even passed their growth potential. However, the evidence is not clear-cut. While there has been strong growth in recent years, labour utilisation has remained low. The same holds for participation and employment rates. Unemployment, even though declining recently, is still high in many countries. There thus seems to be ample space for a larger contribution of labour to growth, mitigating the constraints for a further rise of potential output. At the same time, labour markets in the region are characterised by substantial mismatches.[19] Moreover, labour market disequilibria may be exacerbated by significant migration flows, limiting the supply response to the rise in demand at least in some countries. As a result, the paradox of low labour utilisation and tight labour markets can be observed at the same time.

Theory suggests that in a process of rapid real convergence countries should experience higher overall inflation rates, due to the Balassa-Samuelson effect. However, the recent rise in inflation can hardly be explained by this effect alone. A review of empirical studies on the size of the Balassa-Samuelson effect in Central, Eastern and South-Eastern European countries suggests that the effect is not very large and might even have declined over time.[20] This would suggest that the latest increase in inflation reflects overheating rather than a catching-up phenomenon.

Keeping nominal convergence on track is a major policy challenge in the region. The problem becomes particularly acute in countries which have given up monetary policy independence by choosing an exchange rate target or adopting a currency board arrangement. The key question for these countries is how is it possible to keep inflation under control by pegging the exchange rate, which means adopting de facto the monetary policy of the euro area, especially since the euro area economy is growing at a rate that is less than a third of what a catching-up economy should aim to achieve? In other words, how is it possible to keep inflation under control with very low or even at times negative real interest rates? What are the risks for financial stability of having persistently low real interest rates, much lower than the rate of growth of the economy?

It would go beyond the scope of this chapter to answer these questions in detail. However, it is useful to recall that even in advanced economies periods of low interest rates might fuel financial turbulence, as evidenced by the financial crisis that started in August 2007 although its impact on the Central, Eastern and South-Eastern European countries was not very visible until the second half of 2008.

To be sure, keeping nominal convergence on track is a challenge not only for monetary policy, but also for fiscal and structural policies. Improving supply side conditions and a tight budget can certainly mitigate inflationary pressures stemming from strong domestic demand. One has nonetheless to be realistic in defining the requirements for budgetary, income and structural policies that are consistent with achieving at the same time real and nominal convergence. Thus, the real question to ask is how large should the budget surplus be to counteract the inflationary effects produced by a pro-cyclical monetary policy and would this be acceptable for a catching-up country? How far-reaching, and acceptable to the population, should structural reforms be? All in all, the requirements for the budgetary and structural policies associated with an exchange rate linked to the euro might just be too demanding to counteract the pro-cyclical effects of very low real interest rates. This might lead to boom and bust cycles, with potentially very severe adjustments costs that might delay real convergence.

1.4   Conclusions

Substantial progress in real convergence has been achieved in Central, Eastern and South-Eastern Europe. This has happened with respect to real per capita income but also to economic structures, the business and institutional environment as well as macroeconomic policies. At the same time, the path for catching-up remains large and fraught with risks. The income gap with the euro area, while significantly reduced, is still large. In candidate and potential candidate countries much remains to be done to also advance structural convergence.

A closer analysis of selected aspects of the convergence process in the region showed that signs of overheating have been emerging. After several years of substantial net capital inflows, reflected in high and rising current account deficits, as well as rapid credit growth, economies might react increasingly with price rather than quantity adjustment to strong demand pressures. As a result, keeping nominal convergence on track presents a significant challenge for macroeconomic and structural policies.

Notes

The views expressed in this chapter reflect only those of the author. I thank Eva Katalin Polgar and Adalbert Winkler for their input in the preparation of these remarks.

1. For an overview see Mankiw (1995).
2. See Pritchett (1997).
3. Borrowing from the title of the paper by Sala-i-Martin (1997).
4. However, it could also be argued that European integration is so special that the evidence on convergence in Europe – by way of exception – confirms the rule of divergence. This line of reasoning is further developed in the literature on convergence clubs; see, for example, Baumol and Wolff (1988) and Dowrick and De Long (2003).
5. See Arratibel *et al.* (2007) and Morgese Borys *et al.* (2007).
6. See Young (1995) and IMF (2006).
7. See Merton and Bodie (1995).
8. See, for example, De Gregorio and Guidotti (1992) and Beck *et al.* (2000).
9. See, for example, Bussière *et al.* (2004).
10. Lucas (1990).
11. See also Prasad *et al.* (2007).
12. See Bini Smaghi (2007).
13. The answer by Abiad *et al.* (2007) is a positive one, identifying rapid financial integration of the countries under review as a key factor in explaining the difference from other emerging markets. Financial market differences between countries in the region and other emerging market economies are also stressed by Luengnaruemitchai and Schadler (2007) and Bini Smaghi (2007).
14. See, for example, Adalet and Eichengreen (2005).
15. See Arcalean *et al.* (2007).
16. See Mihaljek (2006) and Moreno and Villar (2005).
17. See Berglöf and Bolton (2002).
18. See, for example, Sachs *et al.* (1996).
19. See Landesmann *et al.* (2004) and Commander and Kollo (2004).
20. See Chapter 4.

Bibliography

A. Abiad, D. Leigh and A. Mody (2007) 'International Finance and Income Convergence: Europe Is Different', IMF Working Paper, No. 64, International Monetary Fund, Washington DC.

M. Adalet and B. Eichengreen (2005) 'Current Account Reversals: Always a Problem?' prepared for the NBER Conference on G7 Current Account Imbalances, Newport, Rhode Island, 1–2 June 2005.

C. Arcalean, O. Calvo-Gonzalez, Cs. Móré, A. van Rixtel, A. Winkler and T. Zumer (2007) 'The Causes and Nature of Rapid Growth of Bank Credit in the Central, Eastern, and South Eastern European Countries', in Charles Enoch and Inci Ötker-Robe (eds), *Rapid Credit Growth in Central and Eastern Europe, Endless Boom or Early Warning?* Palgrave Macmillan, New York.

O. Arratibel, F. Heinz, R. Martin, M. Przybyla, L. Rawdanowicz, R. Serafini and T. Zumer (2007) 'Determinants of Growth in the Central and Eastern European

EU Member States – a Production Function Approach', ECB Occasional Paper Series No. 61.

W. Baumol and E.N. Wolff (1988) 'Productivity Growth, Convergence, and Welfare: Reply', *American Economic Review*, 78(5), 1155–9.

T. Beck, R. Levine and N. Loayza (2000) 'Finance and the Sources of Growth', *Journal of Financial Economics*, 58, 261–300.

E. Berglöf and P. Bolton (2002) 'The Great Divide and Beyond. Financial Architecture in Transition', *Journal of Economic Perspectives*, 16(1), 77–100.

L. Bini Smaghi (2007) 'Global Imbalances and Monetary Policy', *Journal of Policy Modeling*, 29, 711–27.

M. Bussière, M. Fratzscher and G.J. Müller (2004) 'Current Account Dynamics in OECD and EU Acceding Countries – an Intertemporal Approach', ECB Working Paper Series No. 311, European Central Bank, Frankfurt am Main.

S. Commander and J. Kollo (2004) 'The Changing Demand for Skills: Evidence from the Transition', IZA Discussion Paper No. 1073.

J. De Gregorio and P.E. Guidotti (1992) 'Financial Development and Economic Growth', IMF Working Paper, WP/92/101, Washington DC.

J.B. De Long and L.H. Summers (1991) 'Equipment Investment and Economic Growth', *Quarterly Journal of Economics*, 106(2), 445–502.

S. Dowrick and J.B. De Long (2003) 'Globalisation and Convergence', in Michael Bordo *et al.* (eds), *Globalization in Historical Perspective*, University of Chicago Press, Chicago.

IMF (2006) 'Asia Rising: Patterns of Economic Development and Growth', *World Economic Outlook*, September, Chapter 3.

M. Landesmann, H. Vidovic and T. Ward (2004) 'Economic Restructuring and Labour Market Developments in the New EU Member States', The Vienna Institute for International Economic Studies.

R. Levine (1997) 'Financial Development and Economic Growth: Views and Agenda', *Journal of Economic Literature*, 35(2), 688–726.

R.E. Lucas (1990) 'Why Doesn't Capital Flow from Rich to Poor Countries?', *American Economic Review*, 80(2), 92–6.

P. Luengnaruemitchai and S. Schadler (2007) 'Do Economists' and Financial Markets' Perspectives on the New Members of the EU Differ?', IMF Working Paper 07/65, March, Washington DC.

N.G. Mankiw (1995) 'The Growth of Nations', *Brookings Papers on Economic Activity*, 25, 275–310.

R. Merton and Z. Bodie (1995) 'A Conceptual Framework for Analysing the Financial Environment', in D.B. Crane (ed.), *The Global Financial System: A Functional Perspective*, Harvard Business School Press, Boston.

D. Mihaljek (2006) 'Privatisation, Consolidation and the Increased Role of Foreign Banks', in BIS Papers No. 28, 41–65, Basel.

R. Moreno and A. Villar (2005) 'The Increased Role of Foreign Bank Entry in Emerging Markets', in BIS Papers No. 23, 9–16, Basel.

M. Morgese Borys, E.K. Polgar and A. Zlate (2007) 'Real Convergence in Central, Eastern and South-Eastern Europe', ECB mimeo.

A. Musso and T. Westermann (2005) 'Assessing Potential Output Growth in the Euro Area – a Growth Accounting Perspective', ECB Occasional Paper No. 22, Frankfurt am Main.

E. Prasad, R. Rajan and A. Subramanian (2007) 'The Paradox of Capital', *Finance and Development*, 44(1), International Monetary Fund, Washington DC.

L. Pritchett (1997) 'Divergence, Big Time', *Journal of Economic Perspectives*, 11(3), 3–17.

J. Sachs, A. Tornell and A. Velascó (1996) 'Financial Crises in Emerging Markets: The Lessons from 1995', NBER Working Paper No. W5576.

X. Sala-i-Martin (1997) 'I Just Ran Two Million Regressions', *American Economic Review*, Papers and Proceedings, 87, 178–83.

A. Young (1995) 'The Tyranny of Numbers: Confronting the Statistical Realities of the East Asian Growth Experience', *Quarterly Journal of Economics*, 110, 641–80.

2

Fast, but Sustainable? Challenges and Policy Options for the Catching-up Process of Central and Eastern European Countries

Jürgen Stark

2.1 Introduction

The topic of this contribution is 'Fast, but sustainable? Challenges and policy-options for the catching-up process of Central and Eastern European (CEE) countries'. While the focus will be on CEE countries that are member states of the European Union (EU), some of the key points discussed are also of interest to countries in South-Eastern Europe.

Since the fall of the Iron Curtain 18 years ago the CEE countries have made remarkable progress with regard to improving their standards of living. Their income levels have been gradually converging towards those of the euro area. Yet, there continues to be a substantial gap in their income per capita relative to the euro area. Thus, one main policy challenge for the CEE countries is to maintain a strong and sustainable process of catching up with the euro area. That said, the current situation in several countries shows how difficult it is to follow a convergence path that is simultaneously fast and sustainable. In fact, a number of countries currently face substantial as well as rising domestic and external imbalances that may ultimately threaten the sustainability of their catching-up process.

Against this background, a number of important questions arise. What are the available policy options for these countries? What role does the underlying exchange rate regime play in the convergence process? In particular, are certain exchange rate regimes and monetary policy frameworks better suited to ensuring sufficiently stable macroeconomic conditions to make the ongoing catching-up process in the CEE countries sustainable?

2.2   Possible lessons to be drawn from former cohesion countries

Before looking in more detail at the CEE countries, it might be useful to take a quick look at the catching-up experience of the former cohesion countries, namely Greece, Ireland, Portugal and Spain, that are today part of the euro area. What can be learnt from their experiences on their way to joining the euro? In this context, it is important to recall that there are a number of similarities, but also important differences between the cohesion countries at the time when they joined the EU and the CEE countries today. The main similarity is the relatively low GDP-per-capita level at the time of EU accession. Consequently, the cohesion countries also underwent a strong catching-up process in the 1990s, which resulted in high growth and inflation differentials with the more mature EU economies. Moreover, the former cohesion countries also experienced strong credit growth and large current account imbalances.

However, one important difference is that all four cohesion countries were able to make use of their monetary and exchange rate policy to adjust for emerging imbalances. Despite the fact that most cohesion countries participated in the exchange rate mechanism for two or more years, they were able to cushion the inflationary impact of real convergence by allowing the nominal exchange rate to appreciate. Another important difference is that the former cohesion countries had a different time horizon for their catching-up process compared with that currently envisaged for the CEE countries. For all of the cohesion countries, the time span between adopting the *acquis communautaire*, entering the EU, becoming part of the single market, participating in the exchange rate mechanism and eventually joining the euro area was over a decade. This might help to explain why the catching-up process in the cohesion countries appears to have been somewhat smoother than current experiences in some CEE countries.

2.3   Current macroeconomic and financial challenges

Against this background, it is important to briefly outline the main macroeconomic and financial challenges faced by the countries in Central and Eastern Europe. When the countries are grouped according to their underlying monetary and exchange rate regimes, it seems that the countries with hard pegs – that is Bulgaria, Estonia, Latvia and Lithuania – experience rather similar macroeconomic and financial patterns. In recent years, these patterns have appeared to differ significantly from those faced by countries with more flexible exchange rates, namely the Czech Republic, Hungary, Poland, Romania and Slovakia. To give a striking example of macroeconomic performance depending on the underlying exchange rate regime, the countries with hard-peg regimes have recently experienced a very rapid catching-up process, with cumulative real GDP growth standing on average at 18 per cent in the past two years, which is almost twice as fast as the growth rates observed in the countries with flexible regimes. To some extent, this might also reflect the fact that the income level in the fixed exchange rate countries is on average still somewhat lower compared with the countries with flexible rates. Likewise, inflation in the countries with hard-peg exchange regimes was almost one and a half times higher in the past two years compared with the countries with flexible regimes.

The macroeconomic and financial developments in the CEE countries are puzzling in the sense that they are not in line with economic theory, nor do they reflect the empirical findings that are usually observed in other catching-up economies, including the cohesion countries in the 1990s. More specifically, while in the CEE countries the economic performance differs substantially depending on the exchange rate regime, most theoretical models do not support the view that the choice of exchange rate regime should have an impact on macroeconomic performance. In turn, the empirical literature on the impact of the exchange rate regime on inflation basically suggests that countries with hard pegs usually display a better inflation performance compared with countries with floating exchange rates. This can be largely explained by the disciplinary device of the anchor currency and greater confidence, which should result in lower inflation volatility. Likewise, the empirical literature finds a link, although it is somewhat weaker, between the exchange rate regime and growth performance: output growth is assumed to be weaker in countries with fixed regimes than in countries with floating exchange rates. This is explained by higher productivity growth in countries with floating regimes as a result of faster growth in external trade, while productivity growth in fixed regimes might sometimes be reduced by the limited adjustment mechanism and thereby lower economic efficiency. However, these findings are countered by the current macroeconomic performance of the CEE countries, as growth and inflation have been particularly high for a number of years in countries with fixed peg exchange regimes. What are the implications of these findings? In principle, it could be seen as an indication that, for some of these countries, the current situation might not be sustainable. This makes it all the more necessary to look more deeply at the macroeconomic developments and challenges ahead.

What key challenges are the CEE countries currently facing? The countries with hard-peg exchange regimes are currently faced with three main challenges:

- First, inflation is increasing sharply in the countries with hard-peg regimes amidst signs of overheating in the form of labour shortages and strong upward pressures on wages. Growth in unit labour costs has increased dramatically over the past year, mainly driven by strong wage increases. Wage increases have been particularly strong in the construction sector, reflecting labour market bottlenecks, which are aggravated by substantial outflows of migrants.
- Second, the very strong credit growth in past years of well above 40 per cent was to a large extent supported by very favourable financing conditions, including negative real interest rates. Strong credit growth has boosted private domestic demand, inflation and imports. As a result of this, house prices have also boomed, in particular in the Baltic countries, where they have on average doubled since 2004.
- Third, the countries with hard pegs face substantial external imbalances – the four-month moving average of the current account deficit increased strongly over the past two years to around 17 per cent of GDP. The deficit largely stems from robust private consumption growth. Together with high external debt ratios and high foreign currency borrowing, external imbalances of this magnitude make the countries vulnerable to external and financial shocks.

The key challenges for countries with flexible exchange rates – which are currently undergoing a somewhat slower catching-up process – are as follows:

- First, fiscal policy has been very loose, with fiscal deficits standing on average at above 4 per cent of GDP. Fiscal consolidation efforts have been limited in the past and a number of countries are in an excessive deficit situation.
- Second, inflationary pressures continue to be more muted, but are likely to increase once the catching-up process gains momentum and will pick up more strongly than in the past. For a credible monetary policy, this implies standing ready to tighten monetary policy in order to ensure price stability at a time of stronger growth.

2.4 Policy options

What policy options are available to address the macroeconomic and financial challenges? There are basically four areas for possible policy intervention: fiscal policy, structural policy, supervisory and prudential policy and, last, but not least, monetary and exchange rate policy. It goes without saying that the available policy options differ across countries and need to be carefully examined on a case-by-case basis.

On the fiscal side, consolidation efforts need to be intensified, in particular, in the countries with floating exchange rates, and the efficiency of public expenditure improved. Countries with hard-peg regimes, in particular, should avoid pro-cyclical positions, and in some cases their cyclical situation may warrant a quite substantial increase in their budget surpluses in order to contribute to reining in domestic demand. In this context, it is worth keeping in mind that any assessment of the fiscal stance is highly uncertain given the difficulties involved in disentangling the trend from the cycle. As there is some evidence that the size of structural budgetary improvements seems to be constantly overstated, additional prudence is required in the conduct of fiscal policy. Moreover, it is important to prevent wage pressures in the public sector from spilling over into the private sector and to bring the provisions of the tax-benefit system more into line with the requirement to avoid labour market bottlenecks and allow for sufficient flexibility within the economy.

As regards structural policy, there are several ways to improve the supply side conditions and to enhance economic flexibility in the product and labour markets. These measures aim, for example, at improving the wage formation process, fostering labour mobility between sectors and regions and enhancing competition in product markets. To reduce pressures on the housing market, a lower level of regulation, as well as lower tax incentives, might be warranted.

Supervisory and prudential policies can also play a complementary role in reducing strong credit growth and ensuring financial stability. Supervisory action can cover a wide range of measures, from 'softer' measures, like moral suasion, to more intrusive ones, such as laying down additional requirements for risk management.

The availability of monetary and exchange rate policy options obviously differs depending on the underlying exchange rate regime.

The ultimate question for a country is which monetary policy and exchange rate regime is best suited to ensuring a fast and stable convergence process. The relevant question to discuss at this point is not a general discourse about the pros and cons of fixed versus flexible exchange rates – we should not try to apply this more academic debate to the

Central and Eastern European countries as a whole. In the same vein, the opposing argument that is mentioned from time to time, namely that rushing into the euro would solve all the problems experienced by the CEE countries, does not apply. Rather, the relevant question to ask is whether any exchange rate system is better suited for a country to cope with the country-specific challenges arising from real convergence. Obviously, this can only be assessed on a country-by-country basis.

Irrespective of the exchange rate regime, the CEE countries still need to implement all necessary reforms in the areas of fiscal, structural and prudential policies. In fact, these policies should be seen as complementary to the monetary and exchange rate policy.

2.5   Conclusions

To conclude, the CEE countries are currently facing substantial challenges as far as their catching-up processes are concerned. Even if an early adoption of the euro seems unrealistic at the present juncture for most countries, it is wrong to assume that the current problems can be easily solved by joining the euro area before a fully sustainable level of convergence has been achieved. In the end, it is more important for the CEE countries to further build on their impressive achievements than to run the risk of facing additional problems if they enter monetary union too early in their convergence process. A sustainable level of convergence is in the interests of both the applicant country and the euro area as a whole. Notwithstanding the need for high standards for the convergence process, it should be kept in mind that the enlargement of the euro area is an ongoing process. The countries of Central and Eastern Europe have already made substantial progress on their way towards adopting the euro. ERM II has been greatly expanded since 2004, with seven member states currently participating in it. Moreover, a number of countries have already joined or are about to join the euro area since the launch of the euro in 1999. Thus, there is no reason to assume that the door might one day be closed. If the right policies are applied, the CEE countries will master the challenges of convergence in the years ahead.

Note

I thank Carolin Nerlich for her contribution in the preparation of this chapter.

3
Real Convergence in Central, Eastern and South-Eastern Europe: A Production Function Approach

Magdalena Morgese Borys, Éva Katalin Polgár and Andrei Zlate

3.1 Introduction

The countries of Central, Eastern and South-Eastern Europe have made considerable progress in economic transition and integration into the world economy, particularly into the European Union (EU), within less than two decades. Closer economic integration through trade and financial flows, progress in the EU accession process, including EU membership for ten countries by 1 January 2007, and the objective of adopting the euro in the future direct attention to the challenges of real convergence in the region.

This chapter focuses on real convergence – defined as the convergence of per capita income levels towards that of the euro area – and its determinants in the member states that have joined the EU since May 2004 (EU-10) and the candidate and potential candidate countries (C/PC) since 1989. The chapter aims at providing an overview of key facts and figures on real convergence in the countries under review, as well as an analysis of labour markets and investments as determinants of growth. It deliberately refrains from taking up policy issues linked to the convergence process, like inflation and the monetary policy regime, potential growth and economic policy, migration, financial development and financial integration as well as balance of payments developments.

The analysis of this chapter reveals that despite notable improvements in living standards, gaps in terms of income per capita relative to the euro area remain large in the countries under review. This suggests that the challenges of real convergence will remain relevant for the region even in the medium term. However, important cross-country differences can be found. To account for this heterogeneity a distinction is often made between the EU-10, that is, the countries that have already joined the EU, and the C/PC countries that have the status of an EU candidate or potential candidate country. Moreover, as Turkey has not been – in contrast to the other 15 countries under review – a transition country, the analysis of real convergence in candidate and potential candidate countries sometimes distinguishes between Turkey and the remaining countries (C/PC-5). In addition, there is a great degree of heterogeneity among the countries under review in terms of size, the speed of economic reforms and demographic change. Countries were also differently affected by financial and exchange rate crises as well as civil unrest and wars. While these factors arguably had an impact on the speed and timing of convergence, the horizontal nature of the chapter often prevents a deeper analysis of all country specifics.

As the analysis is based on a production function approach, the rest of the chapter is organised as follows. Section 3.2 analyses real convergence patterns focusing on growth rates and relative levels of real output across countries, as well as determinants of growth. Section 3.3 provides an in-depth analysis of labour markets, whereas Section 3.4 highlights the recent patterns of gross fixed capital formation (GFCF) and foreign direct investment (FDI) as determinants of growth. Moreover, as real convergence in the European context has been increasingly defined more broadly than just a convergence of per capita income levels, the chapter also includes a review of the indicators of 'structural convergence' (Padoa-Schioppa, 2002), that is, institutional development and structural reforms.

3.2   Patterns of real convergence

This section provides an overview of growth patterns in the countries under review. It starts with the observation that all transition economies in the group experienced notable output losses in the early 1990s. In general, output per capita reached all-time lows – relative both to the EU-15 and to their own pre-transition levels – around 1993. Thus, 1993 can, at least statistically, be seen as the start of the convergence process. While by 2006 all EU-10 countries surpassed their 1989 levels of total income in real terms, in the C/PC group only the fastest-growing countries – Albania and Croatia – achieved the same performance.

Total factor productivity (TFP) improvement has been the main driver of growth in the region, followed by capital accumulation. Labour productivity improved as well, while labour utilisation declined in most countries relative to the EU-15, reflecting productivity gains and growing mismatches in the labour market. Given that a significant part of TFP growth has been largely triggered by the elimination of inefficiencies of the former central planning regime, a decline to growth rates seen in mature economies can be expected for the future. Therefore, countries face the challenge of improving labour utilisation and fostering capital accumulation to ensure the sustainability of the real convergence process.[1]

3.2.1 Real output growth

Following the collapse of the centrally planned systems and the outbreak of hostilities in the Western Balkans, all countries – with the exception of Turkey[2] – experienced notable recessions during 1990–93 (Table 3.1[3]). The Baltic States, as well as the countries in the Western Balkans seriously affected by the wars of the Yugoslav secession, recorded the largest output losses.

Economic decline in the EU-10 and the C/PC countries reversed after 1993 as macroeconomic stabilisation took hold and structural reforms advanced. As indicated by the European Bank for Reconstruction and Development (EBRD) transition indicators[4] (Figure 3.1, first panel), transition was slower in the C/PC countries in general than in the EU-10. Among the EU-10 countries, Bulgaria and Romania were notably slow reformers during the early and mid-1990s, but started catching up in the late 1990s. Croatia has traditionally been the most advanced among the C/PC-5 group, maintaining a transition pace comparable to that of most EU-10 countries, whereas Bosnia and Herzegovina as well as Serbia and Montenegro have been lagging behind.

After 1993, the speed of recovery differed significantly across countries. In particular, the period between 1994 and 1997 was characterised by the uneven occurrence of recovery and crisis episodes, due to unbalanced progress with reforms, the occurrence of exchange rate and financial crises as well as the differentiated impact of the war in the Western Balkans. While the period 1998–2001 can be characterised as one of consolidation and growth, the years between 2002 and 2005 saw strong growth with signs of an economic boom. Many EU-10 countries experienced their highest growth rates since the beginning of transition. Growth also accelerated in Croatia, whereas Serbia and Montenegro recovered from

Table 3.1   Real GDP growth rates

	1990–1993	1994–1997	1998–2001	2002–2005
EU-10				
Bulgaria	−7.0	−2.5	3.9	5.1
Czech Republic	−3.3	2.9	1.6	3.8
Estonia	−10.2	4.6	5.8	8.4
Hungary	−5.6	2.6	4.6	4.1
Latvia	−13.3	3.7	5.7	8.1
Lithuania	−11.6	2.2	4.2	8.0
Poland	−2.6	6.4	3.7	3.4
Romania	−7.8	2.2	0.5	5.7
Slovakia	−5.4	5.7	2.7	4.9
Slovenia	−4.9	4.5	4.0	3.6
C/PC				
Albania	−5.7	5.1	9.3	5.0
Bosnia and Herzegovina	−19.6	24.9	9.0	4.0
Croatia	−12.0	6.4	2.2	4.7
FYR Macedonia	−7.6	−0.1	1.9	2.6
Serbia and Montenegro	−19.6	5.5	−1.2	5.0
Serbia	–	*9.0*	*−1.5*	*5.6*
Montenegro	–	*9.1*	*0.0*	*2.8*
Kosovo	–	–	–	*2.5*
Turkey	6.0	4.1	−0.4	7.5
Weighted averages				
CEE/SEE	−2.5	4.2	1.9	5.5
EU-10	−5.4	3.9	3.2	4.4
C/PC	1.9	4.6	0.2	7.0
C/PC-5	−11.7	7.8	3.1	4.5
C/PC-4 (without BA, TK)	−15.0	5.2	1.6	4.7
EU-15	1.2	2.5	3.0	1.5

Note: The growth rates for Bosnia and Herzegovina and Serbia and Montenegro are assumed to be equal for the period between 1990 and 1993.

Source: ECB staff calculations, based on the GGDC Total Economy Database, January 2007, using Total GDP in 1990$ (converted at GK* PPP). EBRD data for Serbia and Montenegro as separate entities (covering 1996–2005), Eurostat for Kosovo (2002–04). *Geary-Khamis, see Box 3.2.

slow growth and the recession linked to slow reforms and the Kosovo war. As a result, by 2006 all EU-10 countries surpassed their 1989 level of output in real terms,[5] to an extent ranging from 159 per cent (Poland) to 101 per cent (Bulgaria). By contrast, among the C/PC-5 countries only the fastest-growing economies – Albania and Croatia – managed to surpass their pre-transition level of per capita income.

Box 3.1 Transition and growth

In general, the speed of economic recovery has been positively related to the pace of transition. Advanced reformers in 1993, 1997 and 2001 achieved higher annual growth rates in the subsequent periods than slow reformers.

Figure 3.1 (second panel) plots the EBRD transition scores (see endnote 4) for the years 1993, 1997 and 2001 (on the horizontal axis) against the average annual growth of total gross domestic product (GDP) over the subsequent four-year time intervals (1994–97, 1998–2001 and 2002–05, on the vertical axis) for the transition countries under review. Simple regression analysis shows that the coefficient estimate on the EBRD transition indicator is positive and statistically significant (estimate = 4.58, standard error = 0.91).

Notable exceptions from the trend can be linked either to post-war recoveries in the Western Balkans (Bosnia and Herzegovina in 1998–2001, Serbia in 2002–05) or to financial turbulence, such as in the Czech Republic during 1994–97 and in Romania in 1998–2001.

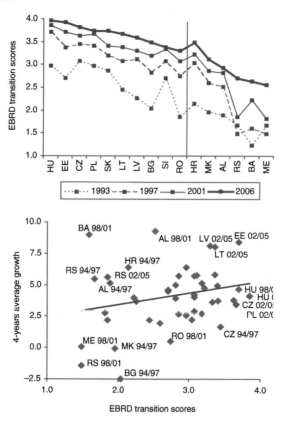

Figure 3.1 Structural reforms and economic growth

Note: For informative purposes, country and time labels have been provided for data points representing exceptions from the trend. Bosnia and Herzegovina in 1994–97 represents an unusual outlier (with 25 per cent average annual growth of total GDP, due to the recovery of unusually large output losses during the war), and was omitted from the chart.

Source: EBRD Transition Indicators, May 2007 (for reform scores) and GGDC (for growth rates).

3.2.2   Income per capita levels

In most countries, output per capita declined sharply relative to the EU-15 average after 1989, reaching all-time lows in the period between 1992 and 1994, followed by a steady recovery thereafter. However, in Serbia and Montenegro and the former Yugoslav Republic of Macedonia income per capita – relative to the EU-15 average – reached its lowest point in 1999 (the year of the Kosovo conflict) and 2002 (the year after the security crisis), respectively (Table 3.2; caveats on the potential bias in cross-country comparisons are described in Box 3.2).[6]

Between 1993 and 2005, average income per capita increased relative to the EU-15 average, although at a slower pace in the C/PC than in the EU-10. By 2005 the EU-10 average reached almost 40 per cent, whereas the C/PC level of income per capita rose to only 34 per cent of the EU-15 average in PPP terms. As the EU-10 and the C/PC countries started their recovery from almost the same level of income per capita in 1993 (32 vs 31 per cent), the catch-up of the C/PC was relatively slow. However, closer analysis reveals that the C/PC average is to a large extent influenced by developments in Turkey, by far the largest economy among candidate and potential candidate countries. Since Turkey was not a transition economy, it did not experience economic collapse after 1989 and fast recovery afterwards. For this reason, it is useful to focus on growth of income per capita in the C/PC-5 countries. While their performance remains below that of the EU-10, the C/PC-5 countries' income per capita rose on average by 6 percentage points relative to the EU-15, that is from 16 per cent in 1993 to 22 per cent in 2005.

On average, total output growth was roughly similar in the EU-10 and the C/PC countries between 1993 and 2005 (58 vs 56 per cent cumulated growth), while income per capita growth was slower in the C/PC (61 vs 37 per cent). This is due to the positive population growth in the C/PC (+13.8 per cent, mainly driven by Turkey), compared with –0.2 per cent in the EU-10. Excluding Turkey, both total output and per capita income increased more rapidly in the C/PC-5 than in the EU-10.[7]

3.2.3   Initial per capita income and growth

Countries with a lower level of income are expected to grow faster than richer ones (*absolute convergence*), provided that the steady state level of income is the same for all countries. This is a strong assumption, as the investment rate, the institutional setup, macroeconomic and financial variables vary across countries, implying that the steady state level will

Table 3.2 Real convergence, GDP per capita (GGDC)
(EU-15 = 100; GGDC dataset, GDP per capita in GK* PPPs, 1990$)

	1989	1993	1997	2001	2005
EU-10					
Bulgaria	39.8	30.7	26.5	29.0	34.9
Czech Republic	57.6	48.6	50.2	48.3	53.3
Estonia	75.2	50.1	57.9	67.2	90.7
Hungary	44.2	34.3	35.1	38.4	43.3
Latvia	61.6	33.7	37.6	43.6	58.4
Lithuania	57.5	33.6	33.5	35.6	46.7
Poland	36.4	31.2	36.5	38.0	41.4
Romania	25.2	17.7	17.8	16.4	19.5
Slovak Republic	51.1	38.9	44.1	44.0	50.5
Slovenia	76.2	59.6	64.9	68.3	74.9
C/PC					
Albania	15.8	11.0	11.9	15.0	17.0
Bosnia and Herzegovina	26.0	11.5	26.5	29.4	30.3
Croatia	50.7	29.5	35.0	34.4	38.8
FYR Macedonia	28.3	19.4	17.2	16.3	17.0
Serbia and Montenegro	36.0	13.3	14.5	12.4	14.3
Turkey	32.5	37.1	37.3	31.0	37.6
Weighted averages					
CEE/SEE	36.6	31.3	33.3	31.7	36.8
EU-10	40.5	31.6	34.1	35.0	39.9
C/PC	31.4	31.0	32.4	28.0	33.5
C/PC-5	28.8	16.2	19.8	19.8	22.1
EU-25	90.7	89.2	90.0	90.4	91.3
Standard deviations					
CEE/SEE	17.8	14.2	15.2	16.7	21.1
EU-10	16.5	12.0	14.2	15.8	20.1
C/PC	11.6	10.8	10.8	9.5	11.1
C/PC-5	13.0	7.8	9.5	9.7	10.6

Note: In cross-country comparisons, the GGDC dataset may suffer from a bias, described in detail in Box 3.2. For example, the relative level of GDP per capita in 2005 is most likely overestimated for Estonia and probably underestimated for the Czech Republic, Hungary and Romania.

Source: ECB staff calculations, based on the GGDC Total Economy Database, January 2007, using Total GDP in 1990$ (converted at GK* PPP). *Geary-Khamis method, see Box 3.2.

Box 3.2 Accounting for the bias in cross-country comparisons of income per capita

Cross-country comparisons of per capita income must be treated with caution, as their relative levels might vary depending on the methodology used to express real income in terms of purchasing power parity (PPP).

The Groningen Growth and Development Centre (GGDC)'s Total Economy Database provides data on income per capita for the EU-10 and the C/PC countries measured in PPP terms following the Geary-Khamis (GK) method. This method may produce biased results because the aggregation uses reference price or reference volume structures that do not properly reflect countries' consumption patterns. For instance, the method does not take into account that consumers switch their expenditure towards products that become relatively cheaper during the reference period (OECD, 2007; Rao, 2001; Rao and Timmer, 2000). While this bias is not relevant when assessing countries' performance over time relative to their initial levels of wealth (to the extent that the country-specific bias stays constant over time), the impact on cross-country comparisons may be significant. For example, in Table 3.2 the relative level of GDP per capita in 2005 is most likely overestimated for Estonia and probably underestimated for the Czech Republic, Hungary and Romania.

The dataset provided by the Vienna Institute for International Economics (WIIW) avoids this bias by applying the Elteto-Koves-Szule (EKS) method, also used by the OECD-Eurostat PPP Programme. It uses neither a reference price structure nor a volume price structure when estimating real expenditures (OECD, 2007). Thus, it allows for a more reliable comparison of the countries' level of income per capita relative to each other in one given year (Table 3.3).

The data show that the 2005 per capita GDP relative to the EU-15 average was significantly higher in the EU-10 than in the C/PC (that is, 46 vs 26 per cent). Notable differences persisted across the EU-10 countries. In 2005 Slovenia came closest to the EU-15 level (with 73 per cent), followed

Table 3.3 Real convergence, GDP per capita (WIIW)
(EU-15 = 100; WIIW dataset, GDP per capita in EKS PPPs)

	1990	1993	1997	2001	2005
EU-10					
Bulgaria	29.8	27.7	23.2	25.5	29.2
Czech Republic	57.3	56.9	62.9	60.0	67.3
Estonia	35.6	30.1	35.0	39.9	54.8
Hungary	45.6	44.5	45.3	51.8	55.9
Latvia	43.1	26.8	29.4	33.8	42.9
Lithuania	51.2	33.9	33.3	36.6	47.3
Poland	28.2	29.8	40.2	42.0	45.4
Romania	25.7	24.2	25.6	23.9	31.6
Slovak Republic	37.7	33.6	42.3	44.3	50.0
Slovenia	59.6	58.3	64.5	67.3	73.3

Continued

Table 3.3 Continued					
	1990	1993	1997	2001	2005
C/PC					
Albania	9.5	11.4	14.4	16.8	18.7
Bosnia and Herzegovina	–	–	–	22.4	23.2
Croatia	37.1	29.3	37.2	37.7	44.4
Macedonia	27.1	23.1	23.2	21.9	23.3
Serbia and Montenegro	–	–	–	–	–
Serbia	–	–	–	*19.9*	*24.7*
Montenegro	–	–	–	*20.6*	*21.8*
Turkey	26.3	29.1	29.1	24.1	25.9
Weighted averages					
CEE/SEE	–	–	–	32.6	36.4
EU-10	34.6	33.3	38.4	39.8	45.4
C/PC (*)	–	–	–	24.0	26.3
C/PC-5 (*)	–	–	–	23.8	27.6
C/PC-4 (**)	26.3	28.1	28.8	24.5	26.6
C/PC-3 (***)	26.1	22.4	27.0	27.6	31.6
EU-25	–	–	86.4	86.9	88.0
Standard deviations					
CEE/SEE	–	–	–	14.9	16.6
EU-10	12.0	12.4	14.3	14.0	13.9
C/PC (*)	–	–	–	7.3	9.0
C/PC-5 (*)	–	–	–	8.1	10.1

Note: (*) C/PC-5 and C/PC include RS rather than SM. (***) C/PC-3 includes Albania, Croatia and the former Yugoslav Republic of Macedonia. (**) C/PC-4 includes the C/PC-3 and Turkey.

Source: WIIW Handbook of Statistics, 2006, with the exception of total GDP for Turkey (Eurostat), population and employment for the EU-15, Cyprus, Malta and Turkey (GGDC).

by the Czech Republic (67 per cent) and Estonia (55 per cent). The lowest levels of income per capita relative to the EU-15 were recorded in Bulgaria and Romania (with 29 and 32 per cent, respectively). Among the C/PC countries, a two-tier hierarchy existed. Croatia's per capita income stood at about 44 per cent of the EU-15 countries' average, almost reaching the average level of the EU-10, while the remaining countries had levels that ranged between one-fifth and one-quarter of the EU-15 average.

The key disadvantage of the WIIW dataset is that it covers a much shorter time period than the GGDC dataset, especially for Bosnia and Herzegovina and Serbia and Montenegro. This significantly constrains the analysis within the group of candidate and potential candidate countries. For this reason, the analysis in this section, focusing on developments in countries over time, is largely based on the GGDC dataset. By contrast, when explicitly focusing on a cross-country perspective, the analysis relies on the WIIW dataset.

be different. Against this background, *conditional convergence*, accounting for these differences, has become one of the most tested propositions of growth theory. However, given the similar post-transition experience and the current (and potential) status of EU membership of the countries under review, it may be justifiable to assume a sufficient degree of homogeneity, providing the basis for an analysis of absolute convergence, at least as a first approximation.[8]

The results suggest that absolute convergence generally holds for the EU-10 for the entire period between 1993 and 2005 (with the exception of Bulgaria and Romania). For the group of C/PC countries, however, absolute convergence can only be observed for the more recent interval between 1999 and 2005 (Figure 3.2).[9] Due to political turmoil and the slow pace of reforms, the former Yugoslav Republic of Macedonia and Serbia and Montenegro, countries which in 1993 were below the average level of C/PC income per capita, had sluggish rates of growth during subsequent years. By contrast, Albania and Bosnia and Herzegovina were among the C/PC countries with the lowest levels of income per capita relative to the EU-15 in 1993, and recorded the highest rates of economic growth relative to the C/PC average during the catching-up.

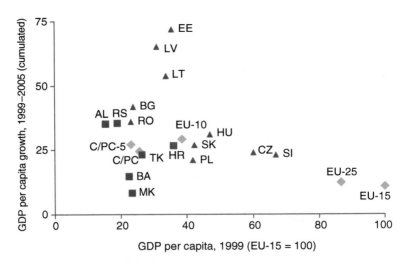

Figure 3.2   Absolute convergence (EU-15 = 100; WIIW dataset, GDP per capita in EKS PPPs)

Source: WIIW, Handbook of Statistics, 2006; Eurostat for total GDP in EKS PPPs (EUR million, current prices) and population of Turkey; GGDC for real growth of GDP per capita.

3.2.4 Labour productivity

Large gaps in income per capita still exist between the EU-10, the C/PC and the EU-15 countries. To analyse the nature of these gaps, the following decomposition of income per capita can be used:

$$\frac{GDP}{Population} = \frac{GDP}{Employment} \frac{Employment}{Population},$$

where the ratio of GDP to employment serves as a measure of labour productivity, and the ratio of employment to population measures the degree of labour utilisation (Arratibel *et al.*, 2007).[10]

Between 1999 and 2005, labour productivity – measured as real output per worker – improved in all countries relative to the EU-15, although notable gaps remained. The pattern reflects not only the expanding shares of more productive sectors in total output (that is, services in particular[11]), but also the decline of overall employment triggered by emerging mismatches in the labour markets – namely between the increasing demand and the short supply of skilled workers – trends which are inherent in the process of economic restructuring in transition economies (see, for example, Commander and Kollo, 2004).

Figure 3.3 (first panel) plots labour productivity in the EU-10 and C/PC-5 countries in 1999 (horizontal axis) and 2005 (vertical axis), expressed in percentage terms relative to the corresponding EU-15 averages. The method illustrates graphically the process of real convergence in terms of labour productivity in the transition economies under review: plots above the diagonal show an improvement in labour productivity relative to the EU-15 average between 1999 and 2005. Among the EU-10 countries, the two most recent member states – Bulgaria and Romania – had the lowest levels of labour productivity (34 per cent of the EU-15 average in 2005), and did not exceed significantly the C/PC-5 average (38 per cent). The frontrunners were Slovenia (70 per cent), the Czech Republic and Hungary (65 per cent each), coming closest to the average level in the EU-15 in 2005. Despite the improvement in labour productivity in the C/PC countries relative to the EU-15 level, in 2005 significant gaps persisted even between the C/PC-5 and the EU-10 countries. By 2005, C/PC-5 average productivity reached roughly one-third of the EU-15 average (37 per cent), significantly less than the EU-10 (51 per cent). Nevertheless, Croatia stands out with a level of labour productivity exceeding the EU-10 average. However, this result may be partly driven by the low level of labour utilisation in Croatia relative to the EU-10 group.

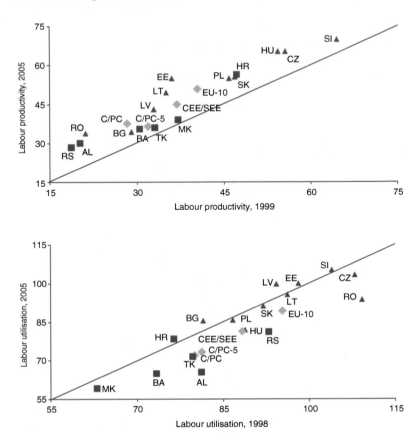

Figure 3.3   Labour productivity and labour utilisation relative to the EU-15 countries (EU-15 = 100; WIIW dataset, GDP per capita in EKS PPs, 1990$)

Source: WIIW Handbook of Statistics, with the exception of total GDP in EKS PPPs (EUR million, current prices) for Turkey (Eurostat); population and employment for the EU-15 and Turkey (GGDC).

3.2.5   Labour utilisation

Labour utilisation – measured as total employment per population[12] – declined significantly between 1998 and 2005 in almost all countries under review relative to the EU-15 (Figure 3.3, second panel). The decline probably reflects growing sectoral and regional mismatches in the labour market, such as the increase of demand for skilled labour and the geographical reallocation of economic activity inside countries. Moreover, there are substantial differences in the level of labour utilisation between the EU-10 (89 per cent of the EU-15 average) and the C/PC countries (72 per cent of the EU-15 average). Among the EU-10 countries, labour utilisation in Slovenia, the Czech Republic and Estonia exceeded the EU-15 level in 2005, whereas Albania, Bosnia and Herzegovina and the former Yugoslav Republic of Macedonia recorded the lowest rates, close to or even below 65 per cent of the EU-15 level.

In addition to labour market frictions, the large size of the informal sector may explain the low levels of official labour utilisation in the C/PC countries, since a large shadow economy may imply an understatement of real employment relative to official figures. In 2003 the size of the shadow economy in C/PC countries was relatively larger in countries with low labour utilisation rates: the shadow economy was estimated at 34 per cent of GDP in Turkey, at roughly 35 to 37 per cent of GDP in Albania, Bosnia and Herzegovina, Croatia and the former Yugoslav Republic of Macedonia, and at as much as 39 per cent in Serbia and Montenegro, significantly exceeding the corresponding estimates for the majority of the EU-10 countries[13] (Schneider, 2004). The figures suggest a negative correlation between the share of the shadow economy in the GDP and the ratio of employment to total population, indicating that the size of the informal sector may be among the factors responsible for pushing labour productivity to artificially high levels in some C/PC countries.

3.2.6 Contributions of total factor productivity, labour and capital to growth

Between 1997 and 2006, TFP growth was the main contributor to economic growth in the countries under review, followed by capital accumulation.[14] By contrast, labour had only a marginal or – in particular for the C/PC countries – even negative contribution (Figure 3.4).[15] The contribution of labour was negative particularly in countries where employment may be notoriously underreported due to the large shares of the informal sector within the economy, such as in Albania, Bosnia and Herzegovina and Serbia and Montenegro (Schneider, 2004).

Besides TFP, and in contrast to labour, capital accumulation has been an important driver of growth in several countries. For instance, our calculations show that the capital stock growth accounted for more than one-third of the cumulated effect on output growth in Bulgaria and Latvia during the last decade (1997–2006), as well as in Croatia, Serbia and Montenegro and Turkey during the most recent years (2002–06).

Given their status as transition economies, all countries under review had been expected to show TFP growth – in the form of a more efficient use of inputs in production and better management – contributing considerably to output growth. Structural reforms, such as privatisation, deregulation of product and labour markets, openness to trade and FDI and technology transfers were deemed to drive TFP growth (Arratibel *et al.*, 2007).

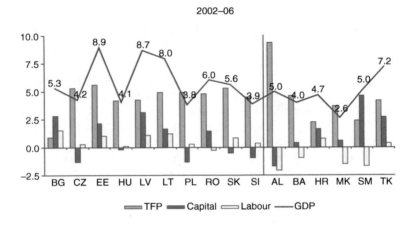

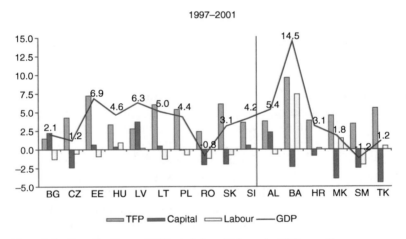

Figure 3.4 Contributions of TFP, capital and labour to GDP growth

Notes: For AL, BA and MK, averages cover the intervals 1997–2001 and 2002–05 only, for SM, 1998–2001 and 2002–05.

Sources: GGDC (for real GDP and employment growth); ESA 95 (for GFCF for the EU-10 countries, in national currencies at constant prices); IMF (for GFCF/GDP and real GDP growth, used to compute real GFCF growth for AL, BA, HR, MK, SM and TK following $GFCF_t/GFCF_{t-1}=(GDP_t/GDP_{t-1}) \times (GFCF_t/GDP_t)/(GFCF_{t-1}/GDP_{t-1}))$; UNCTAD World Investment Report (for GFCF/GDP for BA in 1996 and 1997, as well as for SM in 1997 and 1998).

However, TFP growth might decline once the inefficiencies of central planning are completely eliminated (Iradian, 2007). Thus, we find that the contribution of TFP to economic growth declined notably over the last decade, whereas the importance of capital accumulation increased – without always matching that of TFP growth.[16] The contribution of labour to output growth became positive in the EU-10, whereas it remained negative in the C/PC countries over the decade.[17] The result reflects the more advanced status of the EU-10 relative to the C/PC countries in dealing with unemployment and labour market mismatches, as well as the relatively larger share of the informal sector in the C/PC economies.

Therefore, we conclude that the sustainability of rapid TFP growth is questionable and alternative sources of economic growth will be necessary to keep the growth momentum. In particular, improvements in employment and faster capital accumulation are expected to play a more important role in the future.

3.3   Labour markets

Labour market performance directly affects the degree of labour utilisation, with important consequences for economic growth and per capita income levels. High employment and participation rates, a skilled workforce and the efficient allocation of labour are crucial ingredients for facilitating economic growth and real convergence in countries in the region. Against this background, this chapter provides an overview of the main developments in the labour markets of the countries under review, analyses changes in the composition of employment by sector and reviews the available evidence on labour market mismatches, including long-term and youth unemployment.

3.3.1   Labour market indicators

On average, labour markets in the region are characterised by higher unemployment and lower employment and participation rates compared with the euro area (Table 3.4).[18]

Moreover, there are substantial differences between the EU-10 and the C/PC countries, with unemployment rates substantially higher and employment rates much lower in the latter. Differences have become even more pronounced over time, as – comparing averages between 1997 and 2006 – unemployment continued to rise in the C/PC countries, but dropped in the EU-10, while employment rates rose in the EU-10 and declined in the C/PC.

Table 3.4   Selected labour market indicators (in per cent)

	Unemployment rate		Employment rate		Participation rate	
	1997	2006	1997	2006	1997	2006
EU-10						
Bulgaria	14.0	9.0	43.9	58.6	64.4	64.2
Czech Republic	4.8	7.1	68.6	65.3	72.0	70.4
Estonia	9.6	5.9	65.3	68.1	73.0	72.5
Hungary	9.0	7.5	52.4	57.3	57.1	61.8
Latvia	14.3	6.8	59.9	66.3	69.6	71.1
Lithuania	13.2	5.6	62.3	63.6	72.2	67.6
Poland	10.9	13.8	58.9	54.5	66.2	66.3
Romania	5.3	7.3	65.4	58.8	71.5	64.1
Slovakia	12.6	13.4	60.6	59.4	69.3	68.7
Slovenia	6.9	6.0	62.6	66.6	67.4	71.2
C/PC						
Albania	14.9	14.0	59.0**	49.7*/**	71.1	65.1*
Bosnia and						
Herzegovina	40.9	41.0	na	29.7**	72.2	74.4*
Croatia	9.9	12.0	57.1	55.0*	64.3	64.2*
FYR Macedonia	36.1	36.0	36.5	34.1*	60.7	60.6*
Serbia	13.3	21.6	57.8	51.0*	na	63.6
Montenegro	21.8	30.3*	38.0**	34.8*/**	na	49.9*/**
Serbia and						
Montenegro	13.8	20.8	57.0	na	62.0	65.5*
Simple averages						
CEE/SEE	14.3	14.9	56.3	54.0	66.8	65.2
EU-10	10.1	8.2	60.0	61.9	68.3	67.8
C/PC	20.5	23.5	50.0	42.9	77.2	61.4
Euro area	10.5	7.9	58.4	64.5	65.9	70.3

Notes: C/PC average is calculated depending on the data availability as indicated in the table. (*) indicates 2005 data, (**) indicates working age population defined as 15 years and over.
Source: Eurostat, Statistical Offices, WDI.

In recent years, however, strong growth has had a positive impact on labour market developments in all countries under review. Unemployment rates declined or at least stabilised. In several countries, participation rates have been increasing as well, including Bosnia and Herzegovina and Serbia and Montenegro among the C/PC countries.

3.3.2   Structure of employment

The ongoing process of economic restructuring is captured by the changes in employment shares. In most countries, the share of services has been steadily increasing, while the shares of industry and especially agriculture have been decreasing (Table 3.5). This trend has been very pronounced in most EU-10 countries, but can also be observed in some of the C/PC economies. Exceptions include the former Yugoslav Republic of Macedonia – where the shares of services and industry have declined, while the share of agriculture has increased – and Bosnia and Herzegovina, where a shift has taken place from industry to agriculture.

Compared with the euro area, the share of agriculture in total employment is still high in some countries, especially in Albania (59 per cent) and Romania (36 per cent), but also in Bosnia and Herzegovina,

Table 3.5 Employment shares by broad economic sectors

	Services		Industry		Agriculture	
	1996	2005	1996	2005	1996	2005
EU-10						
Bulgaria	52.9	51.6	36.8	27.0	10.1	21.4
Czech Republic	52.6	57.9	41.2	38.1	6.1	4.0
Estonia	56.7	61.0	33.6	33.7	9.7	5.3
Hungary	58.6	62.7	33.0	32.4	8.4	4.9
Latvia	56.2	62.3	26.7	26.5	17.2	11.2
Lithuania	51.7	57.1	28.3	28.9	20.1	14.0
Poland	42.7	55.4	31.2	27.0	26.1	17.6
Romania	30.3	33.9	34.3	29.9	35.5	36.2
Slovakia	54.4	62.6	37.6	33.7	8.0	3.7
Slovenia	47.5	54.5	38.9	35.4	13.6	10.1
C/PC						
Albania	20.2	28.0	9.6	13.5	70.3	58.5
Bosnia and Herzegovina	45.2	48.7	51.1	30.8	3.7	20.5
Croatia	50.9	63.0	29.1	31.2	19.9	5.9
FYR Macedonia	59.1	48.4	32.7	32.4	8.3	19.6
Serbia and Montenegro	45.1	55.5	49.6	40.3	5.3	4.3
Turkey	34.3	48.2	22.3	26.2	43.4	25.6
Simple averages						
CEE/SEE	47.4	53.2	33.5	30.4	19.1	16.4
EU-10	50.4	55.9	34.2	31.3	15.5	12.8
C/PC	42.5	48.6	32.4	29.1	25.1	22.4
Euro area	66.4	70.4	28.1	25.2	5.5	4.3

Note: For Serbia and Montenegro (2004), Bosnia and Herzegovina (2006, 1991), Romania (2002) and Poland (1995).

Source: Eurostat (SM, RS and ME from WIIW).

the former Yugoslav Republic of Macedonia, Bulgaria and Turkey (20–26 per cent). In addition, the share of industry in total employment is significantly higher and the share of the services sector lower relative to the euro area average. Regional disparities have also emerged, as big cities as well as areas located close to EU borders and other main trading partners have experienced economic booms. By contrast, economic activity has been declining in other areas, previously active in agriculture or heavy industries, leading to sizeable labour market mismatches.

3.3.3   Labour market mismatches

The process of economic restructuring, leading to a shift from employment in agriculture and industry to services, had important consequences for the labour market as a whole. Jobs have been created in more productive sectors of the economy, while the demand for labour has been reduced in less productive areas. This resulted in a decrease in demand for lower-skilled workers, which in turn led to high unemployment rates among people with primary or secondary education. Table 3.6 provides evidence of existing mismatches of this kind, especially in the EU-10 countries. While the share of unemployed people with primary education amounts to 12 per cent of the labour force in the euro area, it is 49 per cent in Slovakia and close to 25 per cent in Poland and the Czech Republic. In these countries educational attainment has become an increasingly important factor in determining the employment status.

In the C/PC countries, probably due to the less advanced stage in transition, the unemployment rate for people with only primary education is below the levels of the euro area (with the exception of Croatia and the former Yugoslav Republic of Macedonia). This may reflect the fact that there is still a relatively large share of employment in industry and agriculture, sectors that have traditionally demanded lower-skilled labour. This situation is likely to change though, as the experience of the EU-10 countries suggests.

Labour market mismatches may be exacerbated by the increasing labour migration to EU countries following the opening of labour markets. This phenomenon can be observed in some of the EU-10 countries, where highly skilled workers (and also low-skilled ones with demanded skills such as construction, etc.) often prefer to relocate. Heinz and Ward-Warmedinger (2006) note that so far, in spite of a noticeable increase after the EU accession, the number of workers from the EU-10 countries employed in the EU-15 constitutes a relatively small share of the overall working age population (ranging between 0.1 per cent in France and the Netherlands to 1.4 per cent in Austria and 2 per cent in

Table 3.6 Unemployment rates by the level of education attained (2006) and by the type of unemployment (2005)

| | Unemployment rates | | | | | |
| | By education | | | By the type of unemployment | | |
	Primary	Secondary	Tertiary	Total	Youth	Long-term
EU-10						
Bulgaria	20.5	7.7	4.0	11.5	22.3	6.0
Czech Republic	24.8	6.4	2.5	7.9	19.2	4.2
Estonia	13.5	6.3	3.3	7.9	15.9	4.2
Hungary	16.7	6.9	2.8	7.2	19.4	3.2
Latvia	14.9	6.3	3.8	8.7	13.6	4.1
Lithuania	10.6	6.5	2.6	8.3	15.7	4.3
Poland	23.7	15.0	6.0	17.7	36.9	10.2
Romania	9.0	7.9	3.8	5.8	20.2	4.4
Slovakia	48.6	11.8	3.3	16.2	30.1	11.7
Slovenia	8.4	6.6	3.3	6.5	15.9	3.1
C/PC						
Albania	7.5**	6.3**	0.3**	14.5	26.8***	13.1
Bosnia and Herzegovina	7.9	21.8	1.4	42.0	8.8*	26.8
Croatia	13.0**	15.0**	6.2**	12.7	32.0	7.4
FYR Macedonia	18.9	14.8	2.9	37.3	71.3	34.6
Montenegro	5.8**	25.8**	3.3**	30.3	7.7	25.9
Serbia	4.4	14.5	1.8	21.8	47.7	17.0
Turkey	6.0**	2.9**	1.2**	10.2	19.3	4.1
Simple averages						
CEE/SEE	14.1	11.3	3.0	16.9	25.7	12.0
EU-10	19.1	8.1	3.5	9.8	20.9	5.5
C/PC	9.1	14.4	2.4	24.1	30.5	18.5
Euro area	11.5	8.1	5.1	8.3	17.7	3.8

Notes: (*) indicates 2006 data; (**) indicates 2005 data; (***) indicates 2002 data. Unemployment rates by education have been calculated as a percentage of working age population, 15–64 years, except for Albania, the former Yugoslav Republic of Macedonia and Montenegro, where they have been calculated relative to the overall labour force. The youth unemployment rate stands for unemployed persons aged 15–24 as a percentage of the labour force; long-term unemployment rate is the number of people in unemployment status of 12 months or more as a percentage of the labour force.

Source: Eurostat; except for the unemployment rates by education in Albania and Turkey (ILO's LABORSTA), in Bosnia and Herzegovina, the former Yugoslav Republic of Macedonia, Montenegro and Serbia (national statistical offices).

Ireland). Their analysis suggests that, while the migration of workers from the EU-10 countries may be a transitional phenomenon, it is likely to create some bottlenecks in their labour markets.[19]

Additional evidence of skill mismatches in labour markets may be derived from an analysis of youth and long-term unemployment (Table 3.6).

While the average long-term unemployment rate in the euro area (unemployment lasting over 12 months) is 4 per cent, it is 5.5 per cent in the EU-10 and 18.5 per cent in the C/PC countries, pointing to a low rate of exit from unemployment and signalling that some groups of unemployed have a minimal chance of finding employment.[20] However, particularly high rates in the C/PC countries may be biased by the extent of unregistered employment in the informal economy.

Another sign of significant labour market mismatches is the high degree of unemployment among 15–24 year-olds. While youth unemployment rates are generally higher than those for overall unemployment in the euro area (18 vs 8 per cent) and this difference is similar in relative terms in the EU-10 and many C/PC countries, in absolute terms the difference is especially high in the former Yugoslav Republic of Macedonia (71 vs 37 per cent), but also in Albania, Croatia, Serbia, Poland and the Slovak Republic (27 to 48 per cent vs 13 to 22 per cent). This may reflect an environment where seniority is important, in particular in large enterprises, creating entry barriers for the young (see, e.g., Nesporova, 2002). However, particularly high unemployment rates in this group may also result from the prevalence of the informal economy.

3.4   Capital accumulation

This chapter reviews the main determinants, trends and prospects for capital accumulation in the EU-10 and the C/PC countries, for both physical and human capital. The main results can be summarised as follows:

1. Investment as a share of GDP has increased significantly in the C/PC-5 countries, matching the corresponding indicator in the EU-10. Moreover, it has exceeded the euro area average. However, in contrast to the EU-7,[21] there has not yet been an overall shift of investment away from industry and towards services in C/PC countries.
2. In both sub-regions, the contribution of FDI to gross fixed capital formation has increased, indicating their continued attractiveness to foreign investors. In the EU-10, FDI has remained strong, with its structure changing from equity capital to reinvested earnings and other capital. This is also expected to happen in the C/PC countries after privatisation is completed.
3. There is a need for improvements in the quality of human capital in order to benefit from possible technology spillovers from FDI. However, public expenditures on education and R&D have remained low in both country groups.

4. Significant progress has been made towards reducing the administrative burden and creating a more business-friendly environment. However, there are still areas in which both groups of countries need further progress, especially in business regulation, competition policy and corruption.

3.4.1 Growth and capital accumulation

Economic literature has highlighted the positive link between investment rates and economic growth across countries (DeLong and Summers, 1991; Mankiw, 1995). In turn, the speed of capital accumulation – and implicitly growth – is influenced by the quality of a large set of institutional factors related to the rate of exit and entry of firms, the rate of introduction of new products, the registration of patents, tax credits and R&D grants among others (Nicoletti and Scarpetta, 2003; Alesina *et al.*, 2003; Arratibel *et al.*, 2007).

Investment rates have varied substantially across time and countries. In the EU-10, excluding Bulgaria and Romania, investment was already strong between 1996 and 2000, exceeding the euro area average (21 per cent of GDP) and indicating their advanced stage in the transition process (Table 3.7). During 2001–05 investment growth consolidated in most countries, while further acceleration could be observed in Estonia and Latvia. In Bulgaria and Romania, as well as in most C/PC countries, a substantial rise in investment occurred between 2001 and 2005, with investment levels notably strong in Albania, Bosnia and Herzegovina and Croatia, ranging between 21 and 27 per cent of GDP on average.[22] Turkey represents an exception to trends observed in the other countries, as the investment ratio declined from around 25 per cent of GDP in the late 1990s to less than 20 per cent in the early 2000s, following the economic downturns of 1999 and 2001.

Services have been attracting an increasingly large share of total investment in the EU-7, while the pattern of investment showed a higher degree of heterogeneity in the C/PC-5[23] (Table 3.7). During the early 2000s, the share of services in total investment was roughly 60 per cent or higher in the Czech Republic, Hungary and Slovenia. Within the C/PC countries, the share of services in total investment increased in the former Yugoslav Republic of Macedonia and Montenegro, but declined in Croatia and Serbia, due to rising investment in industry, particularly in construction and manufacturing. Despite the mixed overall picture, some of the C/PC-5 countries reported notably large shares of services in total investment relative to the EU-7 average – for example, 60 per cent in Croatia in 2001–04 and 67 per cent in Montenegro

Table 3.7   Investment-to-GDP ratios and investment shares by sectors

| | Investment-to-GDP ratios | | Investment shares by sector | | | |
| | | | Services | | Industry | |
	1996–2000	2001–2005	1996–2000	2001–2004	1996–2000	2001–2004
EU-10						
Bulgaria	13.7	20.1	55.2	56.2	42.2	40.8
Czech Republic	28.8	26.9	59.6	61.8	40.8	35.3
Estonia	26.8	28.3	–	–	–	–
Hungary	22.9	23.0	62.0	64.8	33.3	30.2
Latvia	21.4	25.8	–	–	–	–
Lithuania	21.9	21.3	–	–	–	–
Poland	23.4	19.2	55.0	58.1	42.5	39.9
Romania	19.8	21.9	41.0	45.6	51.0	47.0
Slovak Republic	31.6	26.6	64.3	56.5	32.6	40.4
Slovenia	24.5	24.0	56.0	59.9	42.9	39.0
C/PC						
Albania	17.0	23.1	–	–	–	–
Bosnia and Herzegovina	28.2	20.8	–	–	–	–
Croatia	22.6	27.0	62.5	60.1	34.4	37.3
FYR Macedonia	17.0	17.5	38.4	42.9	56.9	53.8
Serbia and Montenegro*	11.5	15.4	62.1	–	31.8	–
Serbia	–	–	–	*57.9*	–	*36.9*
Montenegro	–	–	–	*67.0*	–	*30.6*
Turkey	24.1	17.5	–	–	–	–
Weighted averages						
CEE/SEE	23.6	20.9				
EU-10	24.0	22.2				
C/PC	22.8	18.4				
C/PC-5	17.8	21.9				
EU-25	20.2	19.7				
Euro area	20.8	20.3				

Note: (*) For Serbia and Montenegro, investment shares by sectors have been computed based on data between 1998 and 2000; for Montenegro the shares have been computed based on data for 2003–2004.

Source: ECB staff calculations, based on the World Investment Report of UNCTAD (for the investment-to-GDP ratio) and WIIW data (for investment shares by sectors). Industry includes Mining; Manufacturing; Energy, Gas and Water Supply; and Construction.

during 2003–04 – also highlighting the importance of the tourism sector in those countries.

3.4.2 Developments in foreign direct investment

Domestic capital accumulation can be financed via domestic or foreign savings, with the latter taking the form of FDI, reinvested earnings or other capital flows.[24] Cross-border capital flows are expected to originate in countries where capital is abundant and head towards economies where capital is scarce, offering correspondingly higher rates of return. Moreover, FDI is often mentioned as a driver of investment and economic growth, in particular TFP growth, by fostering the internationalisation of production, increasing trade openness, stimulating the diffusion of foreign technology and fostering effective corporate governance and enterprise restructuring (Arratibel *et al.*, 2007).

FDI inflows have become an increasingly important component of total investment in both country groups. Between 1996 and 2005, the share of FDI in total investment rose from 19 per cent to 22 per cent in the EU-10 and from 4 per cent to more than 11 per cent in the C/PC. Despite a notable opening during 2001–05, FDI continued to have a relatively small contribution to total investment in Turkey (less than 10 per cent), while FDI accounted for more than 20 per cent of investment in all the C/PC-5 countries except Albania during 2001–05.

Net FDI flows have been increasing steadily in the EU-10 since the early years of transition. By contrast, in the C/PC an increase in FDI flows can be observed only starting in 1999–2000 (except for Croatia). This may be attributed to a relatively fast and successful macroeconomic stabilisation policy, rapid progress in structural reforms and EU accession as well as positive characteristics in terms of human capital and R&D in most of the EU-10 countries. Moreover, in the early to mid-1990s most C/PC countries were characterised by political instability and wars. According to 2006 data, FDI inflows remained strong in the EU-10 despite new investment opportunities created in the C/PC countries. While privatisation is largely completed in the EU-10, it is still a significant source of FDI in some C/PC countries.

In 1996–2000 net FDI flows have been particularly high in the Czech Republic, Estonia, Latvia and Hungary (Table 3.8).[25] In 2001–05, Estonia in particular, but also Bulgaria, the Czech Republic and Slovakia, stand out as having relatively high ratios of FDI as a percentage of GDP. Poland, ranking seventh in terms of net FDI flows as a percentage of GDP in 2001–05, has been the top recipient in absolute terms. In the C/PC countries for which comparable data are available across time, a

Table 3.8   Net FDI inflows

	Net FDI flows (percentage of GDP)		Net FDI inflows by form, 2006 (percentage of total FDI)		
	1996–2000	2001–2005	Equity capital	Reinvested earnings	Other capital (loans)
EU-10					
Bulgaria	1.5	3.3	51.1	7.7	41.2
Czech Republic	2.6	3.6	26.4	61.0	12.7
Estonia	2.5	4.4	11.6	65.8	22.6
Hungary	3.0	2.2	28.6	18.5	52.9
Latvia	2.5	1.4	35.7	43.1	21.2
Lithuania	1.7	1.4	58.9	37.8	3.3
Poland	1.9	1.5	21.3	40.4	38.3
Romania	0.9	1.9	45.1	21.5	33.3
Slovakia	1.5	3.1	45.2	20.2	34.6
Slovenia	0.6	1.1	79.6	−0.2	20.6
C/PC					
Albania	0.7	1.5			
Bosnia and Herzegovina	0.9*	1.4	47.9	14.1	37.9
Croatia	2.3	2.5	62.9	24.7	12.4
FYR Macedonia	0.8	1.6			
Simple averages					
CEE/SEE	1.3	2.2	47.9	25.5	26.6
EU-10	1.9	2.4	40.4	31.6	28.1
C/PC	0.8	2.0	55.4	19.4	25.1

Note: (*) indicates an average of 1999–2000.

Source: WIIW, ECB staff calculations.

significant increase in net FDI flows can be observed in Albania, Bosnia and Herzegovina and the former Yugoslav Republic of Macedonia.[26] All countries have experienced a steady increase in FDI stocks as a percentage of GDP, averaging 24 per cent in 2005. Estonia stands out with an FDI stock of more than 90 per cent, while the FDI stock in Turkey has remained broadly stable at around 10 per cent of GDP.[27]

The literature has identified several key determinants of FDI inflows into emerging markets, including the transition economies, for example: market size, agglomeration (clusters), openness, labour costs, business climate, and more recently also the quality of institutions.[28] Campos and Kinoshita (2003) find that FDI into transition countries is driven mainly by agglomeration, large market size, low labour cost and abundant natural resources. Moreover, countries with greater trade openness, fewer restrictions on FDI flows and good institutions are likely to receive more FDI.[29]

The importance of the quality of institutions, proxied by the overall EBRD transition indicator, is confirmed also in our sample of countries. More specifically, high scores in terms of the overall EBRD transition indicator in 2000 seem to have a positive impact on FDI developments in the following years, 2000–05 (Figure 3.5).[30] More specifically, there seems to be a positive correlation between the quality of institutional reforms and the ability to attract FDI inflows. Countries that have managed to attract a higher than average amount of FDI relative to their EBRD indicator score include Bulgaria, the Czech Republic, Estonia and Slovakia in the EU-10 and Croatia and Serbia and Montenegro in the C/PC.

FDI inflows have first taken the form of equity capital, either related to privatisation or as greenfield investment. Later, FDI inflows have been increasingly channelled through reinvested earnings and other capital. Indeed, in 2006 reinvested earnings and other capital combined exceeded the share of equity capital in the overall FDI inflows in seven of the EU-10 countries (Table 3.8). The structure of FDI inflows in Croatia is similar to that of the EU-10 countries, with equity capital and reinvested earnings playing the dominant role. On the other hand, in Bosnia and

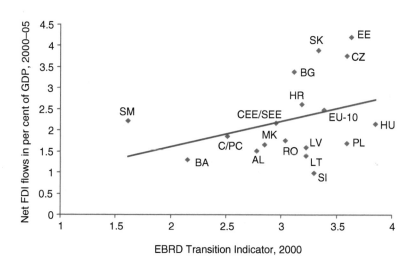

Figure 3.5 EBRD transition indicators and net FDI flows as a percentage of GDP

Note: For Serbia and Montenegro we use FDI inflows as a percentage of GDP.

Source: WIIW and EBRD, ECB staff calculations.

Herzegovina equity capital amounts to the largest share of overall FDI inflows (76 per cent), followed by other capital (24 per cent).

3.4.3 Human capital endowment

Investment in 'knowledge', defined as investment in R&D and education, is a necessary condition for strong economic growth and real convergence.[31] More specifically, infrastructure (capital that can facilitate and support the operational side of the technological progress) and a labour force capable of adapting the new technologies to the local environment are crucial for a successful adoption of technologies.[32] Three indicators are commonly used in order to summarise investments in 'knowledge': total expenditure on education, total expenditure on R&D as a percentage of a country's GDP and the share of 20 to 24-year-olds in the population who have completed at least upper secondary education.

In the EU-10 countries, public expenditures on education as a percentage of GDP are still quite low (Table 3.9). In 2004 only Hungary, Lithuania, Poland and Slovenia did better than the EU-25 average. Public sectors in the C/PC countries allocate an even smaller share of GDP to education. A similar picture emerges when total expenditure on research and development is considered (Table 3.9). In 2002 this amounted to 1.9 per cent of GDP on average in the euro area. In the region, it exceeded 1 per cent of GDP only in Slovenia, the Czech Republic, Croatia and Serbia and Montenegro.

EU-10 countries and some of the C/PC countries (e.g., Croatia and Serbia) score better than the euro area average in terms of the share of 20 to 24-year-olds in the population who have completed at least secondary education. While this average is 74 per cent for the euro area, it is 85 per cent in the EU-10 countries and 73 per cent in the candidate and potential candidate countries. This is in line with Landesmann *et al.* (2004). In addition, they argue that in the EU-10 countries among the 'medium-educated' there is a larger proportion of those who have completed vocational training programmes rather than general upper secondary education as compared with the EU-15, making this labour force particularly suitable for employment in medium-skilled industries. However, the ongoing structural changes and productivity catch-up, in particular, tend to reduce employment in industry. In addition, as voiced by Feldmann (2004), there is a concern that the system of secondary education in transition countries is not able to prepare adequately to face the changing market conditions. This would suggest that the quantitative indicators on the level of education in the countries under review have to be interpreted with care.

Table 3.9 Total public expenditures on education and R&D (Percentage of GDP)

	Education			R&D
	1997	2004	2004/1997***	2002
EU-10				
Bulgaria	2.7	4.6	72.5	0.5
Czech Republic	4.5	4.4	−0.9	1.2
Estonia	5.9	5.1	−14.0	0.7
Hungary	4.6	5.4	17.0	1.0
Latvia	5.4	5.1	−6.4	0.4
Lithuania	5.5	5.2	−4.6	0.7
Poland	4.8	5.4	13.4	0.6
Romania	4.4*	3.3	−25.2	0.4
Slovakia	4.8	4.2	−12.8	0.6
Slovenia	na	6.0		1.5
C/PC				
Albania	3.3	3.2	−3.0	na
Croatia	na	4.5	na	1.1
FYR Macedonia	na	3.4**	na	0.3
Serbia	4.0	3.5	−12.5	1.2
Turkey	2.9	3.8	29.3	0.7
Simple average				
CEE/SEE	4.1	4.6	12.3	0.7
EU-10	4.7	5.4	14.9	0.8
C/PC	3.4	3.7	8.8	0.6
EU 25	4.8	5.1	6.9	1.9****

Notes: (*) indicates 1998 data, (**) 2003 data, (***) indicates change in percentage points, (****) indicates the euro area average.

Source: Eurostat and WDI.

.4.4 Institutional environment

here is a broad agreement that the quality of the institutional envir-
nment has a strong impact on investment and growth.[33] Measuring
ıe degree of market deregulation is not an easy task since there is no
andardised way of comparing institutional developments among
ɔuntries. One such attempt is provided by the EBRD, which publishes
ıe so-called transition indicators, covering nine main areas. The EBRD
ansition indicators suggest that the EU-10 countries have achieved the
:vel of standards and performance of advanced industrial economies
ı terms of price liberalisation and trade and foreign exchange system
ʃable 3.10). Substantial progress has been made in the area of small-scale

Table 3.10 EBRD's transition indicators (2007) and WB's governance indicators (2005)

	Privatisation		Enterprise restructuring	Price liberalisation	Trade and Forex system	Competition policy	Banking reform and interest rate liberalisation	Securities markets and non-bank financial institutions
	Large-scale	Small-scale						
EU-10								
BG	4.0	4.0	2.7	4.3	4.3	2.7	3.7	2.7
CZ	4.0	4.3	3.3	4.3	4.3	3.0	4.0	3.7
EE	4.0	4.3	3.7	4.3	4.3	3.7	4.0	3.7
HU	4.0	4.3	3.7	4.3	4.3	3.3	4.0	4.0
LV	3.7	4.3	3.0	4.3	4.3	3.0	3.7	3.0
LT	4.0	4.3	3.0	4.3	4.3	3.3	3.7	3.0
PL	3.3	4.3	3.7	4.3	4.3	3.0	3.7	3.7
RO	3.7	3.7	2.7	4.3	4.3	2.7	3.0	2.0
SK	4.0	4.3	3.7	4.3	4.3	3.3	3.7	3.0
SI	3.0	4.3	3.0	4.0	4.3	2.7	3.3	2.7
C/PC								
AL	3.0	4.0	2.3	4.3	4.3	2.0	2.7	1.7
BA	2.7	3.0	2.0	4.0	3.7	1.7	2.7	1.7
HR	3.3	4.3	3.0	4.0	4.3	2.3	4.0	3.0
MK	3.3	4.0	2.7	4.3	4.3	2.0	2.7	2.3
ME	3.3	3.0	2.0	4.0	3.3	1.0	2.7	1.7
RS	2.7	3.7	2.3	4.0	3.3	1.7	2.7	2.0
Simple averages								
CEE/SEE	3.4	3.9	2.8	4.2	4.1	2.4	3.3	2.6
EU-10	3.8	4.2	3.2	4.3	4.3	3.1	3.7	3.1
C/PC	3.1	3.7	2.4	4.1	3.9	1.8	2.9	2.1

	Voice and accountability	Political stability	Government effectiveness	Regulatory quality	Rule of law	Control of corruption
EU-10						
BG	0.59	0.16	0.23	0.63	-0.19	-0.05
CZ	1.01	0.69	0.94	1.04	0.70	0.42
EE	1.05	0.68	1.03	1.43	0.82	0.88
HU	1.10	0.79	0.79	1.11	0.70	0.63
LV	0.89	0.83	0.68	1.03	0.43	0.33
LT	0.90	0.88	0.85	1.13	0.46	0.26
PL	1.04	0.23	0.58	0.82	0.32	0.19
RO	0.36	0.03	-0.03	0.17	-0.29	-0.23
SK	1.04	0.69	0.95	1.16	0.41	0.43
SI	1.08	0.94	0.99	0.86	0.79	0.88
C/PC						
AL	0.08	-0.68	-0.49	-0.27	-0.84	-0.76
BA	-0.11	-0.78	-0.53	-0.53	-0.74	-0.32
HR	0.51	0.32	0.44	0.45	0.00	0.07
MK	0.03	-1.04	-0.28	-0.20	-0.38	-0.50
SM	0.12	-0.91	-0.31	-0.53	-0.81	-0.55
TK	-0.04	-0.54	0.27	0.18	0.07	0.08
Simple averages						
CEE/SEE	0.50	-0.01	0.28	0.39	-0.02	0.02
EU-10	0.91	0.59	0.70	0.94	0.41	0.38
C/PC	0.10	-0.61	-0.15	-0.15	-0.45	-0.33
Euro area	1.27	0.77	1.46	1.35	1.43	1.50

Notes: Regarding the EBRD transitions indicators, score 4.3 characterises standards and performance typical of advanced industrial economies; 4.0 is given if a country has achieved substantial convergence with the advanced industrial economies. The shaded cells indicate that the country has achieved a score of at least 4.0. Regarding the WB's governance indicators, all scores are between –2.5 and 2.5, with higher scores indicating better governance. The shaded cells indicate when the C/PC or EU-10 countries reach or exceed the level of the euro area.

Source: EBRD and the World Bank.

privatisation and to a lesser extent in large-scale privatisation. More progress is needed in terms of banking reform and interest rate liberalisation, where only three countries are characterised by well-functioning banking competition and banking supervision. Most EU-10 countries also need substantial improvements in the area of securities markets and non-bank financial institutions, including regulatory changes and improvements in market capitalisation and liquidity, governance and enterprise restructuring, competition policy and overall infrastructure reform. In the C/PC-5, more limited progress has been achieved.

The Fraser Institute provides a more subjective measure of the institutional environment, consisting of indicators for the administrative burden in seven crucial areas. Indicators on the administrative burden on the private sector, for example, show that the countries under review have all recorded significant progress in recent years, but there are areas in which they are lagging behind the euro area average. These include in particular price controls and irregular payments.

According to the World Bank's (WB) Governance Indicators, in 2005 the countries in the region still lagged behind the euro area average in terms of the quality of governance (Table 3.10). The scores for the six governance indicators range between –2.5 and 2.5, with higher scores indicating better governance. In five out of six indicators the C/PC average was negative, indicating relatively low quality of governance, especially in terms of political stability and the rule of law. Although none of the EU-10 averages was below zero, the scores were particularly low in terms of the control of corruption and the rule of law. On average, the EU-10 nevertheless strongly outperforms the C/PC, also reflecting the adoption of the *acquis communautaire* as a prerequisite for EU entry.

In conclusion, significant progress has been made in terms of the institutional environment in the countries under review. However, more progress is needed, especially concerning the rule of law and the control of corruption, as well as business regulation and competition policy.

3.5   Conclusions

All countries in Central, Eastern and South-Eastern Europe have seen a strong recovery, following notable output losses during the early 1990s. However, by 2006 only the EU-10 countries and Albania and Croatia had managed to surpass their 1989 levels of total income in real terms. For the period 1993–2005, absolute convergence only holds for the EU-10, but not for the Western Balkans, as C/PC-5 countries experienced wars, severe political instabilities and a slow pace of reforms for most of the

1990s. Thus, for the region as a whole, absolute convergence emerged only after 1999, when almost all countries saw strong growth fostered by structural reforms, investment and FDI.

Labour productivity has improved in most countries, as the share of productive sectors in total output rose and overall employment declined. TFP growth has been the main driver of convergence, whereas labour has contributed only marginally to economic growth. After the elimination of inefficiencies linked to the former regime of central planning, sustained TFP growth may be more difficult to achieve. Thus, further improvements in capital accumulation and capital efficiency are needed to contribute more to sustain convergence in the future.

Central, Eastern and South-Eastern European countries have experienced adverse developments in their labour markets, namely falling employment and participation rates, triggered initially by severe output losses and later by shifting production patterns. These negative trends have been gradually reversing, although at a different speed depending on the countries' overall economic recovery and the effectiveness of the introduced reforms. While the employment rates have been slowly increasing, on average they are still at significantly lower levels than in the euro area. Similarly, unemployment rates, especially in the C/PC, are much higher on average than in the euro area countries.

Structural changes have resulted in, at least temporarily, increasing labour market mismatches. In most countries there has been a noticeable shift of employment from agriculture and industry to employment in the services sector. While this shift signals that the countries under review have been converging to the economic structure observed in mature economies, strong and increasing demand for skilled labour is only partly matched by supply. Therefore, workers with the highest education levels are characterised by the lowest unemployment rates. Higher unemployment rates among the youth as well as high long-term unemployment rates provide additional evidence of existing labour market mismatches and a still high degree of labour market inflexibility in many Central, Eastern and South-Eastern European countries.

Investment rates have been rising rapidly in recent years. While in the EU-10 countries there has been a shift of investment away from industry and towards the services sector, a similar development has not yet taken place in the C/PC-5 countries. FDI has been found to have a positive impact on total investment. More specifically, countries that received more FDI relative to total investment also reported a larger level of investment relative to GDP. Therefore, FDI flows continue to provide a good basis for further investment growth, leading to improvements in capital accumulation and its efficiency. In the EU-10 countries FDI inflows are increasingly channelled in the form of reinvested earnings and other capital. A similar shift has started to take place in some of the C/PC countries and it can be expected to continue once privatisation is largely completed.

Investment in human capital proxied by the share of expenditure on education in total GDP is still at a relatively low level compared with the euro area average. Similarly, spending on R&D constitutes only a small share of GDP. Given the need for strong economic growth allowing for real convergence towards the euro area, a rise in human capital investment seems to be warranted. This holds even though most countries are characterised by a relatively well-educated labour force, which is indicated by the high percentage of 20–24-year-olds with at least secondary education.

Substantial progress has been made in improving the institutional framework, in particular in terms of removing administrative barriers and creating a more business-friendly environment. Areas in which further improvements are needed include business regulation, competition policy and corruption. Therefore, continued reforms in these areas would enhance the potential for further economic growth and capital accumulation.

In conclusion, Central, Eastern and South-Eastern European countries have been experiencing strong economic growth and improvements in the labour markets, as well as buoyant investment, including strong increases in FDI inflows. In order to sustain these positive developments in the medium to long-term and experience continued real convergence to the euro area, further improvements are needed in terms of labour productivity and utilisation, as well as in terms of capital accumulation. To the extent that recent overall growth has been mainly driven by TFP and not by capital accumulation and labour, it is key to emphasise the importance of further reforms and economic restructuring aiming at improving labour markets, as well as facilitating strong investment growth.

Notes

The authors would like to thank H.-J. Klöckers, C. Nerlich, F. Moss, L. Rawdanowicz, A. Winkler as well as country experts in the EU Neighbouring Regions Division of the ECB for useful comments. To a large extent, the chapter has been inspired by the analysis in the ECB Occasional Paper No. 61 (Arratibel *et al.*, 2007), also used as a reference.

1. By way of comparison, the example of emerging Asia suggests that strong capital accumulation is needed for a sustained catching-up with advanced economies (IMF, 2006c), given that TFP growth rates can be assumed to be rather similar in advanced and emerging economies in a non-transition context.
2. The growth process in Turkey, the only non-transition economy in the sample, has been interrupted by three sharp recessions in 1994, 1999 and 2001, following financial and exchange rate crises and natural disasters.
3. Regional averages are GDP-weighted averages. Calculating unweighted averages yields similar results, in line with the general patterns described in the text. The only exception is the C/PC group, where differences are sometimes significant given the large weight of Turkey, a non-transition economy. This is accounted for by focusing on the C/PC-5 and Turkey separately throughout the analysis when appropriate.
4. The EBRD transition indicator summarises progress in structural reforms that are usually carried out at an early stage of the transition process – small-scale privatisation, price liberalisation, trade and foreign exchange liberalisation – and structural reforms of a more long-term nature, such as large-scale privatisation, governance and enterprise restructuring, competition policy, development of the banking sector, security markets, non-banking financial institutions and infrastructure reform. The EBRD is assigning numerical scores to indicators corresponding to these reform areas. The scores range from 1 (little or no change from a planned economy) to 4.3 (the standard for an advanced market economy).
5. Calculations were based on the GGDC-based levels of total output relative to 1989, which are generally in line with those reported in EBRD (2006), with two notable exceptions. The relative level of income per capita in Bosnia and Herzegovina is much higher in the GGDC-based calculations (2005: 153 vs only 70 per cent reported by the EBRD). To a smaller extent, the same is true for Albania (164 vs 137 per cent, respectively). For the remaining countries the difference in the GGDC and EBRD 2005 per capita income levels does not exceed 5 percentage points.
6. Table 3.2 provides data for 1989, 1993, 1997, 2001 and 2005 only. References in the text for intermediate years are based on the GGDC dataset.
7. Given the lower level of initial income per capita in the C/PC countries in 1993, the pattern is in line with what theory predicts. However, it should be noted that growth of income per capita in the C/PC-5 also reflects the sizeable post-war recovery in Bosnia and Herzegovina during the late 1990s.
8. Previous studies have also investigated and validated empirically the concept of absolute convergence across entities linked by various degrees of political and economic integration, such as the US states (Barro and Sala-i-Martin, 2004), Japanese prefectures (Barro and Sala-i-Martin, 1992), regions within EU countries (Barro and Sala-i-Martin, 1991), Indian states (Cashin and Sahay, 1995) and South Pacific countries (Cashin and Loayza, 1995).
9. Cross-sectional dispersion of income per capita has been stable in the EU-10, while it increased in the C/PC countries, contradicting sigma convergence (Table 3.3). Sigma convergence is a corollary of absolute/conditional convergence. As countries with a lower level of income are expected to grow faster than richer ones, the dispersion of per capita income across countries should fall over time.

10. It would be desirable to study labour productivity in terms of output per total hours worked, since it captures the differences in working times across countries. However, due to data unavailability for the C/PC countries, the analysis is performed on the basis of 'the number of employed people'. It covers the period 1998–2005 in order to avoid incongruous results, such as the low labour utilisation and the artificially high labour productivity in Bosnia and Herzegovina in the mid-1990s due to the war.

11. Labour productivity is the highest in the services sector in almost all countries under review, with agriculture being the least productive sector in most cases. For example, in the EU-10 (C/PC-5), productivity in services exceeded on average by about 20 per cent (30 per cent) the level of overall productivity in the economy in 2005.

12. The definition of labour utilisation is distinctly different from the definition of participation in the labour market. In principle, labour utilisation should always be lower than the participation rate, as it does not take into account the unemployed in the nominator, while having the total population, and not only the working age population (15–64-year-olds), in the denominator (see note 18 below for the definitions of the labour market indicators).

13. The share of shadow economy exceeded 35 per cent of GDP only in Bulgaria, Estonia, Latvia and Romania.

14. Assuming a classic Cobb-Douglas production function, we have computed TFP growth as follows:

$$\frac{TFP_t}{TFP_{t-1}} = \frac{\dfrac{GDP_t}{GDP_{t-1}}}{\left(\dfrac{K_t}{K_{t-1}}\right)^{\alpha}\left(\dfrac{L_t}{L_{t-1}}\right)^{1-\alpha}}$$

where K and L represent the capital stock and employment, α and $(1-\alpha)$ are the corresponding shares of capital and labour in GDP. In the absence of reliable and comparable data on capital stocks in the countries reviewed, we have approximated them by the perpetual inventory method as in Arratibel *et al.* (2007). In particular, we have assumed $\alpha = 0.35$, and have estimated the capital stocks using the perpetual inventory method, that is $K_t = K_{t-1}$ $(1 + i_t - d)$, where i_t is the rate of investment growth between t and $t-1$ estimated from GFCF growth as in Arratibel *et al.* (2007), and d is the annual rate of depreciation of the capital stock, assumed to be $d = 0.07$.

15. While similar results have been found by Doyle *et al.* (2001), European Commission (2004) and IMF (2006a), a possible underestimation of employment and the capital stock might be responsible for an artificially high contribution of TFP to economic growth. Thus, we also performed a robustness test by assuming that the capital stock at the beginning of transition was zero (that is 1989 year-end). We then applied the law of motion of capital ($K_t = (1-d)K_{t-1} + i_t$), with data on real gross fixed capital formation starting in 1990 available for all transition countries but the Baltic states, Bosnia and Herzegovina, Serbia and Montenegro and Turkey. Using this approach, the role of TFP growth and capital accumulation in driving growth was more balanced for most countries, as the contribution of capital

accumulation to economic growth was at least as large as that of TFP growth during 2002–06.

16. Our calculations show that the share of TFP in total growth declined in the EU-10 and C/PC country groups, from 140 and 192 per cent during 1997–2001, to 84 and 94 per cent, respectively, during 2002–06. On average, the share of capital accumulation in total growth increased from –31 and –188 per cent to 6 and 27 per cent, respectively. However, the results are sensitive to the method used for the capital stock estimation (see note 15 above).

17. The share of labour in total growth changed from –29 and –7 per cent during 1997–2001 to 11 and –21 per cent, respectively, during 2002–06.

18. *Employment rate* = Employment / Working Age Population; *Unemployment rate* = Unemployment / Labour Force; *Participation rate* = Labour force / Working Age Population, where *Labour Force = Employed + Unemployed* and the *Working Age Population* refers to the number of 15–64-year-olds in the overall population (unless otherwise indicated). *Euro area* means throughout the chapter the euro area as of 1 January 2001 (with 12 members, not yet including Slovenia).

19. Mansoor and Quillin (2006) provide an overview of migration patterns in the region. Moreover, it should be stressed that labour mobility and migration are also associated with benefits for the sending countries, for example those arising from remittances and training of workers abroad (see, e.g., Arratibel *et al.*, 2007 and Dos Santos and Postel-Vinay, 2003).

20. In some countries, certain ethnic groups are characterised by higher unemployment. For example, unemployment rates in the former Yugoslav Republic of Macedonia varied significantly between various ethnic groups. While it was 28 per cent for ethnic Macedonians, it was about 41 per cent for Turks, 51 per cent for Albanians and 72 per cent for Roma (IMF, 2006b).

21. WIIW data on investment at the sectoral level does not cover the Baltic States.

22. However, it should be noted that compared with other emerging market economies, in particular those in emerging Asia, investment rates are not extraordinarily high.

23. Data are available only for Croatia, FYR Macedonia, Serbia and Montenegro.

24. In contrast to catching-up processes in other parts of the world, the process of real convergence in Central, Eastern and South-Eastern Europe has been accompanied by significant and in several countries widening current account deficits. According to Abiad, Leigh and Mody (2007), Europe has been different as it benefited from rapid financial integration, allowing a convergence process in line with the predictions of standard economic theory.

25. In the remainder of this section both net FDI flows and FDI stocks are analysed in relative terms as a percentage of GDP to avoid distortions due to differences in country sizes. Developments and the ranking of net FDI flows and FDI stocks in per capita terms are broadly similar to the ones observed for FDI as a percentage of GDP.

26. Compared also with other emerging markets, FDI flows to the region have been high, for example – as a share of GDP – exceeding those of emerging markets in Asia (Herrmann and Winkler, 2007).

27. Indeed, in less than twenty years the countries under review have achieved – on average – a level of inward FDI stock, expressed as a percentage of GDP, that is comparable to or even higher than in other emerging and developing countries.
28. The importance of institutions is noted for example by Mauro (1995) and La Porta *et al.* (1998).
29. In addition, Bevan and Estrin (2004) argue that EU announcements about accession prospects increase FDI inflows to countries that are evaluated positively.
30. This indicator is calculated as a simple average of nine indicators developed by the EBRD to measure progress in transition. See note 4 for more details on the indicators.
31. For an overview see Hanushek and Wößmann (2007).
32. Van den Berg (2001) argues that human capital is essential for technological progress, including adopting foreign technologies. Analysing the potential for FDI spillovers, Blomström and Kokko (2003) stress that potential benefits of FDI are only realised if the initial level of education and human capital is sufficiently high. Borensztein *et al.* (1998) find that the impact of FDI on growth depends on the level of human capital in the host country. In particular, they show that there is a strong positive relationship between FDI and educational attainment.
33. See for example IMF (2003) and Alesina *et al.* (2003). A different opinion is provided by Glaeser *et al.* (2004).

Bibliography

A. Abiad, D. Leigh and A. Mody (2007) 'International Finance and Income Convergence: Europe is Different', IMF Working Paper No. 64, International Monetary Fund (IMF), Washington.

A. Alesina, S. Ardagna, G. Nicoletti and F. Schiantarelli (2003) 'Regulation and Investment', NBER, Working Paper No. 9560.

O. Arratibel, F. Heinz, R. Martin, M. Przybyla, L. Rawdanowicz, R. Serafini and T. Zumer (2007) 'Determinants of Growth in the Central and Eastern European EU Member States – a Production Function Approach', ECB Occasional Paper Series No. 61.

R.J. Barro and X. Sala-i-Martin (1991) 'Convergence across States and Regions', Brookings Papers on Economic Activity No. 1, 107–82.

R.J. Barro and X. Sala-i-Martin (1992) 'Regional Growth and Migration: A Japan-United States Comparison', *Journal of the Japanese and International Economies*, 6, 312–46.

R.J. Barro and X. Sala-i-Martin (2004) *Economic Growth*, 2nd edition, Cambridge, MA, MIT Press.

A. Bevan and S. Estrin (2004) 'The Determinants of Foreign Direct Investment into European Transition Economies', *Journal of Comparative Economics*, 32, 775–87.

M. Blomström and A. Kokko (2003) 'Human Capital and Inward FDI', CEPR Discussion Paper No. 3762.

E. Borensztein, J. De Gregorio and J.-W. Lee (1998) 'How Does Foreign Direct Investment Affect Economic Growth?', *Journal of International Economics*, 45, 115–35.

N.F. Campos and Y. Kinoshita (2003) 'Why Does FDI Go Where It Goes? New Evidence from the Transition Economies', IMF Working Paper No. 228.

P. Cashin and N. Loayza (1995) 'Paradise Lost? Growth, Convergence and Migration in the South Pacific', IMF Working Paper No. 28.

P. Cashin and S. Ratna (1995) 'Internal Migration, Center-State Grants and Economic Growth in the States of India', IMF Working Paper No. 66.

P. Cashin and R. Sahay (1995) 'Internal Migration, Centre State Grants and Economic Growth in the States in India', IMF Working Paper No. WP/95/66.

S. Commander and J. Kollo (2004) 'The Changing Demand for Skills: Evidence from the Transition', IZA Discussion Paper No. 1073.

J.B. DeLong and L.H. Summers (1991) 'Equipment Investment and Economic Growth', *Quarterly Journal of Economics*, 106(2), 445–502.

S. Djankov and P. Murrell (2002) 'Enterprise Restructuring in Transition: A Quantitative Survey', *Journal of Economic Literature*, 40, 739–92.

M. Domingues Dos Santos and F. Postel-Vinay (2003) 'Migration as a Source of Growth: The Perspective of a Developing Country', *Journal of Population Economics*, 16(1), 161–75.

P. Doyle, L. Kuijs and G. Jiang (2001) 'Real Convergence to EU Income Levels: Central Europe from 1990 to the Long Term', IMF Working Paper No. 146.

EBRD (2004) 'Spotlight on South-Eastern Europe. An Overview of Private Sector Activity and Investment', European Bank for Reconstruction and Development, London.

EBRD (2006) 'Transition Report 2006. Finance in Transition', European Bank for Reconstruction and Development, London.

European Commission (2004) 'Catching Up, Growth and Convergence of the New Member Economies', CEPR Discussion Paper No. 3798.

H. Feldmann (2004) 'How Flexible Are Labour Markets in the EU Accession Countries Poland, Hungary and the Czech Republic?', *Comparative Economic Studies*, 46(2), 272–310.

E.L. Glaeser, R. La Porta, F. Lopez-de-Silane and A. Shleifer (2004) 'Do Institutions Cause Growth?', NBER Working Paper No. 10568.

E.A. Hanushek and L. Wößmann (2007) 'The Role of Education Quality in Economic Growth', World Bank Policy Research Paper No. 4122.

F. Heinz and M. Ward-Warmedinger (2006) 'Cross-Border Labour Mobility within an Enlarged EU', ECB Occasional Paper No. 52.

S. Herrmann and A. Winkler (2007) 'Real Convergence, Financial Development and the Current Account – Emerging Europe versus Emerging Asia', mimeo.

G. Hunya (2006) 'WIIW Database on Foreign Direct Investment in Central, East and Southeast Europe', The Vienna Institute for International Economic Studies.

IMF (2003) 'Growth and Institutions', World Economic Outlook, April 2003.

IMF (2006a) 'Growth in the Central and Eastern European Countries of the EU – a Regional Overview', IMF Occasional Paper No. 252.

IMF (2006b) 'Former Yugoslav Republic of Macedonia, Selected Issues', IMF Country Report No. 06/345, October 2006, Washington DC.

IMF (2006c) 'Asia Rising: Patterns of Economic Development and Growth', *World Economic Outlook*, September, Chapter 3.

G. Iradian (2007) 'Rapid Growth in Transition Economies: Growth-Accounting Approach', IMF Working Paper No. 164.

J. Kornai (1992) *The Socialist System: The Political Economy of Communism*, Princeton, NJ, Princeton University Press.

R. La Porta, F. Lopez-de-Silanes, A. Shleifer and R.W. Vishny (1998) 'Law and Finance', *Journal of Political Economy*, 106(6), 1113–55.

M. Landesmann, H. Vidovic and T. Ward (2004) 'Economic Restructuring and Labour Market Developments in the New EU Member States', The Vienna Institute for International Economic Studies.

N.G. Mankiw (1995) 'The Growth of Nations', *Brookings Papers on Economic Activity*, 1995(1), 25th Anniversary Issue, 275–326.

A. Mansoor and B. Quillin (2006) 'Migration and Remittances – Eastern Europe and the Former Soviet Union', The World Bank, Washington DC.

P. Mauro (1995) 'Corruption and Growth', *Quarterly Journal of Economics*, 110(3), 681–712.

A. Nesporova (2002) 'Why Unemployment Remains So High in Central and Eastern Europe?', International Labour Organization (ILO).

G. Nicoletti and S. Scarpetta (2003) 'Regulation, Productivity and Growth: OECD Evidence', *Economic Policy*, April, 11–72.

OECD (2007) 'PPP', FAQs, Statistics Directorate.

T. Padoa-Schioppa (2002) Structural Challenges and the Search for an Adequate Policy Mix in the EU and in Central and Eastern Europe, Speech at the 2002 East-West Conference, Vienna, 4 November.

P. Rao (2001) 'Weighted EKS and Generalized CPD Methods for Aggregation at Basic Heading Level and above Basic Heading Level', Joint World Bank – OECD seminar on Purchasing Power Parities, Washington DC, 20 January – 2 February 2001, http://www.oecd.org/dataoecd/23/22/2424825.pdf

P. Rao and M. Timmer (2000) 'Multilateralisation of Manufacturing Sector Comparisons: Issues, Methods and Empirical Results', Research Memorandum GD-47, Groningen Growth and Development Centre, July 2000, http://www.ggdc.net/pub/gd47.pdf

F. Schneider (2004) 'The Size of the Shadow Economies of 145 Countries All over the World: First Results over the Period 1999 to 2003', IZA Discussion Paper No. 1431, December 2004.

H. Van den Berg (2001) *Economic Growth and Development*, Singapore, McGraw-Hill.

4
The Link between Real and Nominal Convergence: The Case of the New EU Member States

Sarah Lein, Miguel Leon-Ledesma and Carolin Nerlich

4.1 Introduction

The new EU member states (EU-9)[1] have made remarkable progress in past years in terms of real economic convergence with the euro area, that is, their standards of living and income levels have gradually increased towards those of the euro area. Still, the EU-9 countries display GDP per capita and price levels which are considerably below those of the euro area. Thus, the catching-up process will need to continue for some time. Income level convergence is usually accompanied by a continuous rise in the price level, which under certain conditions and also depending on the underlying exchange rate regime implies a higher inflation rate than in the euro area. Thus, the process of real convergence in the EU-9 is expected to continue playing an important role for future inflation developments in these countries. The interdependence of real and nominal convergence becomes particularly relevant, as the EU-9 are expected to join the euro area, for which *inter alia* the Maastricht inflation criterion needs to be fulfilled in a sustainable manner. From the perspective of the euro area, potentially higher inflation rates in the EU-9 countries would imply higher inflation differentials. Although the impact on the euro area inflation rate will most likely be limited due to the relatively low economic weight of the EU-9 compared with the euro area, this may nevertheless complicate the conduct and communication of a common monetary policy within an enlarged euro area.

Against this background, there is a need to analyse in more detail the link between real and nominal convergence. How can the long-term process of real convergence affect the price level and possibly inflation dynamics in the EU-9 countries? What are the channels through which this link works? Do the channels vary across countries and what determines them? How is the link between real and nominal convergence expected to change in the years to come?

So far there is only little information about the various channels through which real convergence is affecting the price level and subsequently inflation in the EU-9 countries. In the literature, a few channels are discussed. The Balassa-Samuelson effect is certainly the most prominent one, which is also at the centre of policy discussions when it comes to the EU-9 countries. But there are also other important real convergence-related factors that can be expected to affect the price level and drive inflation developments in these countries. In this chapter, we concentrate on six channels that we expect to be the most relevant ones for the non-euro area EU countries. Besides productivity growth developments, we look at changes in the consumption pattern towards more non-tradeable goods, which is expected to have an upside impact on the price level. Moreover, as a result of real convergence energy intensity is assumed to decline, which in turn could have a favourable impact on prices, in particular as long as energy price increases are above average. A decline in the frequency and size of macroeconomic shocks in gradually maturing economies can also be expected to have a favourable impact on prices. Lower volatility is likely to help to anchor inflation expectations and achieve price stability. Another potential channel works through credit growth, which is expected to increase in a catching-up environment. The impact of higher credit growth on prices, however, is not clear, as it can work in both directions. A rise in trade openness due to real convergence is also likely to affect the price level in both directions.

In this chapter we focus on the six channels mentioned above, which we expect to be the most relevant ones for the EU-9 countries. However, there might be also other channels through which real convergence could impact on inflation in the EU-9 countries. These are, for example, the impact of quality improvement, changes in the endowment ratio or the role of administered prices, which can change in a catching-up environment and would determine the price level.

Real convergence can affect the price level and subsequently inflation in both directions. Moreover, depending on the country-specific structural features and settings of the respective EU-9 countries, the countries can be assumed to be differently affected by real convergence. This is in particular the case for the underlying exchange rate regime, which varies considerably across the EU-9 countries. Countries with a fixed exchange rate regime are obviously not able to use the nominal exchange rate for a real appreciation, so that the adjustment can only take place through prices. Moreover, the flexibility of labour and product markets and the soundness of macroeconomic policies also play a crucial role on how real convergence is affecting nominal convergence.

The focus of this chapter is on the link between catching-up and the price level in the EU-9 countries, that is, how the ongoing process of convergence can affect inflation dynamics. We do not look at the external side of this question, namely how real convergence leads to a real appreciation. Moreover, we abstract from possible policy reactions that inflationary pressures may trigger in these countries, in particular the impact of potential monetary policy reactions on inflation, as we are precisely interested in how real convergence may pose challenges for inflation stabilisation policies. Unfortunately, with the current framework of the analysis, we are not able to quantify the relative importance of the different channels for each country, which is expected to differ across countries. Finally, although we ask how the channel will develop over time, we do not try to answer the question of how the link between real convergence and inflation would change after the EU-9 countries joined the euro area. This would go far beyond the scope of this chapter, while it might be a potential area for future research.

The chapter is organised as follows. The next section contains some stylised facts on the catching-up in income and price levels in the EU-9 compared with the euro area. In Section 4.3 we discuss the most important channels through which real convergence can affect the level of inflation in the EU-9 countries and how these channels are likely to develop in the years to come. Section 4.4 offers some conclusions.

4.2 Real convergence: Stylised facts and prospects

In the past decade, the EU-9 made considerable progress in catching-up with income levels in the euro area (Figure 4.1). Between 1995 and 2007, the GDP per capita level in PPP terms in the EU-9 increased from 36 per cent of the euro area to around 52 per cent.[2] In fact, within this period, the GDP growth rates in the EU-9 stood on average at 5 per cent, compared with around 2 per cent in the euro area. Moreover, the progress in catching-up varied considerably across countries, with the largest increase being experienced by the Baltic States.

Looking ahead, real convergence is expected to gain further momentum in the long run, in particular as EU and euro area memberships are

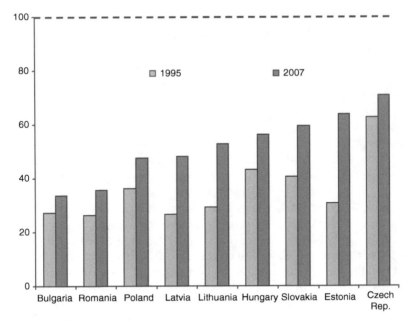

Figure 4.1   GDP per capita in the EU-9 (in per cent of euro area average in PPP terms)

Source: Eurostat.

assumed to add some further stimulus.[3] Nevertheless, real convergence is a very gradual process and will most likely continue for the next decades. Depending on the speed at which the income gap between the EU-9 and the euro area is assumed to be reduced each year – in our example we used for demonstration purposes catching-up rates between 7 and 3 per cent[4] – it will take roughly between 12 and 31 years for the EU-9 as a whole to reach on average a level of at least 80 per cent of the euro area (Figure 4.2).

The average price level in the EU-9 countries, calculated on the basis of the private consumption deflator, stood in 2007 at around 56 per cent of the euro area, compared with 38 per cent in 1995 (Figure 4.3).[5] There are, however, some differences across countries, with the Baltic States and Romania experiencing the strongest pick-up in the price level (by around 30 percentage points) during the last decade. Higher increases in the price level relative to a benchmark country are usually associated with a higher inflation rate relative to the benchmark country. Thus, a further catching-up in price levels implies that the inflation

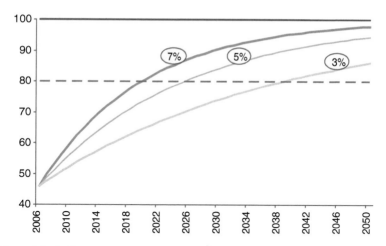

Figure 4.2 Different scenarios of catching-up in real income (GDP per capita in PPP terms, in per cent of euro area average)

Notes: The catching-up rate indicates the speed by which the gap the GDP per capita levels between in the euro area and the EU-9 is expected to shrink each year. In this figure we used rates of 3, 5 and 7 per cent. The higher the catching-up rate, the faster is real convergence. By looking at the catching-up rate we implicitly assume that the GDP growth rate differentials between the EU-9 and the euro area and therefore the speed of real convergence will gradually decline over time as real convergence advances.

Source: Eurostat and own calculations.

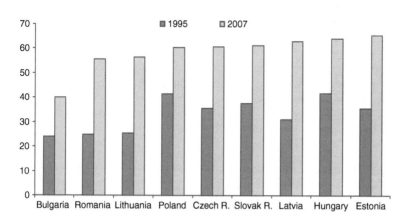

Figure 4.3 Price levels in the EU-9 (Private consumption deflator in per cent of euro area average)

Source: Eurostat.

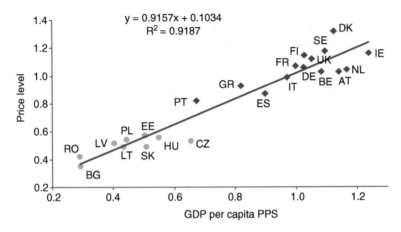

Figure 4.4 GDP per capita and price levels in the EU countries (Average 2000–06)

Notes: EU-27 countries excluding Luxembourg; GDP per capita and price levels in per cent of the euro area average. Price levels are based on the private consumption deflator.

Source: Eurostat, own calculations.

rates in the EU-9 countries will most likely be above the inflation rate of the euro area.

According to the literature, there is strong empirical evidence for a positive relationship between the price level and GDP per capita.[6] For the EU countries, we obtain an elasticity of the relative price level to the relative GDP per capita level (expressed in PPP terms) of around 0.92 for the period 2000 to 2007, that is, a 1 per cent increase in relative GDP per capita implies a 0.92 per cent increase in the relative price level (Figure 4.4). Around 92 per cent of the variation in the relative price level can be explained by changes in the relative income level and a constant. In fact, most of the countries that made large progress in real convergence during the past decade also displayed stronger increases in their relative price level.

4.3   Potential channels of real convergence affecting price levels

In this section we discuss the main potential channels through which real convergence is likely to affect the price level in the EU-9. In the academic literature, reference is mainly made to the Balassa-Samuelson effect. But there are also other important real convergence-related factors that can be expected to drive inflation developments in these countries and which are worth examining in more detail. Besides the productivity growth channel, we look in this chapter in particular at changes in the consumption patterns towards more non-tradeable goods, the gradually declining energy intensity of production, lower macroeconomic volatility, higher credit growth and an increasing degree of external openness. All these channels can be expected to influence the level of inflation, although not necessarily in the same direction or magnitude. We also discuss in this chapter how the importance of each of these channels is likely to develop over time with real convergence progressing. While there might also be additional channels through which real convergence could impact on inflation,[7] we concentrate on those that can be expected to be the most relevant ones for the EU-9. Yet, the ordering of the different channels in this section does not necessarily reflect their empirical importance for the countries. In fact, given that each channel is analysed separately, such a ranking of importance across channels is not possible within this framework. Finally, it is important to keep in mind that we discuss here the potential impact of various real convergence-related factors on the price level and possibly also on inflation. Yet, depending on the underlying exchange rate regime, it can be assumed that countries would react differently to real convergence. Thus, to get an idea of the exact impact on the price level and on inflation in each country it would be crucial also to take the exchange rate developments into account. This, however, is far beyond the scope of this chapter. Thus, when discussing the impact of the various real convergence-related factors on inflation, we abstract from the potential impact that real convergence might have on the nominal and real exchange rate and we also do not discuss potential policy reactions.

4.3.1 Productivity growth and the Balassa-Samuelson effect

According to the well-known Balassa-Samuelson (B-S) effect, a catching-up economy is assumed to experience more rapid convergence of productivity levels in the tradeable goods sector than in the non-tradeable goods sector. Stronger productivity growth in the tradeable goods sector pushes up wages in this sector. Under the assumption of perfect labour mobility across sectors, wages rise in the whole economy. As the productivity growth in the non-tradeable sector is assumed to be relatively lower, higher wages in this sector translate into higher prices of non-tradeable goods and hence an increase in the overall price level. This is often referred to as the internal version of the B-S effect,[8] while the external version of the B-S effect compares productivity growth differentials between the tradeable and non-tradeable sectors and its inflationary impact across countries. Assuming that the nominal exchange rate is determined by purchasing power parity in the tradeable sector, an increase in the price level in the catching-up economy following an increase in productivity will *ceteris paribus* result in an appreciation of the CPI-based real exchange rate in the EU-9. In this chapter, however, we focus only on the internal version of the B-S effect.

In contrast to the B-S effect, which assumes a positive impact of productivity growth on prices, there are also good reasons to argue that higher productivity growth in the tradeable sector can have a dampening impact on inflation. In fact, rising productivity growth in the tradeable sector may lead to higher product variety and increased aggregate supply, which would imply more competition in this sector. Higher competition, however, would force firms to reduce their mark-ups, which in turn would impact favourably on inflation.[9] This so-called competition effect would be even more important in countries with a high degree of trade openness (see also Section 4.3.6).

There is ample empirical evidence in the literature for the existence of the B-S effect in the EU-9 countries.[10] According to Lein *et al.* (2008) this effect seems to be attenuated if countries open up to international trade and thereby more competition. Estimates of the internal version of the B-S effect, that is, the impact of higher productivity growth in the tradeable sector on the relative price of non-tradeable goods, vary considerably across studies, depending on the applied methodology, the respective countries, the included control variables and the sample period. In the selected studies summarised in Table 4.1, estimates of the B-S effect range widely between close to zero and around 3 percentage points per annum. Estimates are usually lower with panel analysis than with time series analysis. In most studies the panel estimates are clearly below 1 percentage point per annum. Country-specific estimates of the B-S effect vary widely across countries. Yet, when looking at Table 4.1, there seems to be a pattern across countries. For the Czech Republic and Slovakia the estimated B-S effect is relatively low in most studies (on average between 0 and 2 percentage points per annum), while the B-S effect seems to play a relatively larger role in Hungary and Poland (on average the effect is estimated to be in the range of 1 and 3.5 percentage points per annum).

The Balassa-Samuelson effect has been often criticised for its underlying assumptions. This relates in particular to the assumption of perfect labour mobility across sectors, the argument of rather low productivity growth in the service sector and the law of one price in the tradeable

Table 4.1 Selected studies on the Balassa-Samuelson effect in the EU-9 countries

Authors (Year)	Time and cross-sectional dimension (EU-9)	Methodology	Dependent variable	Explanatory variable	Estimate of the BS effect*
Halpern and Wyplosz (2001)	1991–1999 CZ, EE, HU, LV, LT, PL, SK, SI (among others)	GLS	Non-tradeable to tradeable goods price ratio	Productivity in tradeable sector, productivity in non-tradeable sector	2.4 (Panel)
Egert (2002)	1993–2001 CZ, HU, PL, SK, SI	Cointegration Test, VAR	Inflation Differential (vis-à-vis DM) in non-traded goods	Relative productivity	0.2–0.6 (CZ) 2.6–3.5 (HU) 1.5–3.3 (PL) −0.2– −0.4 (SK)
National Bank of Hungary (2002)	1993–2001 CZ, HU, PL, SK, SI	Accounting	CPI-based real exchange rate	Relative productivity	1.6 (CZ) 1.9 (HU) 1.0–2.0 (SK)
Mihajlek and Klau (2003)	1992–2001 CZ, HU, PL, SK, SI	OLS	Non-tradeable to tradeable goods price ratio	Domestic productivity growth differential	0.3 (CZ) 1.6 (HU) 1.4 (PL) 0.6 (SK)
MacDonald and Wojcik (2003)	1995–2001 EE, HU, SK, SI	DOLS	Inflation differential (vis-à-vis Austria) in non-traded goods	Relative productivity	0.5–0.6 (Panel)
Blaszkiewicz et al. (2004)	1995–2003 CZ, EE, PL, LT, SK, (among others)	Panel (FMOLS and PMG)	Non-tradeable to tradeable goods price ratio	Relative productivity	0.4–0.6 (Panel) 0.5–0.6 (CZ) 0.8–1.0 (EE) 0.8–0.9 (LT) 1.2–1.3 (PL)
Coricelli and Jazbec (2004)	1990–1998 CZ, EE, HU, LV, LT, PL, SK, SI (among others)	Fixed effects	Non-tradeable to tradeable goods price ratio	Relative productivity	0.9 (Panel)
Mihajlek and Klau (2005)	1995–2005 CZ, HU, PL, SK, SI	OLS	Non-tradeable to tradeable goods price ratio	Domestic productivity growth differential	0.3 (CZ) 0.2 (HU) 0.2 (PL) 0.0 (SK)

Note: (*) Impact of productivity growth in the tradeable and non-tradeable sectors on the relative price of non-tradeable goods, expressed in percentage points per annum (internal BS effect).

sector.[11] From an empirical point of view, the data on job flows as well as relative wage developments do not support the assumption of perfect labour mobility in the EU-9 countries (Égert, 2007). On sectoral productivity growth, there is some evidence of productivity growth in the tradeable sector being higher than in the non-tradeable sector in most EU-9 countries. However, technological advances can be expected to strongly improve productivity in the service sector, in particular in the banking and insurance sector (Rogoff, 1996). Moreover, it is worth noting that the estimates of the B-S effect could be distorted due to difficulties in distinguishing between tradeable and non-tradeable goods. Many items that are usually considered as tradeable goods also contain a non-tradeable component. In addition, frequent changes in administered prices affect relative prices and could thereby disfigure the actual size of the B-S effect, as mainly non-tradeable goods and services are administered.[12] In the EU-9, most administered prices have been gradually increased closer towards cost-recovery levels,[13] which can partly explain the higher inflation rate in the service sector in the past years, in particular as the share of administered prices in the consumer basket appears to be still relatively high in the EU-9 countries compared with the euro area.

With real convergence advancing, how will the Balassa-Samuelson effect develop in the coming years? While it is obvious that the B-S effect will disappear once the process of real convergence is concluded, the short- to medium-term prospects for the B-S effect are less clear. Some rough indication can be derived from the empirical studies listed in Table 4.1, which suggest that the estimated size of the B-S effect is on average lower in those studies that focus on a later period, in which the GDP per capita levels are already somewhat higher. However, the relationship between the B-S effect and real convergence might not be linear, as suggested by the opposing arguments below:

- The main argument suggesting that the B-S effect is likely to gain further importance with real convergence advancing is the assumption that the share of non-tradeable goods is likely to increase in the consumer price basket (see Section 4.3.2). A higher weight of non-tradeable goods would *ceteris paribus* imply a higher leverage of the B-S effect, which would result in higher overall inflation.
- On the other hand, it can be argued that the B-S effect might become less important due to faster productivity growth in the non-tradeable sector, which would result in a gradually declining productivity growth differential in the tradeable relative to the non-tradeable

sector. Anecdotal evidence suggests that FDI inflows are increasingly oriented towards the non-tradeable sector (namely the banking, insurance and IT sector), which can be assumed to contribute to stronger productivity growth in this sector. For the distribution sector in the EU-9 there is in fact already empirical evidence that substantial FDI inflows led to strong productivity growth in this sector and changes in relative prices (MacDonald and Ricci, 2001; MacDonald and Wojcik, 2003).

- Moreover, as product market reforms need to be advanced further, this might lead to higher productivity growth in the non-tradeable sector and, as a consequence of higher competition, to a reduced mark-up and smaller relative price changes. Labour market reforms aimed at improving wage differentiation across sectors are likely to diminish the B-S effect, while measures to increase labour mobility would per se have the opposite effect.

While the productivity channel described above reflects an equilibrium adjustment process of relative prices, real convergence might be also accompanied by developments which are not equilibrium-based. In particular, it is possible that in the context of the catching-up process pressures emerge for wage levels to converge at a non-sustainable pace.[14] It could be even argued that the risk of wage growth exceeding productivity growth might increase with the EU-9 eventually becoming part of an enlarged euro area. This relates to the so-called demonstration effect, which assumes that with a common currency wage levels become more comparable across countries so that trade unions might aim to more strongly equalise wage levels upwards across the member countries (Demertzis and Hallet, 1995; Jackman, 1997). However, for the current euro area countries there is no strong empirical evidence supporting this hypothesis (Mora *et al.*, 2005) and for the EU-9 the risk of unsustainable wage level convergence might be further limited as collective bargaining seems to be weak in most of these countries (Arratibel *et al.*, 2007).

4.3.2   Changes in the consumption pattern

While the Balassa-Samuelson effect is a supply side phenomenon, real convergence can affect the price level also through the demand side. This relates mainly to changes in the consumption pattern, as it can be expected that with higher wealth the demand for non-tradeable goods and services will increase relative to tradeable goods. This phenomenon is known as the Linder hypothesis (Linder, 1961).[15] With respect to its inflationary impact, an increase in the consumption of non-tradeable goods is assumed to result in a higher overall price level and from a dynamic perspective a rise in inflation, due to, first, higher prices of non-tradeable goods at least in the short run, and, second, a gradually increasing weight of non-tradeable goods in the consumer price basket. With respect to the first aspect, a higher income level is expected to result in higher absolute and relative demand for non-tradeable goods.[16] Under the assumption of inelastic supply in the short run, this is expected to lead to higher price increases of non-tradeable goods.[17] Several empirical studies confirm a positive relationship between the consumption of non-tradeable goods and relative prices.[18] With respect to the second aspect, an increasing weight of non-tradeable goods in the HICP consumption basket would affect overall inflation to the extent that relative inflation of non-tradeable goods is higher. In addition, a higher HICP weight of non-tradeable goods is likely to amplify the inflationary impact of the Balassa-Samuelson effect (see Section 4.3.1).

Looking at the EU-9, there seems to be empirical support for the Linder hypothesis. Figure 4.5 shows a positive relationship between real GDP per capita and the consumption of services relative to goods in

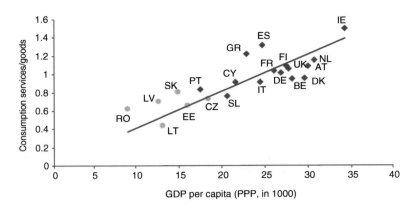

Figure 4.5   Consumption of services relative to goods and GDP per capita (PPP)

Notes: The definition of the consumption of goods and services follows the definition of the HICP breakdown. The relative consumption ratios are calculated for all EU countries (excluding Luxembourg) for which all 39 HICP sub-groups are available. Bulgaria, Hungary, Malta and Poland are not included. Data refers to 2006 (except for Denmark, Portugal and the UK data refer to 2004 and for Cyprus, Latvia, Lithuania, the Netherlands and Slovenia data refer to 2005).

Source: Eurostat and own calculations.

the EU countries.[19] The higher the countries' GDP per capita level, the more people seem to consume services relative to tradeable goods.[20] At the same time, it appears that the consumption patterns in the EU-9 are still very different from those in the more mature euro area countries. If one takes Germany as a benchmark country, the difference in the consumption pattern between the respective EU-9 countries and Germany can be measured by constructing a deviation coefficient.[21] This coefficient calculates the difference of consumption expenditures on various groups of goods in comparison to the reference country.[22] The deviation coefficient is particularly high in Romania and Lithuania, that is, the consumption pattern in Romania and Lithuania seems to differ substantially from that in Germany (Figure 4.6). This points to a positive relationship between the income gap and the deviation coefficient, that is, the more similar the GDP per capita level of the country is to the benchmark country, the more similar seems to be the consumption pattern. However, it should be borne in mind that country-specific tastes can also influence the consumption pattern irrespective of the GDP per capita level.

Thus, the consumption pattern in the EU-9 countries can be assumed to gradually converge towards the one in the more advanced euro area

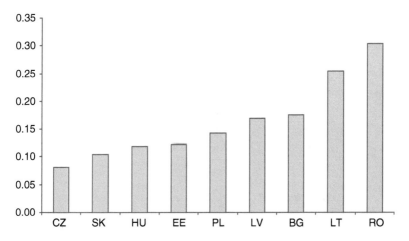

Figure 4.6   Deviation coefficient in the EU-9 relative to Germany (2006)

Notes: The deviation coefficient calculates the difference of consumption expenditures on various groups of goods in comparison to the reference country Germany (see endnote 21). A low coefficient indicates a rather similar pattern with the reference country Germany. Data refer to 2006, except for Bulgaria, Latvia and Lithuania it is 2005.

Source: Eurostat and own calculations.

countries.[23] As regards the development of the deviation coefficient over time, the coefficient decline was most pronounced in countries with a relatively low GDP per capita level in the mid-1990s, that is, in Bulgaria, Latvia, Lithuania and Romania, while it remained broadly constant in the Czech Republic and Hungary (Figure 4.7). As a declining deviation coefficient implies that the composition of a country's consumption basket gradually converges towards the benchmark's consumption basket, it can be argued that a lower coefficient points to a higher share of non-tradeable goods in the country's consumption basket. Assuming dual inflation, that is, higher inflation of non-tradeables compared with tradeables, a decline in the deviation coefficient points to an upward impact on the country's price level. As this is likely to be a continuous process it is likely also to affect inflation. Thus, with respect to the EU-9, at least part of the underlying inflationary pressures in the low-income countries could in principle be related to changes in their consumption pattern towards more non-tradeable goods.

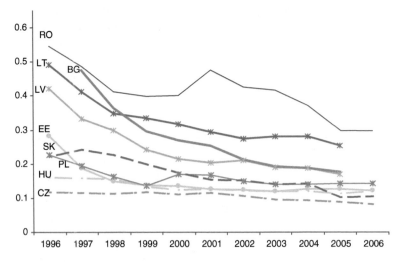

Figure 4.7 Development of the deviation coefficients over time in the EU-9 (1996–2006)

Notes: The deviation coefficient calculates the difference of consumption expenditures on various groups of goods in comparison to the reference country Germany (see endnote 21). A low coefficient indicates a rather similar pattern with the reference country Germany. Data refer to the period 1996–2006, except for Bulgaria (1997–2005) and Latvia and Lithuania (1996–2005).

Source: Eurostat and own calculations.

Looking ahead, adjustments of the consumption pattern are likely to continue mainly in those EU-9 countries which have still a relatively low GDP per capita level, such as Bulgaria and Romania, but also in Latvia, Lithuania and Poland. This might impact on price level convergence and possibly inflation in these countries. The impact on the price level is, however, likely to decline over time, as the income elasticity of the relative consumption of services to goods is expected to gradually decline with a higher GDP per capita level.

4.3.3 Energy intensity and production costs

Real convergence might have a dampening effect on price level convergence of the EU-9 countries as a continuous decline in energy consumption is likely to result in a lower increase in production costs. With real convergence progressing, the countries' total energy consumption usually increases. However, energy intensity, defined as the ratio of energy consumption to GDP, is likely to converge towards the lower levels usually observed in more mature economies due to efficiency gains.[24] In fact, more advanced economies can better afford to implement energy-saving technologies in the production process, transportation and for private consumption. Moreover, energy intensity might decline if real convergence triggered a change in the countries' production structure. As the countries' comparative advantage changes over time, the predominant role of the (heavy) industry sector can be expected to be gradually overtaken by the less energy-intensive service sector.

Overall, a decline in energy intensity implies *ceteris paribus* lower production costs. This, in turn, would have a dampening effect on price level convergence if the decline in production costs were passed on to the consumers. With respect to the EU-9 countries, energy intensity is considerably higher than in the euro area countries (Figure 4.8). In 2004, the EU-9 countries needed on average around five times more energy than the euro area to produce one unit of real GDP, with the relative energy intensity ranging from 2.8 in Hungary to 8.7 in Bulgaria compared with the euro area. Yet, energy intensity has declined noticeably in the EU-9 countries since the beginning of transition. Between 1995 and 2004, energy intensity fell by 29 per cent for the EU-9 average, compared with a decline of around 9 per cent in the euro area.[25] It can therefore be assumed that the sharp decline in energy intensity in the EU-9 countries had a dampening impact on production costs in these countries. Yet, whether this was passed on to consumers depends also on the countries' degree of product market competition and labour market flexibility. Moreover, the sharp increase in energy prices and

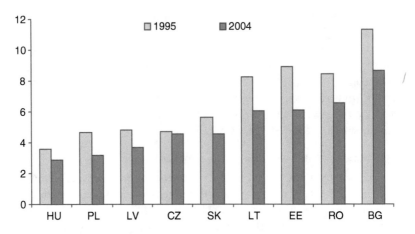

Figure 4.8   Energy intensity in the EU-9 (in relation to the euro area)

Notes: The figure shows energy intensity in the EU-9 in relation to energy intensity in the euro area in 1995 and 2004. Energy intensity is measured as the ratio of gross inland energy consumption, expressed in tonnes of oil equivalent, to real GDP.

Source: Eurostat.

other cost factors such as wages suggest that the dampening effect on production costs was limited in the past. The main reasons for energy price inflation being so high in these countries refer not only to the sharp increase in world oil prices but also to structural reasons such as the deregulation in the energy sector which brought energy prices closer to cost-recovery levels and the fact that excise taxes on household energy, gas and fuel prices need to converge towards the minimum level required by the EU legislation.[26]

Higher energy efficiency should in principle also be reflected in a lower weight of the energy-related items in the HICP basket (such as transport, water, electricity, gas and fuels). This in turn would also have a dampening impact on price level convergence, assuming that energy prices are above average inflation. Looking at the EU-9 countries, the HICP basket weights of energy-related items are still well above those of the euro area and inflation of the energy-related items exceeded overall HICP inflation. In the past years, the energy-related weights declined in a number of countries due to efficiency gains in energy consumption, which suggests a dampening impact on inflation and price level convergence. In some countries, however, the HICP weight of energy-related items increased as the rise in energy consumption must have outpaced any efficiency gains.

Looking ahead, with real convergence progressing energy intensity is likely to converge further towards the level observed in the euro area, although country-specific factors will remain. This might have, in principle, a dampening impact on production costs and thereby on price level convergence. Yet, this also depends on energy price inflation, structural features and the degree of energy consumption. Energy prices are likely to remain above average inflation due to a continuous shortage in energy resources in view of increasing world demand for energy. Moreover, further structural reforms and deregulation in the energy sector in the EU-9 countries is likely to bring energy prices further towards their cost-recovery levels. Also excise taxes on household energy need to be increased further. Yet, with real convergence progressing further, the relevance of the energy-intensity channel will diminish over time.

4.3.4 Reduced macroeconomic volatility

With real convergence advancing, the frequency and size of macroeconomic shocks are likely to decline in the EU-9 economies. Lower macroeconomic volatility is in turn assumed to have a favourable impact on anchoring inflation expectations and therefore achieving price stability.[27] Due to this, reduced macroeconomic volatility can be argued to have a favourable impact on the price level.

The dampening impact of real convergence on macroeconomic volatility is to a large extent related to the fact that the EU-9 countries underwent a major transformation process from a centrally planned to a market-based economy in the early years of transition. The restructuring of the economies and the implementation of same far-reaching structural reforms generated a strong degree of macroeconomic volatility in the countries. At the same time, sound macroeconomic policies had to be implemented, and it usually takes time for them to gain credibility. Macroeconomic volatility started to decline in recent years, with the adjustment process being largely completed by now and as increasingly sound macroeconomic policies are in place in the EU-9 countries. In addition, inflation volatility is likely to decline in the EU-9 countries as the weights of the most volatile HICP items in the consumer basket, such as food, which are still considerably higher than in the euro area, will converge towards those prevailing in the euro area, reflecting changes in the consumption pattern. Taking all these factors together, it can be argued that gradually declining macroeconomic volatility can be expected to have a favourable impact on anchoring inflation expectations and therefore achieving price stability, as it would help to improve the signalling mechanism of prices. Moreover, lower inflation volatility would facilitate for agents in an economy to formulate their pricing strategies, reduce contracting costs and decrease the costs of borrowing. At the same time, it can be argued that the causality could also be the other way around, namely that a decline in inflation volatility could facilitate the process of real convergence. In fact, some studies show that a high degree of inflation volatility might have a negative impact on output and investment (Blanchard and Simon, 2001; Judson and Orphanides, 1996).

In the EU-9 countries the degree of macroeconomic volatility appears to be still considerably higher than in the euro area, when looking at the standard deviation of industrial production and HICP inflation as a proxy for macroeconomic volatility (Figure 4.9). It should be noted, however, that to some extent the higher degree of volatility in the EU-9 compared with the euro area can be also explained by the fact that most of the EU-9 are small and open economies, which are usually more exposed to external shocks. Moreover, the respective EU-9 countries are differently affected by exchange rate developments, due to their different exchange rate regimes in place. This might also explain the country differences in macroeconomic volatility. Generally speaking it is worth noting that a certain degree of macroeconomic volatility is warranted as it partly also reflects the ability of the economy to adjust to economic shocks.

Looking ahead, further progress with real convergence can be assumed to lower macroeconomic volatility in the EU-9 countries. Thus, by helping to anchor inflation expectations real convergence is likely to contribute to lower inflation. Some of the factors that have been responsible for rather large macroeconomic volatility in the EU-9 countries, such as the need for a substantial restructuring of the economy and the imperfect access to capital markets, have disappeared or improved. Moreover, inflation volatility is likely to decline as changes in the consumption pattern will bring the weight of the most volatile HICP components in the consumer basket closer to that in the euro area. Moreover, countries with higher per capita levels usually experience less frequent changes in administered prices and indirect taxes, which have also been a source of inflation volatility in the EU-9 countries.

4.3.5   Higher credit growth

Real convergence usually comes along with financial deepening and strong credit growth. According to the 'financial deepening argument', credit growth increases more rapidly than output during the

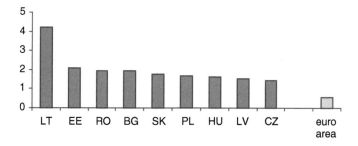

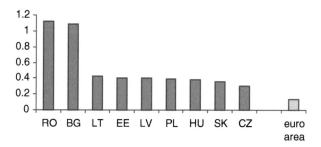

Figure 4.9 Volatility of industrial production and HICP inflation in the EU-9 (1998–2007)

Notes: Macroeconomic volatility is measured by the average of the quarterly standard deviation of industrial production and HICP inflation (monthly data, 1998–2007). For industrial production, seasonal and working-day adjusted data (for Bulgaria from 2000 onwards).

Sources: Eurostat and own calculations.

catching-up phase of an economy (King and Levine, 1993), as improved financial conditions of the private sector in form of higher expected income and profits allow for higher levels of indebtedness. Moreover, firms may want to maintain the ratio between internal and external capital as the economy is growing. At the same time, banks are usually more willing to lend to the private sector in regions with good growth potential (Kiss *et al.*, 2006).

The impact of higher credit growth on price level convergence and inflation is ambiguous, depending on a number of factors, namely the sectoral composition of credit growth and the equilibrium level of the stock of credit which is largely determined by fundamentals such as the level of economic development (Égert *et al.*, 2006). On the one hand, it can be argued that higher credit growth limits the effect of demand pressures on inflation, as economic agents have less liquidity constraints to finance investments, which would subsequently result in higher output (Blinder, 1987; Calza and Sousa, 2005; McCallum, 1991). Thus, under these circumstances rising credit growth would have a dampening impact on inflation. On the other hand, however, credit growth far beyond what would be in line with economic fundamentals can be expected to trigger financial bubbles and strong demand pressures, which would subsequently result in higher inflation. This also depends on the sectoral composition of credits to the private sector. In particular, rapid growth in household loans mainly used for consumption purposes can be expected to foster consumption far beyond equilibrium, which would cause inflationary pressures. Moreover, in the long run risks to price stability might also emerge in case of strong growth in mortgage credits to the extent that this triggers a boom in housing prices.

With respect to the EU-9 countries, credit growth to the private sector was strong in a number of countries, especially in the Baltic States, which seemed to be partly correlated with their lower level of economic development (Figure 4.10).[28] So far, however, there is only little evidence that credit growth caused inflationary pressures in the EU-9 countries. This might also reflect that most countries had a very low starting point in terms of financial depth. Only for the Baltic countries has there been some indication that the strong growth in credit in recent years contributed to price dynamics (Backé and Zumer, 2005; Terrones and Mendoza, 2004). According to the literature, the credit-to-GDP ratio in Estonia and Latvia already exceeded their equilibrium levels determined by the level of economic development, while credit growth seemed to be already close to equilibrium in Hungary (Égert *et al.*, 2006). Yet, inflationary pressures arising from credit growth also depend largely on the sectoral composition of credit growth and their relative importance. In this context it is important to note that growth in consumer credit was particularly strong in the Baltic States and Slovakia (around 60 per cent and above in 2006), but reversed partly during 2007.

In the long run and irrespective of temporary interruptions, credit growth in the EU-9 is likely to be high and in some countries to increase even further as the degree of financial deepening is expected to gradually converge closer to that of more mature economies. Stronger credit growth can be expected to cause some inflationary pressures in the EU-9 in the coming years, in particular if the countries' credit-to-GDP ratios exceed their equilibrium levels and if most of the credit expansion relates to consumer credits.

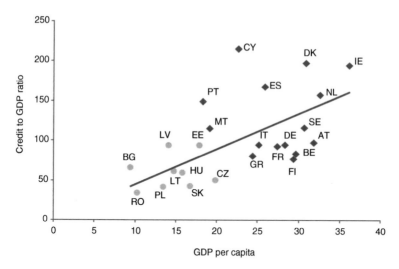

Figure 4.10 Credit to the private sector and real convergence in EU countries (2007)

Note: GDP per capita in PPP terms. EU countries excluding Luxembourg, Slovenia and the United Kingdom.

Source: Eurostat and BSI.

4.3.6 Greater openness

Real convergence might lead through increased specialisation and productivity expansion to a higher degree of trade openness, as firms are likely to become more export-intensive with a higher share of import penetration.[29] This in turn would affect the pass-through of international prices, which could influence inflation developments in the EU-9.

Greater openness can have an impact on the price level in both directions.[30] On the one hand, greater openness might generate higher price levels, to the extent that prices of tradeable goods catch up with international prices through the law of one price (Kravis and Lipsey, 1988; Maier, 2004). Moreover, the structure of imported goods might change over time, as with real convergence countries are likely to import goods of higher quality. This in turn could imply higher prices for tradeable goods. On the other hand, however, there are several arguments to assume that higher openness will have a dampening effect on prices (Chen *et al.*, 2004, 2007; Romer, 1993; Terra, 1998). First, higher trade integration contributes to higher competition in domestic markets and supports the relocation of production of many internationally traded goods to countries with a comparative advantage. This in turn reduces

mark-ups and lowers prices. Second, openness reduces the inflationary bias. Incentives for policy makers to create surprise inflation are
expected to be lower in more open economies, as the ability to temporarily stimulate domestic output is smaller because of the relatively
smaller share of non-tradeable goods in consumption and the induced
exchange rate depreciation.

With respect to the EU-9 countries, the direction in which openness
is affecting inflation hinges to a large extent on the country-specific circumstances, such as the price level of tradeable goods, the underlying
monetary policy regime and the scope for further trade integration.
There is empirical evidence that increased openness leads to reduced
mark-ups and costs and therefore can have a negative impact on prices
(Lein *et al.*, 2008). Looking ahead, it should be borne in mind that the
degree of openness is generally already rather high in the EU-9 countries, standing in 2007 at a weighted average of around 123 per cent
compared with 80 per cent in the euro area (Figure 4.11). Therefore, it
can be assumed that the future impact of real convergence on openness is likely to be rather small, although joining a common currency
area might provide some further impetus for openness due to lower
exchange rate risks and transaction costs.[31]

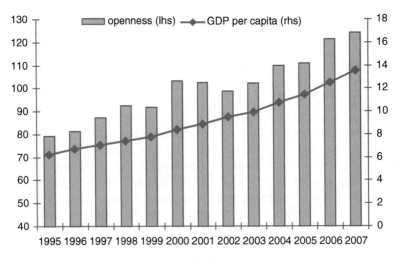

Figure 4.11   Real convergence and openness in the EU-9 (1995–2007)

Note: Openness is measured as exports plus imports as a percentage of GDP (weighted
average); real convergence is measured as GDP per capita (in PPP terms, in 1000).

Source: Eurostat.

4.4 Conclusions

The chapter discusses the impact of real convergence on prices in the EU-9 and how this is likely to develop in the coming years. Several channels are analysed in detail, through which real convergence could affect nominal convergence. These are the Balassa-Samuelson effect, changes in the consumption pattern, decline in energy intensity, lower macroeconomic volatility, higher credit growth and greater openness.

A number of conclusions can be drawn from the analysis. First, the current level of real convergence is assumed to have at present an upward effect on inflation, but its overall magnitude is highly uncertain, in particular given the fact that not all channels point in the same direction. Productivity growth and changes in the consumption pattern are assumed to have an upward impact on prices in the EU-9 countries. The decline in energy intensity and lower macroeconomic volatility are expected to have a dampening impact on prices and credit growth and openness can affect inflation in both directions. Second, the relative importance of the convergence-related variables for inflation seems to largely differ across countries. Besides their different starting positions, the high degree of heterogeneity across countries might reflect differences in the conducted macroeconomic policies and in the underlying monetary and exchange rate regimes as well as in the importance of structural rigidities in the respective countries. Consequently, the risk of second-round effects stemming from the inflationary impact of real convergence can be expected to vary considerably across the EU-9. Third, the inflationary impact of real convergence is expected to decline over time. The Balassa-Samuelson effect is assumed to diminish with relatively stronger productivity growth in the non-tradeable sector, which is partly supported by FDI inflows into this sector. As regards changes in the consumption pattern, the inflationary impact is expected to decline as the consumption patterns of the EU-9 converge closer to those of the euro area. Also the potentially dampening impact of lower energy intensity on inflation is likely to gradually lose speed, with the production structures converging more towards those in the euro area. Furthermore, macroeconomic volatility might gradually approach the degree observed in the euro area, while the inflationary impact of credit growth might continue for some time but will largely depend on the sectoral composition of credit. The importance of openness for explaining future inflation developments is likely to fade, given that the EU-9 have already reached a very high degree of openness.

Some policy recommendations can be drawn from the analysis. It can be assumed that the process of real convergence will continue to affect price developments in the EU-9 although the catching-up process is currently temporarily interrupted. Whether this would trigger any second-round effects, which could bring inflation developments far beyond a sustainable level, hinges to a large extent on the conduct of macroeconomic policy and structural rigidities. In fact, it seems to be crucial for policy makers to follow a policy directed towards macroeconomic stabilisation to avoid excessive domestic demand. Likewise, it is important that the catching-up process is accompanied by structural reforms to further improve the supply side conditions, enhance competition and reduce existing bottlenecks. With respect to euro adoption it appears advisable that the EU-9 join the euro area only if the inflationary impact of real convergence is sufficiently limited with relatively low costs of the adjustment process, so that those policy instruments that remain available for euro area members, in particular fiscal policies and structural policies, are sufficient to prevent unsustainable price developments. Thus, the findings on the inflationary impact of real convergence underline the importance of focusing on sustainable real convergence.

Notes

1. The term EU-9 refers to the nine non-euro area EU member states that have joined the EU since May 2004.
2. Expressed in EUR exchange rates, the GDP per capita levels in the EU-9 increased on average even more during the same period. In fact, the currencies of most of the countries with flexible or semi-flexible exchange rate regimes appreciated against the euro during the past decade.
3. Ireland, Portugal and Spain had a similar experience after they had joined the EU and later on the euro area.
4. The catching-up rate indicates by how many per cent the gap of the GDP per capita levels between the euro area and the EU-9 is expected to shrink each year (see also footnote in Figure 4.2).
5. The private consumption deflator is measured by the ratio of private consumption expressed in EUR exchange rates and private consumption expressed in PPP terms.
6. See for example Kravis and Lipsey (1988), Bergstrand (1991), Rogoff (1996). For the EU-9 see Cihak and Holub (2001), De Broeck and Slok (2001) and Herrman and Jochem (2003).
7. For example, to the extent that real convergence is accompanied by substantial quality improvements of domestically produced consumer goods and services that are not properly accounted for, the inflationary impact could be overestimated. Moreover, a rise in the endowment ratio of capital to labour in the EU-9 following, for example, strong capital inflows could result in a higher price level under the assumption that the non-tradeable sector is relatively

more labour-intensive and the tradeable sector is more capital-intensive (see Bhagwati, 1984). While this channel is similar to the Balassa-Samuelson effect, most empirical studies on the Balassa-Samuelson effect assume that the endowment ratio remains constant.

8. The domestic version of the Balassa-Samuelson effect is often referred to as the Baumol-Bowen effect (Baumol and Bowen, 1966).

9. MacDonald and Ricci (2002) developed a new trade theory model and relaxed the assumption of price equalisation and perfect substitutability of tradeables across countries. According to their model, higher productivity growth in the tradeable sector would have two opposing effects. On the one hand, prices in the tradeable sector would decline due to higher competition following larger product variety, which would force firms to reduce their mark-ups. On the other hand, wage equalisation across sectors (just as in the B-S framework) implies an increase in the price of non-tradeables. Assuming an expenditure bias towards domestic tradeables, the negative inflationary impact would dominate the positive one.

10. For a survey of the literature see Mihaljek and Klau (2003), Breuss (2003), Coudert (2004) and European Commission (2002).

11. According to Maier (2004) the price level of tradeable goods in the EU-9 is well below that in the euro area. The expected convergence of tradeable goods prices would result in higher inflation by on average 1.5 to 3.5 percentage points per annum.

12. MacDonald and Wojcik (2003) found that, when regulated prices are included in the analysis, the B-S effect becomes statistically insignificant.

13. This relates in particular to energy-related items, while the recent deregulation of the telecommunication sector in a number of countries led to a sharp decline in telecommunication prices.

14. A similar experience was made, for example, in East Germany after the reunification.

15. See also Bergstrand (1991). The impact of the Linder effect on inflation can be shown by the following equation:

$$p = \alpha + p^{\mathrm{T}} + (1-\alpha)p^{\mathrm{NT}},$$

with the overall price level p being a weighted average of the prices for tradeable (T) and non-tradeable (NT) goods.

16. Consumer tastes are assumed to be non-homothetic with income elasticity of demand for services being greater than 1 and for tradeable goods less than 1 (Bergstrand, 1991). Services are often luxuries in consumption, while tradeable goods include to a large extent necessities in the consumption basket, such as food.

17. See, for example, Evans (1985) for a theoretical model that explains an increase in the price level due to short run capacity constraints in the input factors.

18. This is, for example, shown by Bergstrand (1991) in a cross-country study for OECD countries and by Rawdanowicz (2008) for the EU-9. De Gregorio *et al.* (1994) find evidence for the demand and supply side effects determining relative inflation. Yet, in the long run the impact of demand side factors appears to become less important, while the importance of supply side factors seems to increase.

19. The definition of goods and services follows the definition of the HICP goods/services breakdown.
20. The phenomenon of rising consumption weights of non-tradeable goods was also observed for some of the euro area countries within the period 1980–2003. See also ECB (2003).
21. The deviation coefficient is based on Cihak and Holub (2001) and is calculated as follows:

$$\rho_i = \sqrt{\frac{1}{n}\sum_j e_{ij}(e_{ij} - e_{dej})^2}$$

where e_{ij} is the share of item j in country i in overall individual consumption expenditure and e_{dej} represents the same figure for the benchmark country. This coefficient can be interpreted as a difference in the consumption pattern compared with the benchmark country. A low coefficient indicates that a country has a similar pattern, while a high coefficient represents a very different pattern compared with the benchmark country.
22. The exercise was done for the 12 main HICP groups. Slightly different results for the deviation coefficients can be obtained when using the 39 HICP subgroups. However, these data are not available for Bulgaria, Hungary, and Poland, so that we only report the results on the basis of the 12 main HICP groups.
23. The relationship, however, might not be linear, as an increase of 1 per cent in the GDP per capita of a richer country might lead to a lower increase in the consumption ratio of services to goods in a poorer country. See also Podkaminer (1998) for estimated income elasticities of different groups of goods in transition countries.
24. Yet, energy consumption also reflects country-specific factors (such as, for example, the regional climate or the need for long-distance transport).
25. In the early years of transition, the decline in energy intensity in Central and Eastern Europe was mainly attributed to a decline in private consumption, as energy prices were increased towards cost-recovery levels. Energy intensity also dropped in the industry sector as companies were restructuring, replacing their capital stock and closing inefficient production facilities. In contrast, structural shifts away from the industrial sector were slow within this period and therefore contributed only marginally to the overall reduction in energy intensity (EBRD, 2001).
26. The EU-9 countries have to raise their excise taxes to the minimum level prescribed by the *acquis communautaire* before the transition period expires in 2014.
27. There is empirical evidence for developing countries that less volatility in growth rates of output is associated with less inflation. See also Easterly *et al.* (2000), Ewing and Seyfried (2003).
28. Cottarelli *et al.* (2005) present empirical evidence for the positive relationship between per capita income and financial deepening in the EU-9. Backé and Zumer (2005) argue that credit growth in the EU-9 has been fostered especially by economic growth, higher income and profit expectations and the liberalisation of the financial system.
29. The causality can also be the other way around, namely that increased openness leads to more real convergence, especially if countries share a

single currency, as predicted by the literature on endogeneity of the OCA criteria (see de Grauwe and Mongelli (2005) for a recent survey).

30. See IMF (2006) for a survey. For empirical evidence see Sachsida *et al.* (2003), Gruben and McLeod (2004).

31. In line with the arguments brought forward by Frankel and Rose (1998).

Bibliography

I. Angeloni, M. Flad and F.P. Mongelli (2005) 'Economic and Monetary Integration of the New Member States: Helping to Chart the Route', ECB Occasional Paper No. 36.

O. Arratibel, F. Heinz, R. Martin, M. Przybyla, L. Rawdanowicz, R. Serafini and T. Zumer (2007) 'Determinants of Growth in the Central and Eastern European EU Member States – a Production Function Approach', ECB Occasional Paper No. 61.

O. Arratibel, D. Rodriguez-Palenzuela and C. Thimann (2002) 'Inflation Dynamics and Dual Inflation in Accession Countries: A "New Keynesian" Perspective', ECB Working Paper No. 132.

P. Backé and T. Zumer (2005) 'Developments in Credit to the Private Sector in Central and Eastern European EU Member States: Emerging from Financial Repression – A Comparative Overview', Oesterreichische Nationalbank, Focus on European Economic Integration No. 2.

B. Balassa (1964) 'The Purchasing Power Parity Doctrine: A Reappraisal', *Journal of Political Economy*, 72, 584–96.

W.J. Baumol and W.G. Bowen (1966) *Performing Arts: The Economic Dilemma*, New York: Twentieth Century Fund.

J.H. Bergstrand (1991) 'Structural Determinants of Real Exchange Rates and National Price Levels: Some Empirical Evidence', *American Economic Review*, 81(1), March, 325–34.

J.N. Bhagwati (1984) 'Why Are Services Cheaper in the Poor Countries?', *Economic Journal*, 94(374), 279–86.

O. Blanchard and J. Simon (2001) 'The Long and Large Decline in US Output Volatility', mimeo, MIT.

M. Blaszkiewicz, P. Kowalski, L. Rawdanowicz and P. Wozniak (2004) 'Harrod–Balassa Samuelson Effect in Selected Countries of Central and Eastern Europe', Center for Social and Economic Research (CASE) Network Report No. 57, Poland.

A.S. Blinder (1987) 'Credit Rationing and Effective Supply Failures', *Economic Journal*, 97(386), June, 327–52.

F. Breuss (2003) 'Balassa-Samuelson Effects in the CEEC: Are they Obstacles for Joining the EMU?', IEF Working Paper No. 52, Forschungsinstitut fuer Europafragen, Vienna.

A. Calza and J. Sousa (2005) 'Output and Inflation Responses to Credit Shocks – Are There Threshold Effects in the Euro Area?', ECB Working Paper No. 481.

N. Chen, J. Imbs and A. Scott (2004) 'Competition, Globalisation and the Decline of Inflation', CEPR Discussion Paper No. 4695.

N. Chen, J. Imbs and A. Scott (2007) 'The Dynamics of Trade and Competition', mimeo, London Business School.

M. Cihak and T. Holub (2001) 'Convergence of Relative Prices and Inflation in Central and Eastern Europe', IMF Working Paper No. 01/124.

F. Coricelli and B. Jazbec (2004) 'Real Exchange Rate Dynamics in Transition Countries', *Structural Change and Economic Dynamics*, 15, 83–100.

C. Cottarelli, G. Dell'Ariccia and I. Vladkova-Hollar (2005) 'Early Birds, Late Risers, and Sleeping Beauties: Bank Credit Growth to the Private Sector in Central and Eastern Europe and in the Balkans', *Journal of Banking and Finance*, 29, 83–104.

V. Coudert (2004) 'Measuring the Balassa-Samuelson Effect for the Countries of Central and Eastern Europe?', *Banque de France Bulletin Digest* No. 122.

Z. Darvas and G. Szapáry (2008) 'Euro Area Enlargement and Euro Adoption Strategies', European Commission, Economic Papers 304.

M. De Broeck and T. Slok (2001) 'Interpreting Real Exchange Rate Movements in Transition Countries', IMF Working Paper No. WP/01/56.

P. De Grauwe and F.P. Mongelli (2005) 'Endogeneities and Optimum Currency Areas: What Brings Countries Sharing a Single Currency Closer Together?', ECB Working Paper No. 468.

J. De Gregorio, A. Giovannini and H.C. Wolf (1994) 'International Evidence on Tradables and Nontradables Inflation', *European Economic Review*, 38(6), June, 1225–44.

M. Demertzis and A.H. Hallet (1995) 'On Measuring the Costs of Labour Immobility and Market Heterogeneity in Europe', CEPR Discussion Paper No. 1189.

W. Easterly, I. Roumeen, and J. Stiglitz (2000) 'Shaken and Stirred: Explaining Growth Volatility', World Bank, Annual World Bank Conference on Development Economics.

EBRD (2001) 'Transition Report 2001 – Energy in Transition', European Bank for Reconstruction and Development, London.

ECB (2003) 'Inflation Differentials in the Euro Area: Potential Causes and Policy Implications', European Central Bank, Frankfurt.

B. Égert (2002) 'Estimating the Balassa-Samuelson Effect on Inflation and the Real Exchange Rate during the Transition', *Economic Systems*, 26(1), 1–16.

B. Égert (2007) 'Real Convergence, Price Level Convergence and Inflation Differentials in Europe', Oesterreichische Nationalbank, Working Paper No. 138.

B. Égert, P. Backé and T. Zumer (2006) 'Credit Growth in Central and Eastern Europe: Emerging from Financial Repression to New (Over)shooting Stars?', ECB Working Paper No. 687.

B. Égert, I. Drine, K. Lommatzsch and C. Rault (2002) 'The Balassa-Samuelson Effect in Central and Eastern Europe: Myth or Reality?', William Davidson Working Paper No. 483, July 2002.

European Commission (2002) 'The EU Economy: 2002 Review', Commission of the European Communities, Brussels.

G. Evans (1985) 'Bottlenecks and the Phillips Curve: A Disaggregated Keynesian Model of Inflation, Output, and Unemployment', *Economic Journal*, Royal Economic Society, 95(378), 345–57.

B.T. Ewing and W.L. Seyfried (2003) 'Modeling the Phillips Curve: A Time-Varying Volatility Approach', Texas Tech University, Working Paper 2002–09 (revised version April 2003, http://www3.tltc.ttu.edu/ecowp/working%20paper/ EwingSeyfried.PDF).

J.A. Frankel and D. Romer (1999) 'Does Trade Cause Growth?', *American Economic Review*, 89(3), June, 379–99.

J.A. Frankel and A.K. Rose (1998) 'The Endogeneity of the Optimum Currency-Area Criteria', *Economic Journal*, 108, July, 1009–25.

W.C. Gruben and D. McLeod (2004) 'The Openness-Inflation Puzzle Revisited', *Applied Economics Letters*, 11(8), 465–8.

L. Halpern and C. Wyplosz (2001) 'Economic Transformation and Real Exchange Rates in the 2000s: The Balassa-Samuelson Connection', *Economic Survey of Europe*, No. 1, United Nations Economic Commission for Europe, Geneva.

S. Herrmann and A. Jochem (2003) 'Real and Nominal Convergence in the Central and East European Accession Countries', *Intereconomics*, November/December, 323–7.

IMF (2006) 'How Has Globalisation Affected Inflation?', *World Economic Outlook*, International Monetary Fund, April, Chapter III, 97–134.

R. Jackman (1997) 'EU Labour Markets Inside and Outside the Monetary Union', in P. Welfens (ed.), *European Monetary Union: Transition, International Impact and Policy Options*, Berlin, Springer.

R. Judson and A. Orphanides (1996) 'Inflation, Volatility and Growth', Federal Reserve Bank Working Paper 1996–19.

R.G. King and R. Levine (1993) 'Finance and Growth: Schumpeter Might Be Right', *Quarterly Journal of Economics*, 108(3), August, 717–37.

G. Kiss, M. Nagy and B. Vonnak (2006) 'Credit Growth in Central and Eastern Europe: Trend, Cycle, or Boom?', Paper presented at the Finance and Consumption Workshop: Consumption and Credit in Countries with Developing Credit Markets, Florence.

I.B. Kravis and R.E. Lipsey (1988) 'National Price Levels and the Prices of Tradables and Nontradables', *American Economic Review*, 78(2), Papers and Proceedings of the One-Hundredth Annual Meeting of the American Economic Association, May, 474–8.

S.M. Lein, M.A. León-Ledesma and C. Nerlich (2008) 'How Is Real Convergence Driving Nominal Convergence in the New EU Member States?', *Journal of International Money and Finance*, 27, 227–48.

S.B. Linder (1961) *An Essay on Trade and Transformation*, New York, Wiley.

R. MacDonald and L.A. Ricci (2001) 'PPP and the Balassa-Samuelson Effect: The Role of the Distribution Sector', International Monetary Fund, Working Paper No. 01/38.

R. MacDonald and L.A. Ricci (2002) 'Purchasing Power Parity and New Trade Theory', IMF Working Paper No. 02/32.

R. MacDonald and C. Wojcik (2003) 'Catching Up: The Role of Demand, Supply and Regulated Price Effects on the Real Exchange Rates of Four Accession Countries', CESIfo Working Paper No. 899.

P. Maier (2004) 'EMU Enlargement, Inflation and Adjustment of Tradable Goods Prices: What to Expect?', Dutch Central Bank, DNB Working Paper No. 10.

J. McCallum (1991) Credit Rationing and the Monetary Transmission Mechanism, *American Economic Review*, 81(1), 946–951.

D. Mihaljek and M. Klau (2003) 'The Balassa-Samuelson Effect in Central Europe: A Disaggregated Analysis', BIS Working Paper No. 143.

T. Mora, J. López-Tamayo and J. Suriñach (2005) 'Are Wages and Productivity Converging Simultaneously in Euro-Area Countries?', *Applied Economics*, 37, 2001–8.

NBH (2002) 'On the Estimated Size of the BS-Effect in Five Central and Eastern European Countries', Kovács, M.A. (ed.), National Bank of Hungary, No. 5.

M. Obstfeld and K. Rogoff (1996) *Foundations of International Macroeconomics*, chapter 4, Cambridge, MA, MIT Press.

L. Podkaminer (1998) 'Income Elasticities of Demand for Consumer Goods in Transition Countries', WIIW Monthly Report 7.

L. Rawdanowicz (2008) 'The Enlargement of the Euro Area: Differences in Relative Inflation', *International Review of Applied Economics*, 22(5), September 2008, 623–638.

K. Rogoff (1992) 'Traded Goods Consumption Smoothing and the Random Walk Behaviour of the Real Exchange Rate', NBER Working Paper No. 4119.

K. Rogoff (1996) 'The Purchasing Power Parity Puzzle', *Journal of Economic Literature*, 34(2), June, 647–68.

D. Romer (1993) 'Openness and Inflation: Theory and Evidence', *Quarterly Journal of Economics*, 108(4), 869–903.

A. Sachsida, F.G. Carneiro and P.R.A. Loureiro (2003) 'Does Greater Openness Reduce Inflation? Further Evidence Using Panel Data Techniques', *Economics Letters*, 81(3), 315–19.

C.T. Terra (1998) 'Openness and Inflation: A New Assessment', *Quarterly Journal of Economics*, 113(2), May, 641–8.

M.E. Terrones and E.G. Mendoza (2004) 'Are Credit Booms in Emerging Markets a Concern?', *World Economic Outlook*, International Monetary Fund, April, Chapter IV, 147–66.

Summary of discussion at 2007 ECB Economic Conference on Central, Eastern and South-Eastern Europe

The discussion of the chapter by Lein (University of Zürich), Leon-Ledesma (University of Canterbury) and Nerlich (ECB) started with Jimeno (Banco de España), who approached the issue of real and nominal convergence from a Spanish perspective. In this context he pointed out the need to distinguish between:

i) adjustment in aggregate prices, in relative prices and inflation,
ii) the long-run trends in inflation versus the responses to shocks,
iii) the sources of real convergence and
iv) the quantitative importance of Balassa-Samuelson effects versus other causes of inflation differentials.

Jimeno showed that inflation differentials between Spain and the euro area average have been substantial during the past decade. Yet, the catching-up process in Spain since 1990 was largely driven by a sharp rise in the employment rate mainly reflecting some labour market reforms, while labour productivity growth, total factor productivity growth and the capital-to-labour ratio declined during this period relative to the euro area. This suggests that other factors beyond the Balassa-Samuelson effects seemed to have played a dominant role in determining inflation developments in Spain. Jimeno pointed in this context in particular to the strong growth of mark-ups, especially in the non-tradeable sector. Mark-ups seem to explain a large part of Spain's inflation differentials with the euro area as well as of dual inflation between tradeable and non-tradeable goods. Also rapid wage increases made a significant contribution to Spain's overall inflation, reflecting to a large extent wage rigidities in the wage bargaining mechanism.

Looking at Central, Eastern and South-Eastern Europe, Jimeno argued that there is a wide heterogeneity in initial productivity levels and that countries' path of real convergence varied considerably, which might explain the different inflation developments. On average, their employment rates declined relative to the euro area, while labour productivity increased in these countries relative to the euro area during the period 1998 to 2005. At the same time, however, countries display substantial differences in their employment rates and labour productivity developments. This suggests that the driving forces behind real convergence and consequently also the inflationary impact of real convergence in the Central, Eastern and South-Eastern countries are different. Estimates of the Balassa-Samuelson effect are generally relatively low, ranging in the order of 0.1–1.7 percentage points per annum for most of these countries. Looking at the determinants of GDP growth from an accounting perspective, Jimeno argued that total factor productivity was in all countries crucial for the catching-up process, while the employment rate played only a limited role. Capital accumulation contributed to real convergence in a number of countries although this became mainly relevant in the more recent years. Against this background, Jimeno stressed the importance of structural features in labour and product markets, in particular the wage and price setting in these countries, to explain differences in their inflation developments.

In his discussion, Holub (Czech National Bank) pointed out that in an open economy such as the Czech Republic price level convergence can be achieved via the inflation channel as well as the exchange rate channel. He mentioned that an average GDP growth differential with the euro area of around 3 percentage points per annum gives room for the price level to catch up by about 2 to 2.5 percentage points per annum. Looking at the real exchange rate, the trend appreciation is estimated at around 3–4 per cent per annum for the Czech Republic. Holub argued that the Czech National Bank (CNB) has set its inflation targets such as to leave some room for the catching-up process to take place through the inflation channel beside the exchange rate channel. In past years, however, the CNB inflation targets were often undershot, mainly due to the strong appreciation of the Czech koruna and its dampening impact on inflation. Thus, price level convergence in the Czech Republic took place mainly through the exchange rate channel.

Looking ahead, Holub expects that the room for the future real appreciation in the Czech Republic will continue to be relatively large, also compared with other Central Eastern European countries, such as Hungary and Poland. He explains this mainly with the relatively low price level in relation to GDP.

With respect to euro adoption, Holub discussed a number of challenges that are likely to arise in the context of real convergence. For the Czech Republic in particular a main challenge relates to the currently predominant role of the exchange rate channel for the real appreciation. By adopting the euro, the inflation channel would remain the only channel through which the real convergence can be achieved. This implies that inflation rates are likely to increase in comparison to past years. Together with the elimination of the remaining risk premium after adopting the euro, this will most likely lead to lower real interest rates. In fact, they might even turn negative, given that the equilibrium real interest rate is already low. Holub left it open whether negative real interest rates should be seen as a problem or a benefit of euro adoption.

Mitreska (Central Bank of Macedonia) briefly discussed the driving factors of the rapid disinflation process in Macedonia and illustrated the potential outlook for inflation due to real convergence. Following the introduction of an exchange rate peg in 1995, inflation has been generally low in Macedonia, at times even below the euro area level. Inflation was largely driven by price developments of food, given its predominant weight in the consumption basket of more than 45 per cent, but also by prices for housing and communication. The level of real GDP per capita, as well as the price level, is still considerably below the EU average. Moreover, the inflationary impact of real convergence has been limited so far, as the catching-up process has been fairly slow in the past.

Mitreska mentioned four potential sources of upward inflation pressures in Macedonia, related to real convergence: the Balassa-Samuelson effect, adjustment of regulated prices, cost-push factors from non-tradeable intermediates (such as the distribution sector, the business services sector and rents) and quality increases of domestically produced goods. As regards the Balassa-Samuelson effect, the data currently does not provide empirical evidence that the Balassa-Samuelson effect is at work, due to higher productivity growth in the non-tradeable sector, faster wage increases in the non-tradeable sector and stronger inflation in the non-tradeable sector. Yet, Mitreska asked for this result to be interpreted with caution, as the analysis might be distorted by the short time series and the importance of the shadow economy, which impinges on the accuracy of official statistical data. Moreover, the slow rise in the real effective exchange rate can be largely explained by the large share of tradeable goods in the consumption basket (of around 80 per cent), for which inflation was very low in the past. According to some rough estimates by the National Bank of the Republic of Macedonia, a change in the consumption basket towards the one prevailing in the euro area is likely to increase domestic inflation by 3 percentage points, thus fostering the nominal convergence process.

5
Growth and Economic Policy: Are There Speed Limits to Real Convergence?

István P. Székely and Max Watson

5.1 Introduction

The concept of speed limits to real convergence can be interpreted in two different ways. It can mean factors that limit or enhance potential growth in the recently acceded EU member states (RAMS) – in other words, *speed limits to the potential pace of real convergence*. But it can also mean factors that limit adjustment capacity and/or create market imperfections and rigidities, that is, *speed limits due to vulnerabilities*. Both are important and will be dealt with in this chapter.

Regarding the former, recent research findings offer empirical evidence on the role of several non-traditional growth factors that are of particular importance in RAMS. These include the quality of institutions, the size and efficiency of government, and the development of the financial sector and financial integration.[1]

More attention to non-traditional growth factors reflects the fact that real convergence in RAMS is taking place in a new environment. The differences from previous convergence episodes are attributable to several factors, including financial integration, globalisation and European integration. RAMS also have important characteristics that are different from those of previously converging economies, such as the level of education or cross-border mobility of the labour force.

These differences in environment and characteristics also have important implications for the speed limits due to vulnerabilities. On the one hand, financial liberalisation – which provides a historically unique opportunity to use foreign savings to accelerate real convergence – can also increase the amplitude of certain cyclical elements, while financial integration, in large part due to European integration, can provide the necessary external finance for the kind of current account deficits that these larger deviations may generate. That is, these factors may lengthen the periods during which relative prices are distorted and resources are not reallocated to reach a new equilibrium.

It may be a challenging task for policy makers to achieve fast and steady nominal convergence, a prerequisite for euro adoption, in certain phases of convergence in this new environment. Financial liberalisation and integration may lead to sizeable changes in the composition of final demand, and, through this, considerable movements in the equilibrium real exchange rate. As policies also work rather differently in the new environment, some even arguing that they are ineffective, policy makers may face a double challenge in this regard.

5.2 The convergence process

RAMS are catching up with the average income level in the EU, and with each other, at a relatively rapid pace. The pace of convergence has accelerated since the turn of the century when EU accession became a central scenario for business. At the same time the dispersion of per capita relative income within this group started to decline rapidly, that is, the convergence also gathered pace among RAMS themselves (Figure 5.1).

Both phenomena are mostly explained by the acceleration of convergence in the Baltic countries. These economies kept up with the fastest-growing emerging market economies, while the growth performance of the others has been, overall, more modest (Figure 5.2).

Exports product structures of most RAMS have also improved rapidly, indicating that these countries have a significant potential to absorb modern technology (Igan *et al.*, 2007; IMF, 2006). Given their relatively high educational achievements and the fact that their financial systems are well-developed, this is not surprising. Differences across countries in this regard are, however, also likely to be influenced by the quality of education and, more broadly, by their attractiveness for technology-transferring FDI (Figure 5.3).

Caselli and Tenreyo (2005) call attention to the importance of the initial production and employment structures in explaining the speed of convergence, especially in the early phases of convergence. Indeed, the share of agriculture, particularly if measured by employment, is rather different in RAMS, with Poland, among others, having much higher shares of employment in agriculture (Figure 5.4 Chart on

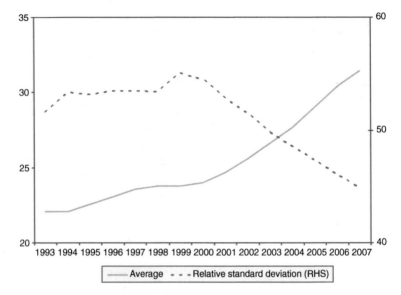

Figure 5.1   Catch-up within Europe and convergence among EU-10 (per capita GDP at 2000 market prices relative to EU-27 average)

Source: Eurostat and own calculations.

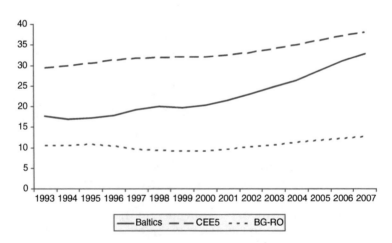

Figure 5.2   Catch-up within Europe (per capita at 2000 market prices relative to EU-27 average)

Source: Eurostat and own calculations.

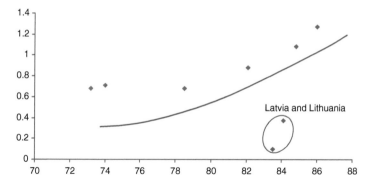

Figure 5.3 RAMS: Educational attainment and change in export unit value, 1999–2004

Note: Percentage of the population aged 25 to 64 having completed at least upper second-ary education in 1999 (horizontal) and change in export unit value in between 1999 and 2004 (vertical).

Sources: Igan *et al.* (2007) and Eurostat.

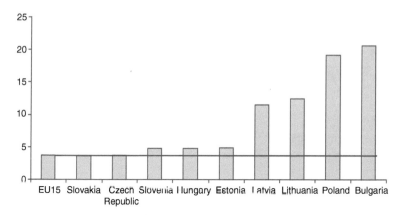

Figure 5.4 RAMS: Share of agricultural employment in 2006

Note: Share in total employment.

Source: Eurostat, for Slovenia the Statistical Office of Slovenia.

agricultural employment). The resulting scope for sectoral shifts can, in principle, be a source of rapid growth in the coming years in these countries, as was the case, for example, in Spain. The issue, however, is broader than just agricultural employment even in Poland. The level of employment, and thus the potential in increasing labour input, is rather different across the RAMS, with the Baltic countries having relatively high employment levels by EU standards (Figure 5.5).

The process of convergence is associated with high current account deficits and rapid real appreciation in several RAMS. The recent experiences of the Baltic countries and Bulgaria are of particular importance in this regard, though the origins, and, thus, the longer-term implications for growth, are likely to be rather different in these cases (Figures 5.6–5.8). The

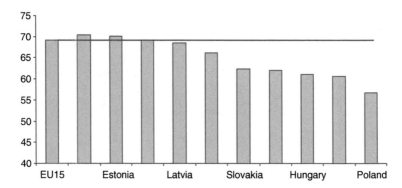

Figure 5.5   RAMS: Employment ratios in 2006
Note: Employment ratios for people aged 15 to 59.
Source: Eurostat.

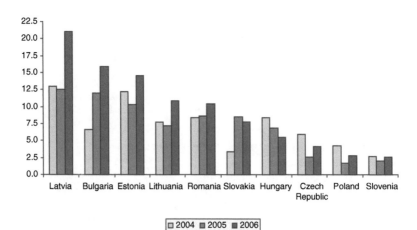

Figure 5.6   RAMS: Current account deficit, 2004–06
Note: In per cent of GDP.
Source: Eurostat and the authors' own calculations.

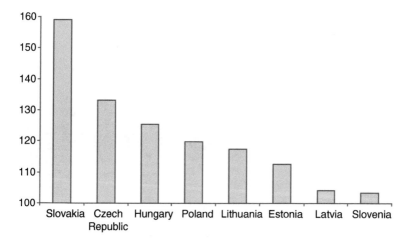

Figure 5.7   RAMS: Real effective exchange rate indices, 2006

Note: Based on CPI, 1999 = 100.

Source: Eurostat.

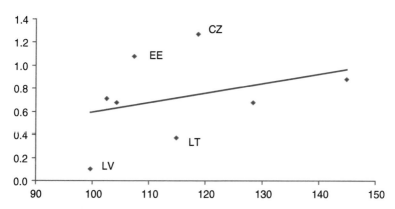

Figure 5.8   RAMS: Change in export unit value and real appreciation, 1999–2004

Note: Change in export unit value (horizontal) and REER index (1999 = 100) between 1999 and 2004 (vertical).

Source: Igan *et al.* (2007) and Eurostat.

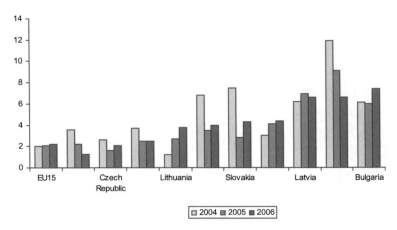

Figure 5.9   RAMS: Rate of inflation, 2004–06

Note: Harmonized indices of consumer prices (2005 = 100) – Annual rate of change.

Source: Eurostat.

flip-side of real appreciation in RAMS with fixed exchange rate regimes is somewhat higher inflation, though a periodic acceleration of inflation is not restricted to these countries (Figure 5.9, Rate of Inflation).

5.3   Theoretical foundations and empirical evidence

Though findings are not always robust and/or theoretically well understood, there are several factors that are consistently found to influence growth performance in empirical studies. In what follows we shall review some of these findings and try to relate them to theoretical models in order to understand the channels through which, and the ways in which, they might influence catch-up potential in the RAMS. We shall also review how these factors might influence the adjustment to a new equilibrium and, through this, the variability of output and macroeconomic vulnerabilities. Of course, with perfect markets, fully informed agents, and flexible prices, theory would suggest no impact of such variability on potential growth. But these assumptions are not necessarily plausible for the RAMS (or other EU member states). Thus major deviations from potential output create vulnerabilities – mostly, though not only, through large external gross financing requirements. Moreover, they also limit growth potential because of extended periods of distorted relative prices and slow responses to relative price changes.

Other things equal, a lower initial income level seems to be associated with more rapid growth: lower-income countries, on average, do converge with higher-income countries. As the RAMS' income level is still significantly lower than that of the rest of the EU (Figure 5.1), this factor will potentially work in their favour, as it has done since the beginning of transition. The evidence for an interaction of this exogenous catch-up factor with policy-determined factors, however, is much scarcer and more recent. Schadler *et al.* (2006) offer some evidence on the interaction with institutional quality and financial integration. These interactions are of particular importance to RAMS because European integration, by design, brings about major improvements in these areas.[2]

Aghion *et al.* (2006) offer a model that can establish a link between domestic savings and growth performance in a small open economy. This is an important, though long overdue, theoretical result. Even though it has been a widely held view in economics that domestic savings matter for growth also in a small open economy, theory has long offered little support for this view. A crucial element of this link in the above model is the capacity of domestic banks to cofinance investments by foreign firms that bring local firms closer to the industry frontier. As monitoring is crucial to ensure efficient use of external financing by firms, the higher domestic savings are – the higher the domestic banks' capacity to cofinance – the higher foreign investment and, thus, the faster convergence to the efficiency frontier will be.

Schadler *et al.* (2006), however, find no evidence of this link to domestic savings for growth rates in the RAMS. Instead, they offer evidence suggesting that higher current account deficits – that is, more reliance on foreign savings – on average, speeds up convergence.[3]

Is this a contradiction, or a finding that reduces the relevance of this model? Not necessarily. The banking sector in most RAMS is dominated by foreign-owned banks that can bring in foreign financing at large scales and that have already developed the necessary capacity to efficiently monitor local firms. In fact, in the early phase, foreign-owned banks mostly specialised in corporate financing and moved into the retail sector only more recently. So, there is a very plausible explanation for the fact that RAMS can easily substitute foreign for domestic savings[4] and, on average, converge fast with the rest of the EU despite relatively low domestic savings (relative to, for example, South-East Asian countries; see Schadler *et al.*, 2006). Large-scale FDI, and, more broadly, openness to foreign ownership, is another factor that makes this channel less relevant. We shall take up this issue below.

In another seminal contribution, Aghion *et al.* (2005) present a model to explain how financial development can enhance the growth potential once it reaches a threshold level.[5] This is an issue that has long been in the centre of attention (Demirgüç-Kunt and Levine, 2001; Greenwood and Jovanovic, 1990; Levine, 1997). This model, however, is of particular interest to RAMS as it explicitly accounts for technological transfer and the role of financial development in this, a central mechanism for the convergence of RAMS. Their model predicts an acceleration of growth once financial intermediation (proxied by the private credit-to-GDP ratio) reaches a threshold level (at around 25 per cent based on their estimates); and they provide empirical evidence to support this prediction of their model.

Though these results would suggest a strong relationship between financial development and growth in the RAMS, empirical evidence is weak. Credit-to-GDP ratios in RAMS are above this threshold level and credit growth is well in excess of nominal GDP growth in most RAMS. Nonetheless, Schadler *et al.* (2006), for example, find no evidence that this factor is serving to enhance growth potential in these economies.[6]

Again, this is not necessarily a contradiction. While increased access to credit is a positive development even if it is used for financing consumption or housing investment (since it allows households to optimise their consumption over a much longer time horizon) the contribution of credit expansion to potential growth is greatly dependent on how the increased credit is allocated. In the model of Aghion *et al.* (2006), this comes down to the assumption that credit finances innovation, or in that of Aghion *et al.* (2005) that finance is essential for the technology transfer – which clearly do not apply to credit that goes to non-productive use, such as durables or housing. And indeed, the share of consumption and housing loans is significant in the RAMS, albeit with important differences among countries (Figure 5.8). Thus, depending on the actual share of credit that finances innovation or technology transfer (more broadly, productive investment) in a given sample, one may or may not find financial development as a direct growth-enhancing factor.[7]

FDI is another important factor that can enhance potential growth and convergence. It can directly finance innovation and/or transfer technology, and thus substitute for local innovation.[8] RAMS have been benefiting from large FDI inflows since the beginning of transition, though to a varying extent. Similarly to debt finance, the structure of FDI is key to understanding its implications for real convergence. FDI that finances or creates a real estate boom, in itself, is clearly not a factor that speeds up the convergence to the production frontier in the receiving country.[9]

Financial development and integration, however, can also increase vulnerabilities, especially if they take place in countries and periods that are characterised by major market imperfections. Improved access to credit by households, especially in countries with large pent-up demand for housing such as Latvia, can increase the demand for non-tradeable goods and shift resources in a dramatic fashion towards non-productive uses even in the medium term. This, in turn, can lead to a sizeable widening of the current account deficit and a considerable real appreciation – comparable in size to, or even larger than, that generated by the B-S effect. Moreover, with sticky prices, the initial deterioration in the current account is significantly higher than with flexible prices, further increasing vulnerabilities (Box 5.1). This mechanism seems key to understanding recent developments in some RAMS with very large current account deficits and rapid asset price inflation, such as Latvia.

Box 5.1 Factors determining real exchange rate trends in converging economies

The discussion on real exchange rate trends in converging economies has so far focused mostly on the possible size of the Balassa-Samuelson (B-S) effect. The general consensus is that this effect is modest (on average, 1–2 per cent annually) (e.g., Kovács, 2002). More broadly, sectoral data for EU-15 countries suggest that even in the euro area (a single market with a common currency) there are several uncertainties surrounding the very basic assumptions underlying the B-S framework, most importantly the one price assumption for tradeable goods. Moreover, recent movements in the real exchange rates of some of the converging economies have been much more dramatic than the estimated extent of the B-S effects, and real appreciation occurred even when TFP growth was mostly generated in non-tradeable sectors (e.g., Latvia).

Recent research in the European Commission, however, provides important insight into alternative mechanisms that might be equally important in determining real exchange rate trends in RAMS. They may also help better understand the recent experience of RAMS that witnessed rapid real appreciation, way beyond the possible extent of the B-S effect. Results of stochastic dynamic general equilibrium model-based simulations (Lendvai, 2007) seem to suggest that financial integration, most importantly increased access for households to credit, can be one such important factor. These results show that removing credit constraint on households, while leaving TFP growth unchanged in both tradeable and non-tradeable sectors, leads to a persistent real appreciation and a widening of the current account deficit in the medium run – just as in the case of the B-S effect. The long run implications are, however, markedly different from those of the B-S effect. The real exchange rate appreciates only temporarily; in the long run it depreciates slightly (relative to the baseline) to generate the current account surplus necessary to service the higher net external debt accumulated in the first phase. That is – unlike in the case of the B-S effect where the appreciation is permanent – the real exchange rate goes through major adjustments twice before a long-run equilibrium is reached again (Figure 5.10).[10]

These results also shed some light on the vulnerabilities rapid financial development and integration can create in RAMS. As one would expect, when prices are sticky, the exchange rate regime matters in the short run: a fixed exchange rate regime generates a larger current account deficit (relative to the baseline) than a flexible exchange rate regime(Figure 5.11). That is, the extent of vulnerability to adjustment risk will depend on several factors, and trade-offs between these. These factors include the stickiness of prices, the extent of unhedged balance sheet exposures, and the degree of nominal flexibility afforded by the exchange rate regime.

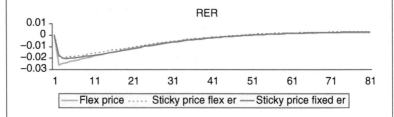

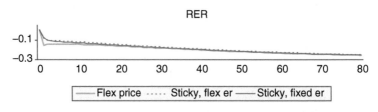

Figure 5.10 Real exchange rate trends under different scenarios: Increased access by households to credit (upper panel) and TFP shock in the tradeable sector (lower panel)

Source: Lendvai (2007).

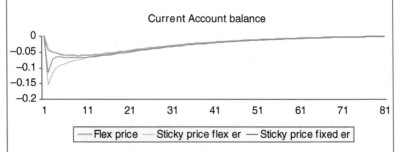

Figure 5.11 Current account developments following an increase in the access of collateral-constrained households to credit

Source: Lendvai (2007).

These findings offer a useful frame of reference for exploring some aspects of economic developments and policy challenges in the converging EU economies. Notably, the two shocks illustrated here may be hard to distinguish initially, so policy makers may face a diagnostic problem. Meanwhile, the adjustment challenge facing the economy will be very different under these alternative scenarios. Under the 'household collateral shock', quite a significant corrective depreciation could be needed over the medium term: how smoothly this is achieved will depend on rigidities in the economy and on the capacity to switch resources and restart strong productivity growth at that stage. The implications for policy of this diagnostic uncertainty and potential adjustment challenge are explored in more detail below.

It is, however, important to note that the distinction between investment in productive and non-productive uses is not necessarily the same as the one between investments in tradeable and non-tradeable sectors. The overall productivity of an economy, and its long-term competitiveness, are not only a function of productivity in the tradeable sectors – an issue that received considerable attention recently in Europe – but also the productivity of the non-tradeable private sector, and that of the government sector. As Blanchard (2006) shows, higher productivity in non-tradeable sectors can enhance the competitiveness of producers in tradeable sectors in the same way as productivity increase in the tradeable sectors does, by keeping wages down in tradeable sectors. In fact, as he argues, for many PAMS – and we would add RAMS – it is much easier to implement reforms that enhance productivity growth in non-tradeable sectors than to attract more investment in high-tech sectors.[11]

Moreover, regarding RAMS, it is also important to keep in mind that the share of foreign ownership in tradeable sectors, particularly in export sectors, is rather high. That is, production technologies and managerial practices in a considerable part of the tradeable sector are likely to be close to the efficiency frontier. In fact, many producers in tradeable sectors are fully integrated into the global production networks of their parent companies. Rapid improvements of export product structure and export unit values in several RAMS, such as Hungary and the Czech Republic, reflect this fact (IMF, 2006). In a way, the catching up is near full in these parts of the economies of RAMS. While this is a very positive development, this also means that productivity growth in RAMS in these sectors will be driven by developments at the frontier and, thus, will be similar to that in the rest of the EU. The catching-up potential is thus related to the increase of the relative size of this part of the economies of RAMS. However, as evidence in Schadler *et al.* (2006)

suggests, this is limited in most RAMS, most likely because of the relative lack of highly skilled labour, and institutional weaknesses that limit the capacity to rapidly reallocate resources. Looking forward, increasing the supply of highly skilled labour will take time and will require major improvements in the educational systems of RAMS, mostly in their higher education. While this is a crucial area for structural policies, private sector involvement is critical to improve allocative efficiency and ensure incentive compatibility.

The size of the government is found by some to influence growth performance, also in RAMS (e.g., Barro, 1991, or more recently Aslund and Jenish, 2005, and for RAMS Schadler *et al.*, 2006). A large government may reduce the growth potential because of the deadweight loss stemming from collecting tax revenue; the larger the size the higher the loss through this channel. And in most RAMS, the government is similar in size to that in the rest of the EU euro area and significantly higher than in countries with similar income levels in other parts of the world, particularly in fast-growing South-East Asian economies. The most damaging means of high tax intake is perhaps a high tax wedge on labour. Most RAMS score rather poorly in this regard (see, e.g., World Bank, 2007) with tax wedges at least twice as high as those of their fast-growing middle-income competitors. The Baltic countries, however, compare favourably in this regard, with an average size of government relative to GDP about 8½ percentage points lower than in the rest of RAMS. It is also important to point out that it is expenditure on social transfers and government consumption that explains most of the difference between RAMS and their competitors in this regard, expenditure items that are generally not found to enhance the growth potential directly (Barro, 1991). Moreover, if social transfer schemes are not well designed, which seems to be frequently the case in RAMS, they can significantly reduce labour market participation and labour supply. Though not only for this reason, employment ratios in RAMS, except the Czech Republic and the Baltic countries, are indeed rather low by international comparison (see, e.g., Schadler *et al.*, 2006).[12]

Nonetheless, size in itself is not necessarily the only, or even the main, factor that determines how the government will influence the convergence potential of RAMS.[13] More recent results by the World Bank (2007) call attention to the quality of government (expenditure), and provide some evidence for transition economies that large government (above a certain threshold size) hinders potential growth only if government is inefficient. They provide important evidence for the efficiency of government spending in education and health care in transition economies and RAMS, and use the size of the government to approximate the impact of resource waste and deadweight cost. As results in Afonso *et al.* (2006) suggest, with the exception of Slovenia, the use of government size as an explanatory variable may not be a major distortion for RAMS (see figure 7 in Afonso *et al.*, 2006).[14]

Macroeconomic policies can be very different, however, if an economy has rigidities that may impede external adjustment. RAMS with fixed exchange rate regimes, currency boards or hard pegs, are indeed growing fast and have major imbalances. Schadler *et al.* (2006) find growth, and partly because of this current account deficit, above equilibrium in some of the Baltic countries. Rapid nominal convergences on interest rates and high inflation are apparent in this group of countries, producing low, in many cases negative, real interest rates, which are in turn thought to lead to a consumption boom (financed by credit) and a shift in investments towards non-tradeable sectors. While these phenomena are apparently present in these countries, it is not clear whether they are exclusively or even in the first place related to the choice on the exchange rate regime. First, euroisation is widespread in countries with fixed exchange rate regimes, more so than in other RAMS, and therefore the low or negative real interest rate on domestic currency-denominated instruments can have little impact on overall resource allocation. Second, as long as the UIP condition holds, the domestic real interest rate will be low in a country irrespective of the exchange rate regime if there is strong real appreciation. Finally, a fixed exchange rate arrangement, including the currency board, is not necessarily more credible than any other arrangement; thus the risk premium is not necessarily lower for 'fixers'. It may be lower if economic fundamentals are stronger and fiscal policy is on a sustainable path.[15] Therefore, it is not surprising that empirical studies find no systematic effect of the exchange rate regime on growth performance.

Implications for vulnerabilities, however, might be different, particularly if a fixed exchange rate regime is combined with rigidities and imperfections. In an ideal economy, once the effects of a shock fade, the economy reaches its new equilibrium and resources will be reallocated accordingly. Therefore, there is no impact on long-term growth performance. For example, regarding the case of removing credit constraints discussed in Box 5.1, as households and other agents reach their desired net wealth positions and restructure their portfolios of financial and real assets and liabilities, the consumption and housing booms end and the economy finds a new equilibrium. With imperfect or missing markets and sticky prices, however, relative prices, including the relative prices of foreign exchange and labour, are persistent and, thus, remain distorted for a considerable period – increasing vulnerability and eventually reducing the convergence potential. Policies, thus, might matter.

5.4   Challenges for policy

In this setting of financial integration and real convergence, the key challenges for policy are two-fold. First, an overarching priority is to foster high potential growth over the medium term, thus raising the speed limits on economic activity. Second, policy makers must engage in suitable risk management, to avoid adjustment stresses that could set back the real convergence process. The framework illustrated above suggests important ways in which policy can contribute to both objectives.

Macroeconomic and structural policies, jointly, will have a key role to play in raising the ceiling on potential growth. A key concern will be to ensure that the scope for gains from financial integration is fully tapped. This requires a strong emphasis on actions to improve resource allocation. Credible macroeconomic policies can help ensure moderate real interest rates. Structural fiscal reforms to increase the efficiency (and thus reduce the size) of government and to rearrange priorities with a view to enhancing human resources, developing infrastructure, and avoiding distortions will enhance potential growth. Labour and product market policies can help shift resources toward new opportunities for productivity gains. Prudential policies can seek to counter capital market imperfections. Overall, the emphasis will be on maximising potential gains from technology so as to raise total factor productivity, with financial integration playing a strong supportive role.

The risk management challenges facing policy makers in containing vulnerabilities and enhancing adjustment capacity are complex. Nonetheless, it seems feasible to map these to challenges for the main branches of policy:

• A first source of uncertainty and potential risk lies in the nature of the shocks that the economy is experiencing. As discussed above, an expansion driven by easier household borrowing constraints will ultimately require a correction of the real exchange rate to divert resources to debt service. During the correction phase, rigidities in the real and financial sectors may prove costly in terms of output foregone. In other words, the expansion will be an equilibrium process but may involve a testing adjustment phase. By contrast, where the drivers of growth are favourable shocks to productivity, then the need for later real depreciation will be lower and the adjustment challenges less. Initially, however, the symptoms of these shocks may be hard to distinguish, leaving policy makers unclear about the magnitude of the challenges ahead.

- A second source of risk lies in distortions and incentive problems. These could cause a misallocation of resources, and move the economic expansion away from an efficient path. Distortions could stem from fiscal programmes that affect financial markets (such as mortgage subsidies) as well as the real sector. Incentive issues may also be significant in the financial sector – for example, where moral hazard results from guarantees of deposit liabilities, or where private sector agents rely unduly on a commitment to exchange rate stability.
- Experience in advanced and emerging market economies points also to the risk that errors in fiscal policy could cause an unintended stimulus during the economic and financial upswing. Public revenues may benefit strongly from the tax-rich composition of activity during a financial boom, and there are risks that policy makers may also underestimate the cyclical position of the economy. Such errors could lead to an unintended fiscal stimulus that impairs resource allocation – including by triggering unwarranted real appreciation. This could also complicate adjustment by reducing the stabilising capacity of fiscal policy when a domestically driven boom loses steam.

These considerations suggest that policy makers need to engage in a comprehensive risk-return strategy – enhancing resource allocation, and thus pushing out the frontier of potential growth, while also safeguarding the economy against adjustment stress.

There is clearly a strong potential for complementarity between the measures required to pursue these twin goals. Nevertheless, it will be valuable to analyse as far as possible the nature of the shocks affecting the economy and hence the potential demands on policy – and especially the adjustment challenges – that may lie ahead. Here, a promising analytical route is to simulate different combinations of shocks to the economy (for example, building on the DSGE approaches illustrated here). This can provide a basis to explore what underlying shocks and patterns of allocation are confirmed by observed trends in incomes, output, prices, the real exchange rate, the external balance and – with particular emphasis – sectoral productivity trends.

In designing policies, moreover, country authorities need to take account of specifics in the EU integration and convergence context. On the one hand, the trade and integration opportunities of EU accession and membership, and the scope for institutional strengthening in line with the *acquis communautaire*, pose unique opportunities to raise the speed limits on growth. At the same time, this environment also fosters accelerated financial integration, thus raising the stakes for policies to the extent that it amplifies both opportunities and, in some ways, costs of policy failure. Moreover, policy makers in the converging economies have faced questions about the efficacy of economic instruments in managing financial risks in a rapidly integrating environment.

This concern about policy efficacy deserves careful exploration. There are certainly potential constraints on policy in this environment. Even where exchange rates are floating, there are limits on the autonomy of monetary policy, including through the prevalence of euro-denominated borrowing. Foreign-owned banks, which account for an overwhelming proportion of financial assets, have deep pockets in terms of capital and liquidity – meaning that prudential measures may have limited traction. And in a setting of ever deeper financial integration, credit controls are not likely to work well: they will tend to divert flows to cross-border or less supervised channels.

Clearly, policy is far from powerless. But effective risk management requires policy makers to internalise four cross-cutting features that are particularly pronounced in this policy environment:

- Policy interactions, as always, can be mutually reinforcing. But with large balance sheet risks they may not operate with the conventional sign. With unhedged foreign currency exposures, nominal depreciation can potentially be deflationary – affecting the desirable fiscal stance to flank devaluation.[16]
- Policy actions may have strong distributional effects: (1) depreciation in the presence of large currency exposures may compress the existing non-trade goods sector, which is unlikely to be hedged; (2) prudential tightening may particularly impact locally owned banks, and firms with less access to diversified funding, and both aspects of this may affect SMEs severely even in economies with relatively well-developed financial systems and (3) monetary tightening and nominal appreciation may need to be sharp where the role of the domestic currency in financial intermediation is modest: the brunt of this will fall unevenly across firms. These distributional considerations underscore the case for fiscal measures to play a full role in the policy mix.
- Lying behind concerns about the 'policy impotence' are two regime-related issues: (1) there is an understandable reluctance to reactivate

monetary policy, and potentially moderate unhedged borrowing, by ending hard-peg regimes; and (2) there is currently something of a vacuum as regards local systemic risks in large foreign-owned establishments – for example, sector concentrations or intra-group funding vulnerabilities. In both cases, there are circumstances in which policy may need to 'think outside the box' to regain full effectiveness. In other words, there are issues of regime design as well as policy calibration.

- Many measures are complementary, with mutually reinforcing benefits for adjustment and growth. This includes the scope for growth-oriented fiscal consolidation. But, in some respects, policy makers face tough trade-offs. This may be true of some measures needed to assure a risk-averse fiscal policy. Equally, the shift from a peg to a flexible rate, or even the very active use of interest rates under a flexible regime, may entail increased short-run volatility in the economy. This may be desirable to dampen excessive risk-taking, and even if costly may still be key to avoiding larger risks to growth in the future.

Therefore, it will be important to rely on quantified macroeconomic scenarios in exploring policy options. These models can also support the design of appropriate stress-tests, which capture compound risks, and help explore the scope of policy interactions. They provide, too, some objective basis on which to discuss difficult inter-temporal trade-offs of the kind highlighted above.

To provide a sound basis for policy making, such scenarios need to build in explicitly a number of financial stability factors:

- The evidence from productivity growth about resource allocation during the boom, and the medium-term implications of different assumptions on this, including for swings in net foreign liabilities and the real exchange rate.
- The impact of balance sheet risks, where vulnerable exposures may lie in any sector of the economy – firms, households, banks, government, and the aggregate external balance sheet – and the interaction of sector exposures can be of key importance.
- Concerning the saving–investment balance of the private sector, the impact on this of rapid financial integration, credit growth and asset price increases: sensitivity analysis could explore how far the external current account might widen as a result, on varying assumptions about the fiscal stance.

- As regards real exchange rate adjustment, an exploration of how adjustment through different channels – nominal exchange rate, wage and price level – may interact with rigidities, such as wage and price stickiness, and balance sheet exposures.

Together with the other issues discussed above, these considerations underscore that policy makers face important analytical challenges. Gaining a better understanding of these issues is essential in the development of effective frameworks and measures.

5.5   Conclusion

This chapter has suggested some elements of a framework for thinking about 'speed limits on growth' in the converging economies of the EU (RAMS). It has distinguished throughout between the challenges relating to potential growth and to adjustment risks. But in both respects it has laid particular emphasis on the interaction of financial integration with real economic convergence.

The factors that may limit the convergence potential most in RAMS seem to be

- resource waste in public sector;
- government policies that reduce labour force participation by distorting the relative price of labour; and
- policies that promote shifting resources to non-productive uses in the private sector, particularly when they are combined with market inefficiencies and sticky prices.

Though to a varying extent, Central and East European RAMS seem to suffer from all these problems, while Baltic RAMS face the latter as a major challenge. Consequently, the most important way of increasing the speed limit on growth potential in the former group is to enhance efficiency of government expenditure, most importantly on government consumption and social transfers, and use most of the efficiency gain not needed to restore fiscal sustainability for reducing the tax wedge on labour. The latter would also help with increasing employment. Since the housing boom in the Baltic countries – which in the short run boosts growth – is still ongoing, the possible negative impact on the convergence potential cannot yet be detected. Moreover, relatively small and efficient governments and increasing labour utilisation will mask any negative effect of this factor. Nonetheless, it may turn out to be an important factor that could reduce an otherwise high growth potential and threaten macroeconomic stability.

Regarding policies, five main conclusions flow from this analysis:

- A key goal for policy frameworks should be to unlock the full potential offered by financial integration, including the interaction of cross-border flows with institutions that are well placed for monitoring credit contracts.
- The nature of shocks to the economy is important. For example, higher productivity in traded goods, or an easing of collateral constraints on households, will have rather different impact on growth prospects and will create different adjustment challenges. But, from the initial symptoms, it may be hard to discern which shocks are actually occurring.
- This argues for a comprehensive approach to policy management: one that aims to foster strong potential growth, to contain vulnerability risks and to enhance adjustment capacity. In such a strategy, measures that promote higher productivity and address rigidities and distortions will take centre stage.
- Policy is far from powerless to influence these outcomes. But the specifics of the EU convergence setting mean that particular attention is warranted to the direction of policy interactions; the sectoral impact of measures; the design of policy regimes; and the inter-temporal trade-offs that may face policy makers.
- The need to evaluate policy options, and also to design realistic stress-tests, argues in favour of developing quantified macroeconomic scenarios. This is one of several areas in which deeper economic analysis can shed light on policy challenges and responses, and can help to articulate persuasive policy approaches.

Notes

This chapter is based on a paper which was presented at the ECB Economic Conference on Central, Eastern and South-Eastern Europe, Frankfurt, 1–2 October 2007. The authors are advisors at the European Commission, DG ECFIN. István P. Székely is on leave from the IMF, and is on the faculty of Corvinus University, Budapest. Max Watson is a Fellow of Wolfson College, Oxford. Views expressed are those of the authors and do not necessarily represent the views of DG ECFIN or the IMF. The authors wish to thank colleagues in DG ECFIN, and notably Julia Lendvai and Werner Roeger, for their great assistance in developing the material on which this chapter is based.

1. Some of these factors might have played an equally important role in previous convergence episodes but received little attention.
2. Schooling, which influences a country's capacity to adopt new technologies (Howitt and Mayer-Foulkes, 2002), does not seem to have a strong explanatory power for the RAMS, perhaps because differences among them in this area are more qualitative than quantitative, as indicated in Figure 5.3.
3. Abiad *et al.* (2007) provide further empirical evidence and argue that Europe (RAMS) is different in this regard. They also make the important distinction between steady state growth and convergence, which might be essential to understand why previous studies for larger sets of low-middle-income countries found no evidence supporting this link (Kose *et al.*, 2006), or found that capital tended to flow 'uphill' (Prasad *et al.*, 2006).
4. For example, in Latvia, foreign borrowing by (mostly foreign-owned) domestic banks amounts to more than half of their total lending (to residents and non-residents), and over two-thirds of their deposit base.
5. Empirical investigations in Aghion *et al.* (2005) and Aghion *et al.* (2006) do not include RAMS as no reliable long-run data are available for these countries, simply because data for pre-transition periods are not very meaningful in this regard. The lack of data for a longer time period, of course, makes it rather difficult to draw any conclusion from empirical work on the nature of the effects these development factors have on the growth or convergence potential of RAMS.
6. It is, however, important to mention that they include variables that measure institutional quality, which might pick up some of the effects of the key mechanism involved in the models in Aghion *et al.* (2005) and Aghion *et al.* (2006), namely enterprise monitoring.
7. For example, the share of loans to households and for real estate development in the increase in loans to the private sector (excluding financial institutions) amounted to 75 per cent in the past year (12 months up to end Q1 2007) in Latvia.
8. In fact, Aghion *et al.* (2006) directly estimate the implication of FDI for the impact of domestic savings on long-term growth and convergence and find that FDI makes this impact smaller, though still important. FDI is equally relevant to the model in Aghion *et al.* (2006).
9. For example, in Latvia, 12 per cent of cumulative FDI went into the real estate sector, and 37 per cent into the financial system, which, at present, seems to finance mostly a real estate boom.
10. In discussing recent experiences of Portugal and Spain, Blanchard (2007) presents a model that can produce a similar outcome, but the shock in his model is a change in preferences, namely increased impatience (decrease in the discount factor). While we have evidence that supports an easing of the credit constraint on households in several RAMS, we have little to suggest a sudden change in preferences in any of the known episodes of rapid real exchange rate appreciation (and consequent widening of the current account deficit) in RAMS.
11. This issue would also deserve more attention in the euro area, as it was lagging behind the US in the past decade mostly because of dismal performance in many non-tradeable sectors.

12. This is another channel through which a large government can reduce the relative income level (though not necessarily the long-term growth rate).
13. There is also a technical issue related to the size of the government in this regard. Productivity is rarely measured in the public sectors and, thus, it is typically imputed by statisticians. A quick look into the data suggests that assumptions on productivity growth in the public sector across EU/OECD countries are rather similar at around 0–½ per cent a year. If so, by design, a larger government (higher share of GDP produced in the public sector) in a country than in another one results in lower growth even if the private sectors (and presumably the public ones as well) grow at the same rate in the two countries.
14. Though it may slightly distort the parameter estimate for this variable if the equation is estimated for a wider set of countries. There is, however, little support in Afonso *et al.* (2006) for threshold size for government (35 per cent of GDP) chosen in World Bank (2007). The finding by Schadler *et al.* (2006) that the size of government has a significant negative impact on growth also suggests that, in general, it is a relatively good proxy for resource waste in government.
15. In economies where the fixed exchange rate regime was adopted in order to make political commitment to sound fiscal policies lasting (commitment device), as in the case of some of the Baltic countries, the exchange rate arrangement and higher credibility (and consequently lower risk premium) are likely to go hand in hand.
16. This is also the case for real effective depreciation with an unchanged nominal rate, but the time-path of the balance sheet impact will be much more gradual.

Bibliography

A. Abiad, D. Leigh and A. Mody (2007) 'International Finance and Income Convergence: Europe Is Different', IMF Working Paper No. 07/64, March 2007.

A. Afonso, L. Schuknecht and V. Tanzi (2006) 'Public Sector Efficiency: Evidence for New EU Member States and Emerging Markets', ECB Working Paper Series No. 581, January 2006.

P. Aghion, P. Bacchetta and A. Banerjee (2004) 'Financial Development and the Instability of Open Economies', NBER Working Paper No. 10246, January 2004.

P. Aghion, D. Comin and P. Howitt (2006) 'When Does Domestic Saving Matter for Economic Growth?', draft, 4 August 2006.

P. Aghion and P. Howitt (2006) 'Appropriate Growth Policy: A Unifying Framework', 2005 Joseph Schumpeter Lecture, *Journal of the European Economic Association*, 4(2–3), 269–314.

P. Aghion, P. Howitt and D. Mayer-Foulkes (2005) 'The Effect of Financial Development on Convergence: Theory and Evidence', *Quarterly Journal of Economics*, 120(1), February, 173–222.

A. Aslund and N. Jenish (2005) 'The Eurasian Growth Paradox?', Peterson Institute for International Economics, Washington DC.

A. Aslund and J. Nazgul (2005) 'The Eurasian Growth Paradox?', Peterson Institute for International Economics, Washington, DC.

R.J. Barro (1991) 'Economic Growth in a Cross Section of Countries', *Quarterly Journal of Economics*, 106(2), 407–43.

R.J. Barro (1997) *Determinants of Economic Growth: A Cross-Country Empirical Study*, Cambridge, MA: MIT Press.

R.J. Barro and X. Sala-i-Martin (1992) 'Convergence', *Journal of Political Economy*, 100(2), April, 223–51.

R.J. Barro and X. Sala-i-Martin (2004) 'Economic Growth', 2nd edition, Cambridge, MA: MIT Press.

O. Blanchard (2006) 'Adjustment within the Euro. The Difficult Case of Portugal', *Portuguese Economic Journal*, 6(1), April 2007, 1–21.

O. Blanchard (2007) 'Current Account Deficits in Rich Countries', NBER Working Paper Series No. 12925.

C. Brezski and E. Ruscher (2007) 'Differences in Price and Cost Competitiveness across Euro Area Member States', mimeo.

F. Caselli and S. Tenreyo (2005) 'Is Poland the Next Spain?', NBER Working Paper Series No. 11045.

A. Demirgüç-Kunt and R. Levine (2001) *Financial Structure and Economic Growth: A Cross-Country Comparison of Banks, Markets, and Development*, Cambridge, MA: MIT Press.

S. Fabrizio, D. Igan and A. Mody (2007) 'The Dynamics of Product Quality and International Competitiveness', IMF Working Paper No. 07/97, April 2007.

J. Greenwood and B. Jovanovic (1990) 'Financial Development, Growth, and the Distribution of Income', *Journal of Political Economy*, 98(5), Part 1, October, 1076–107.

P. Howitt and D. Mayer-Foulkes (2002) 'R&D, Implementation and Stagnations: A Schumpeterian Theory of Convergence Clubs', NBER Working Paper Series No. 9104.

IMF (2006) 'Czech Republic, Republic of Estonia, Hungary, Republic of Latvia, Republic of Lithuania, Republic of Poland, Slovak Republic, and Republic of Slovenia–Export Structure and Credit Growth', IMF Country Report No. 06/414.

M.A. Kose, E. Prasad, K. Rogoff and S.-J. Wei (2006) 'Financial Globalization: A Reappraisal', IMF Working Paper No. 06/189.

M.A. Kovács (ed.) (2002) 'On the Estimated Size of the Balassa-Samuelson Effect in Five Central and Eastern European Countries', NBH Working Paper No. 2002/5.

K. Krajnyák and J. Zettelmeyer (1998) 'Competitiveness in Transition Economies: What Scope for Real Appreciation?', *IMF Staff Papers*, 45(2), June, 309–62.

J. Lendvai (2007) 'Modeling Real Convergence', mimeo.

R. Levine (1997) 'Financial Development and Economic Growth: Views and Agenda', *Journal of Economic Literature*, 35(2), June, 688–726.

R. Levine, N. Loayza and T. Beck (2000) 'Financial Intermediation and Growth: Causality and Causes', *Journal of Monetary Economics*, 46 (August), 31–77.

E. Prasad, R. Rajan and A. Subramanian (2006) 'Patterns of International Capital Flows and Their Implications for Economic Development', paper presented at the symposium 'The New Economic Geography', The Federal Reserve Bank of Kansas City, Jackson Hole, Wyoming, 24–26 August 2006.

S. Schadler, A. Mody, A. Abiad and D. Leigh (2006) 'Growth in the Central and Eastern European Countries of the European Union', IMF Occasional Paper No. 252, IMF, Washington.
World Bank (2007) 'Fiscal Policy and Economic Growth: Lessons for Eastern Europe and Central Asia', The World Bank, Washington DC.

Summary of discussion at 2007 ECB Economic Conference on Central, Eastern and South-Eastern Europe

Following up on Székely and Watson (European Commission), Ancāns (Bank of Latvia) discussed the speed limits on real convergence from a driver's seat perspective, that is, from the perspective of a policy maker in a rapidly converging economy. He started out by emphasising the importance of convergence in labour productivity, which requires further structural shifts in the composition of employment in the region. Focusing on the Latvian example, recent data suggest that Latvian employment is still too much concentrated in relatively low productivity sectors compared with the EU-15. Thus, enhancing labour mobility across sectors may provide a further boost to overall productivity growth, thereby raising the speed limit on real convergence. In combination with wage flexibility, this would also act as an important channel for offsetting relative price distortions facing economies characterised by a rapid removal of liquidity constraints for households. Indeed, many countries in the region benefit from a favourable institutional framework supporting wage flexibility. However, increasing international demand for labour and rising opportunities for migration might counteract this effect by putting upward pressures on wages in the region.

Turning to risks associated with the rapid rise in real estate prices in several countries of the region, Ancāns confirmed concerns about the effects of an unwinding real estate boom on economic activity. At the same time, some mitigating factors have to be taken into account. For example, decreasing profitability and taxing income gained from real estate transactions would most likely change incentives in the direction of channelling resources away from the real estate sector and more into productive activities. Indeed, demand spillover effects of the positive stimulus of mortgage lending might have already propagated to other sectors, including ones deemed 'productive'. In terms of policy conclusions, Ancāns expressed doubts about the benefits of increasing the risk awareness in the economy through activist interest rate policy and increased exchange rate volatility, referring to signs that market players may already be in the process of reassessing risks under the current policy framework.

Cihan (Central Bank of the Republic of Turkey) reviewed the Turkish growth process over the last 20 years from a growth accounting perspective, highlighting the change in total factor productivity growth since 2001 and its impact on the convergence performance of the Turkish economy. The analysis reveals that real convergence had been sluggish until 2001, as economic developments had been characterised by numerous boom–bust phases and underutilisation of resources, reflecting concerns about growth sustainability in the context of external imbalances, a fragile financial system and slow progress in structural reforms. More recently, however, fiscal discipline, central bank independence and substantial reforms in the banking sector have significantly contributed to economic stability. This is reflected in results of a growth accounting exercise suggesting that the Turkish economy has 'switched gears' since 2001, as the contribution of total factor productivity to economic growth has turned from negative to strongly positive, raising the economy's potential growth rate. This supports Székely and Watson in their call for financial stability and a reduction of distortive activities by the public sector as key policy measures raising potential growth. Cihan also noted that the sustainability of future productivity growth will heavily depend on the continuation of both structural and macroeconomic reforms.

Browne (Central Bank and Financial Services Authority of Ireland) focused on the growth and financial stability implications of rapid credit growth. On a more general level, Browne stressed that rapid credit growth per se is not a bad thing. Indeed, following the Aghion model, it may lead to a rise in potential growth if credit is properly allocated to productive sectors. And, even if focused on durables and housing, lending activity may offer expenditure smoothing opportunities contributing to the so-called great moderation of economic fluctuations. In the countries under review, however, the convergence environment is characterised by a specific feature, namely the 'instantaneous' capital and money market convergence following financial liberalisation and the much more sluggish convergence of income and price levels. The example of Ireland in the 1990s suggests that in such an environment the real cost of debt capital may fail to respond to domestic economic fundamentals, thereby suppressing a natural self-correcting mechanism. This may lead to dynamic instability in financial markets, that is, boom and bust cycles, with negative implications for the process of real convergence.

Developments in the housing market serve as a good illustration, as the supply response of the construction industry can be assumed to be limited, at least in the short term. With supply not in the position of meeting rising demand, spurred by rising incomes and/or demographic developments, prices and price expectations accelerate sharply. Expected capital gains and negative real interest rates lower the user cost of capital. As a result, housing demand increases further, leading to prices overshooting their long-run equilibrium values. Their eventual correction could, depending on how abrupt the correction turns out to be, impair financial stability and retard the convergence process.

6
The Impact of Real Convergence on Migration and Labour Markets

Herbert Brücker

Abstract

Migration from the new member states of the European Union (EU) has accelerated in the course of the EU's eastern enlargement. About 250,000 persons per annum moved from the eight new member states (NMS-8) who joined the community in 2004 into the EU-15 during the first three years following enlargement, and another 150,000 persons from Bulgaria and Romania during the same period of time. This migration took place despite a real convergence of per capita GDP levels. In this context, this chapter addresses two questions: first, does real convergence of GDP mitigate migration pressures? Second, what is the impact of migration on convergence and labour markets?

We find, first, that the real convergence of per capita GDP levels can reduce migration levels, but only to a limited extent under reasonable assumptions on real GDP convergence. Second, we find that migration itself supports the convergence of per capita GDP levels, wages and unemployment rates. In the long run, the GDP of the enlarged EU will, however, increase by some 0.6 per cent if 4 per cent of the population of the new member states emigrates into the EU-15. In particular the GDP of Ireland will increase by more than 4 per cent and that of Austria, Germany and the UK by about 2 per cent. These gains dwarf those of a further integration of goods and capital markets. The main winners are the migrants themselves: their income increases by more than 100 per cent. While natives in the sending countries tend to gain on average, the aggregate impact on the income of natives in the receiving countries is neutral or even negative. However, migration has only a negligible impact on the convergence of native income levels between the East and the West. The unemployment rate increases in the immigration countries by less than 0.1 percentage points, but blue-collar workers are particularly affected. Their earnings net of taxes and transfers might decline by 0.2 per cent in the receiving countries at the given skill composition of the workforce from the new member states.

6.1 Introduction

The European Union (EU) admitted eight new member states from Central and Eastern Europe[1] and two other countries (Cyprus and Malta) in 2004. Another two countries – Bulgaria and Romania – joined the EU on 1 January 2007. This eastern enlargement round has changed the economic landscape of the EU. The 15 incumbent EU member states (EU-15) formed a club of wealthy countries with relatively homogeneous income levels before its eastern enlargement. In contrast, the enlarged EU is characterised by marked income differences today: at current exchange rates, the gross national income (GNI) per capita of the ten new member states from Central and Eastern Europe (NMS-10)[2] numbers 21 per cent of that in the EU-15, and – measured in purchasing power parities (PPPs) – some 40 per cent of that in the EU-15 (World Bank, 2007; see Figure 6.1).

Since the end of the transitional recession the GDP growth rate in the new member states has exceeded that in the old member states.

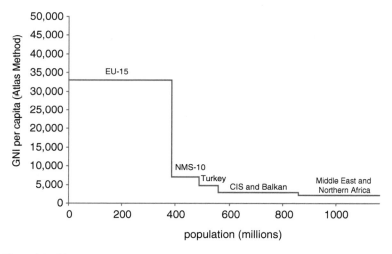

Figure 6.1   The European income gap, 2006

Sources: World Bank (2007); calculations by the author.

On average, the GDP growth rate of the NMS amounted to 5 per cent per annum, while that in the EU-15 numbered about 3 per cent per annum in the period from 1995 to 2006 (World Bank, 2007). The rate of convergence between the old and the new member states of the EU resembles the famous 2 per cent rate found by Robert Barro and Xavier Sala-i-Martin (1991, 1995) in many areas of the world. This implies that an initial gap in per capita GDP levels has a half-life of about 35 years. At this speed of convergence, the economic incentives to migrate remain high for decades. Nevertheless, the convergence of income levels as well as the convergence of labour market conditions can affect the scale of migration flows and stocks.

EU membership involves the free movement of workers within the Common Market. This sets the EU apart from other regional trade areas, such as ASEAN or NAFTA. The free movement of workers was defined as one of the four fundamental freedoms of the Common Market as early as in the Rome Treaties of 1957, and was fully implemented by the six founding members of the Community (whose joint population numbered 180 million) in 1968. Step by step, the free movement has been extended to the 15 EU member states and the three other members of the European Economic Area (EEA)[3] with a joint population of 387 million at the outset of the EU's eastern enlargement. The extension of the free movement to new members of the Common Market has not involved any migration surge in the past. Even with the accession of Greece, Portugal and Spain, migration increased only modestly, if at all. In the EU of today, less than one-third of the foreign-born population stems from other EU member states. However, the income gap between the incumbent and new member states in the case of the EU's eastern enlargement is much larger than in any previous accession episode. As a consequence, the incumbent EU member states concluded agreements with the new entrants for transitional periods of up to a maximum of seven years before the free movement of workers would be extended to apply fully to citizens of the accession states. In 2004, only a minority of the EU-15 countries opened their labour markets. This involves a diversion of migration flows away from the main destinations in the pre-accession period –that is, Austria and Germany – to those destinations which opened the labour market, primarily to the UK and Ireland. Even before their accession, migration from Romania and Bulgaria to Spain and Italy accelerated. Meanwhile, many other EU member states have opened their labour markets for migrants from the NMS-8, which, however, did not involve a migration surge.

The objective of this chapter is to analyse the relationship between real convergence and migration. This is, however, a two-way relationship: income convergence affects migration incentives, while migration affects income convergence. Moreover, other aspects of real convergence, *inter alia* the convergence of unemployment rates, are affected by migration. Ideally, the issue of real convergence would be addressed simultaneously in a general equilibrium framework. We follow here, however, the standard framework and treat the impact of convergence on migration separately from the impact of migration on convergence. This has the advantage that we can exploit the econometric literature on the determinants of migration, which usually treats the wages and unemployment rates as exogenous variables. This is justified by the fact that the impact of migration on wages and unemployment is relatively modest compared with the huge differences in wage levels and labour market conditions which we observe in the enlarged EU of today.

The remainder of this chapter is organised as follows. In order to establish the institutional and the quantitative background, Section 6.2 describes the application of the transitional periods for the free movement and presents the main facts on the east–west migration in the course of the EU's eastern enlargement. Section 6.3 uses a standard econometric model which has been used to forecast migration flows from the NMS into the EU-15 to analyse the effects of real convergence of per capita GDP levels and unemployment rates on the scale of migration. Section 6.4 briefly outlines a simulation model which is used for the evaluation of the migration impact on GDP, wages and unemployment. A detailed description of the model is given in the Appendix. On this basis, Section 6.5 simulates the marginal impact of migration employing different assumptions regarding the flexibility of labour markets, international capital mobility and capital accumulation, and regional differences in wages and employment opportunities. Section 6.6 analyses the short- and the long-run impact of east–west migration in the enlarged EU. Finally, Section 6.7 discusses the implications of the findings for the EU's enlargement policies.

6.2 Migration developments in the course of the EU's eastern enlargement

Against the background of the large income differences between the incumbent EU member states and the accession candidates, and the high degree of uncertainty about the potential scale of migration, the EU-15 countries decided at the European Council to impose transitional periods for the free movement of workers from the NMS. The so-called two-plus-three-plus-two rule allows the individual member states to suspend the free movement of workers from the new member states for a period of up to seven years. Extension of the transitional period is first considered after two years, then for a second time after three years. A second prolongation of the transitional period requires that the member state announces that serious imbalances exist in its domestic labour market. However, the application of transitional periods for the free movement remains a sovereign decision of the individual member state.

This delegation of the decision on the free movement to the individual member states had important policy implications. With the remarkable exception of Austria and Germany, most EU members had planned initially to open their labour markets, or were at least undecided. However, as enlargement came closer, only a few member states removed immigration barriers for workers from the NMS-8 completely (Sweden) or largely (UK, Ireland, Denmark) in 2004. Others opened their labour markets partially either by (small) quotas or for certain sectors based on bilateral agreements (e.g., Austria, Germany, Greece, Netherlands, Spain, Portugal). The majority maintained tough restrictions for labour immigration from the NMS-8 during the first phase.

The selective application of the transitional periods for the free movement of labour resulted in the diversion of migration flows away from countries which pursed a restrictive immigration policy to those which decided to open their labour markets largely or completely during the first phase. Altogether, the 2004 enlargement round has resulted in a distinct increase in migration from the NMS-8 to the EU-15. Migration data are poorly reported in most EU member states, such that some uncertainty surrounds the estimates of the actual scale of east–west migration. Based on the information of those countries which report migration properly, and on the information provided by the European Labour Force Survey for those countries which do not, we can estimate that the number of foreign residents from the NMS-8 in the EU-15 has increased from about 900,000 persons in 2003 to almost 1.8 million in 2007. This corresponds to an annual influx of about 220,000 persons during the first four years following enlargement.

Although this appears moderate relative to the income gap between the incumbent and the new member states of the EU, there has been an important change in the regional structure of migration since enlargement. In 2000, some 70 per cent of the foreign citizens from the NMS-8 residing in the EU were registered in Austria and Germany. This share has fallen to less than 40 per cent in 2007. At a net increase of the foreign population of between 150,000 and 250,000 persons per annum, the UK and Ireland receive between 60 and 70 per cent of the migration flows from the NMS-8 today (Table 6.1).

Thus, the changing regional pattern of migration suggests that the selective application of the transitional periods across the EU has triggered a substantial diversion of migration towards the UK and Ireland. Interestingly enough, this does not hold true for the Scandinavian countries: although Sweden has opened its labour market completely, and Denmark largely, net migration flows into these two countries have been – at some 6,000 persons – almost negligible since enlargement. Language and, perhaps, differences in labour market institutions might have played an important role in shaping the direction of east–west migration flows.

It is striking that there was also a substantial migration flow from Bulgaria and Romania into the EU-15 during the last years, although neither country was part of the EU before 2007. Based on bilateral agreements, Spain has admitted some 600,000 migrants from Romania and Bulgaria between 2000 and 2007 and Italy about 400,000 during the same period of time. Altogether, we observe a net inflow of about 160,000 persons per annum from these two countries from 2000 to 2007, which has not accelerated since their accession in 2007 (Table 6.2). Again, we see a diversion of migration flows: in Germany, which had been the main destination for migrants from these countries in the early 1990s, the number of residents from Bulgaria and Romania has declined from 260,000 to 130,000 during the last decade. Not surprisingly, the emigration rates in Bulgaria and Romania are larger than those from the NMS-8, reflecting the lower per capita income level in these countries.

The diversion of migration flows has influenced two subsequent policy decisions. First, even those countries which opened their labour markets to workers from the NMS-8 at the beginning of enlargement were reluctant to extend this free movement to Bulgaria and Romania upon their accession in 2007. The fear of receiving an extraordinarily high share of migrants from these countries if labour markets were opened has certainly affected the decision to keep the doors closed to Bulgaria and Romania in countries such as Ireland and the UK. Second, most EU member states decided to open their labour markets for the second phase of the transitional periods. Particularly, Finland, Greece, Italy, Luxembourg, the Netherlands, Portugal and Spain decided to apply the Community rules for the free movement of workers during the second phase of the transitional periods. With the remarkable

Table 6.1 Residents from the NMS-8 in the EU-15 and the EEA, 2000–07

	in persons and per cent							
	2000	2001	2002	2003	2004	2005	2006	2007
Belgium[b]	9,667	12,102	14,106	16,151	19,524	25,638	32,199	35,925
in %	0.09	0.12	0.14	0.16	0.19	0.25	0.31	0.34
Denmark[b]	8,394	9,101	9,447	9,805	9,807	11,635	14,282	7,884
in %	0.16	0.17	0.18	0.18	0.18	0.22	0.26	0.14
Finland[b]	12,804	13,860	14,712	15,825	16,459	18,266	20,801	12,777
in %	0.25	0.27	0.28	0.30	0.32	0.35	0.40	0.24
France[c]	37,832	44,946	44,857	39,779	44,848	37,426	39,462	39,755
in %	0.06	0.07	0.07	0.06	0.07	0.06	0.06	0.06
Germany[d]	434,603	453,110	466,356	480,690	438,828	481,672	525,078	554,372
in %	0.53	0.55	0.57	0.58	0.53	0.58	0.64	0.67
Greece[c]	12,114	14,872	16,546	17,432	19,275	17,948	18,144	21,978
in %	0.11	0.14	0.15	0.16	0.17	0.16	0.16	0.20
Ireland[e]	3,535	11,392	9,306	9,451	58,786	111,859	138,939	203,000
in %	0.09	0.30	0.24	0.24	1.46	2.72	3.30	4.70
Italy[b]	34,421	40,433	40,108	54,665	66,159	77,889	91,318	75,758
in %	0.06	0.07	0.07	0.10	0.11	0.13	0.16	0.13
Luxembourg[c]	1,073	683	1,159	1,095	1,059	732	2,804	3,087
in %	0.25	0.16	0.26	0.24	0.23	0.16	0.60	0.65
Netherlands[b]	9,235	10,063	11,152	12,147	13,048	17,814	23,155	20,569
in %	0.06	0.06	0.07	0.08	0.08	0.11	0.14	0.13

Austria[a]	53,683	53,362	54,797	57,537	60,255	68,933	77,264	83,978
in %	0.67	0.67	0.68	0.71	0.74	0.84	0.93	1.01
Portugal[d]	58	58	96	87	185	233	na	na
in %	0.00	0.00	0.00	0.00	0.00	0.00	na	na
Sweden[b]	23,884	22,868	21,376	21,147	23,257	26,877	33,757	18,489
in %	0.27	0.26	0.24	0.24	0.26	0.30	0.37	0.20
Spain[d]	10,557	19,284	29,998	41,471	46,710	61,830	77,772	100,832
in %	0.02	0.03	0.05	0.07	0.08	0.10	0.12	0.16
United Kingdom[c]	57,749	66,293	69,867	99,853	152,165	264,844	464,552	580,973
in %	0.10	0.11	0.12	0.17	0.25	0.44	0.77	0.95
Iceland[d]	1,865	2,232	2,462	2,547	2,644	4,251	7,803	na
in %	0.67	0.79	0.86	0.88	0.91	1.45	2.60	na
Norway[d]	3,366	3,658	4,195	5,166	5,549	7,427	11,240	20,074
in %	0.08	0.08	0.09	0.11	0.12	0.16	0.24	0.43
Switzerland[d]	17,598	18,733	19,997	20,308	20,909	22,060	25,711	na
in %	0.25	0.26	0.28	0.28	0.28	0.30	0.34	na
EU-15[f]	709,610	772,427	803,883	877,135	970,365	1,223,596	1,559,527	1,759,377
in %	0.19	0.20	0.21	0.23	0.25	0.32	0.40	0.45
other EEA and Switzerland	22,830	24,624	26,655	28,022	29,103	33,740	44,757	na
in %	0.19	0.20	0.22	0.23	0.24	0.27	0.36	na

Notes: [a] 2000–2001: Labour Force Survey; 2002–2007: National popoulation statistics; [b] 2000–2006: National population statistics; 2007: Labour Force Survey; [c] Labour Force Survey; [d] National population statistics; [e] 2000–2006: Worker registration numbers (PPSN); 2007: LFS, all data include Bulgaria and Romania; [f] Aggregate series are not comparable over time due to different data sources.

Source: National population statistics and Eurostat Labour Force Survey 2007.

Table 6.2 Residents from Bulgaria and Romania in the EU-15 and the EEA, 2000–07

	in persons and per cent							
	2000	2001	2002	2003	2004	2005	2006	2007
Belgium[b]	3,435	4,642	5,900	6,831	8,238	10,814	14,095	16,404
in %	0.03	0.05	0.06	0.07	0.08	0.10	0.13	0.15
Denmark[b]	1,482	1,580	1,646	1,746	1,834	1,987	2,200	na
in %	0.03	0.03	0.03	0.03	0.03	0.04	0.04	na
Finland[b]	786	854	873	887	909	970	1,089	na
in %	0.02	0.02	0.02	0.02	0.02	0.02	0.02	na
France[c]	5,752	8,761	7,960	20,496	13,826	13,781	28,752	27,523
in %	0.01	0.01	0.01	0.03	0.02	0.02	0.05	0.04
Germany[d]	124,453	126,245	131,098	133,404	112,532	112,196	112,406	131,402
in %	0.15	0.15	0.16	0.16	0.14	0.14	0.14	0.16
Greece[c]	13,319	19,761	32,395	31,881	41,491	46,890	48,466	55,817
in %	0.12	0.18	0.30	0.29	0.38	0.42	0.44	0.50
Ireland[e]	na	na	na	na	na	na	na	na
in %	na	na	na	na	na	na	na	na
Italy[b]	47,224	69,020	81,444	189,279	264,223	315,316	362,124	400,045
in %	0.08	0.12	0.14	0.33	0.46	0.54	0.62	0.68
Luxembourg[c]	na	na	na	na	na	na	na	na
in %	na	na	na	na	na	na	na	na
Netherlands[b]	2,110	2,564	3,168	3,720	4,413	4,944	5,082	na
in %	0.01	0.02	0.02	0.02	0.03	0.03	0.03	na

Austria[a]	16,229	30,229	22,387	24,926	26,802	28,367	29,573	29,958
in %	0.20	0.38	0.28	0.31	0.33	0.35	0.36	0.36
Portugal[d]	185	210	246	298	528	413	13,263	18,106
in %	0.00	0.00	0.00	0.00	0.01	0.00	0.13	0.17
Sweden[b]	3,951	3,300	3,123	3,148	3,170	3,205	3,080	na
in %	0.04	0.04	0.04	0.04	0.04	0.04	0.03	na
Spain[d]	9,441	43,676	97,020	190,185	277,814	410,403	508,776	649,076
in %	0.02	0.07	0.16	0.31	0.45	0.66	0.81	1.02
United Kingdom[c]	na	11,352	21,739	13,029	21,180	28,326	34,608	33,799
in %	na	0.02	0.04	0.02	0.04	0.05	0.06	0.06
Iceland[d]	1,865	2,232	2,462	2,547	2,644	4,251	7,803	na
in %	0.67	0.79	0.86	0.88	0.91	1.45	2.60	na
Norway[d]	3,366	3,658	4,195	5,166	5,549	7,427	11,240	20,074
in %	0.08	0.08	0.09	0.11	0.12	0.16	0.24	0.43
Switzerland[d]	17,598	18,733	19,997	20,308	20,909	22,060	25,711	na
in %	0.25	0.26	0.28	0.28	0.28	0.30	0.34	na
EU-15[e]	228,367	322,194	408,999	619,830	776,960	977,612	1,163,514	1,328,332
in %	0.06	0.09	0.11	0.16	0.20	0.25	0.30	0.34
other EEA and Switzerland	22,830	24,624	26,655	28,022	29,103	33,740	44,757	na
in %	0.19	0.20	0.22	0.23	0.24	0.27	0.36	na

Notes: [a] 2000–2001: Labour Force Survey; 2002–2007: National popoulation statistics; [b] 2000–2006: National population statistics; 2007: Labour Force Survey; [c] Labour Force Survey; [d] National population statistics; [e] Aggregate series are not comparable over time due to different data sources.

Sources: National population statistics and Eurostat Labour Force Survey 2007.

Box 6.1   Were the forecasts of the potential for east–west migration wrong?

The large number of migrants from the NMS-8 moving to UK and Ireland has triggered a public debate over whether migration projections carried out before the EU's eastern enlargement underestimated the migration potential. These studies have relied either on extrapolations of south–north migration in Europe during the 1960s and 1970s, surveys among the population of the new member states, or econometric estimates considering *inter alia* differences in income levels and labour market conditions across countries as explanatory variables. Under the counterfactual assumption that the free movement will be introduced in all EU member states at the same time, the majority of these studies predicted a long-run migration potential of 3–5 per cent of the population from the NMS-8, and a short-run net inflow of about 250,000–400,000 persons per annum (see, e.g., Boeri and Brücker, 2001; Alvarez-Plata *et al.*, 2003; Krieger, 2003; Layard *et al.*, 1992; Bauer and Zimmermann, 1999). There exist also some studies which obtained significantly lower (Dustmann *et al.*, 2003; Fertig, 2001; Fertig and Schmidt, 2001) or higher projections (Sinn *et al.*, 2001).[4]

Thus, the aggregate scale of east–west migration within the enlarged EU does not contradict the predictions of most migration projections, albeit the migration conditions in the first two years following eastern enlargement do not allow a verification or falsification of the forecasts. However, the net increase of the foreign residents from the NMS-8 in UK and Ireland was well above the projections before enlargement (10,000–20,000 persons per annum; see Dustmann *et al.*, 2003; Alvarez-Plata *et al.*, 2003). It is worth noting that those projections relied on the counterfactual assumption that all EU member states would open their labour markets at the same time. It was already anticipated before enlargement that countries which opened their labour markets before others would attract a substantially higher share of migrants than projected under this counterfactual assumption (e.g., Alvarez-Plata *et al.*, 2003). However, there have not been any quantitative estimates of those diversion effects, since no historical precedents exist, and even today it is hardly possible to quantify the scale of diversion. Altogether, there is still a considerable amount of uncertainty surrounding all estimates of migration potential from the NMS.

---

exceptions of Austria, Belgium, Germany and France, all member states have therefore opened their labour markets for workers from the NMS-8 largely or completely. The rationale behind these policies is the expectation that second-mover countries, that is, countries which open their labour markets after the others, receive only a relatively small share of migrants. Given that regional migration patterns are relatively stable over time – due in part to network effects, language barriers etc. – this expectation is not unreasonable. Indeed, the available data from 2006 and 2007 do not suggest that the second-mover countries experienced an immigration surge after opening.

The economic impact of migration depends not only on its scale, but also on the socioeconomic characteristics of the migrant labour force. The available Labour Force Survey data suggest that east–west migrants tend to be concentrated at the medium level of the education spectrum, that is, we observe that mainly young skilled workers with completed vocational training move from the east to the west. This holds for all receiving countries in the EU-15. Average education levels of the migrant population are slightly above the average of the population in the sending countries. Unemployment rates of migrants from the NMS differ largely across the EU: while they are well below those of natives in the UK and Ireland, they are well above in Germany, France and the Benelux countries. As a rule of thumb, those countries which impose tight migration restrictions experience higher unemployment rates among the migrant population from the NMS relative to those which open their labour markets.

6.3   Does real convergence affect potential migration?

The standard approach to explain macro-migration patterns assumes that an equilibrium relationship exists between migration stocks or flows on the one hand, and the expected income on the other hand (e.g. Hatton, 2004; Brücker and Schröder, 2006). Following the famous Harris–Todaro (1970) model, income expectations are formed on basis of wage levels and employment rates, which determine the probability of employment. Thus, real convergence affects macro-migration stocks or flows by two channels: first, via the expected convergence of wage levels, which determine expectations of income levels, once employed; second, via the convergence of labour market conditions, which in turn affect employment probabilities.

It is worthwhile to note that macro-migration models can be distinguished in flow and stock models. Flow models rely at least implicitly on the assumption of a *representative* agent. Consequently, net migration flows do not disappear before expected income levels in the receiving and sending countries have converged to a certain threshold level, where the expected returns to migration equal expected costs for the *representative* agent (Hatton, 2004). In contrast, stock models are derived from the assumption that agents differ with respect to their preferences or productivity. This has important implications for the macro view on migration: net migration flows can cease even if wages and employment opportunities between the sending and the receiving countries do not converge. More precisely, net migration flows cease when the expected benefits from migration equal expected costs for the *marginal* agent. Although the empirical evidence is not unambiguous, cointegration tests suggest that an equilibrium exists between migration stocks and the explanatory variables rather between migration flows and the explanatory variables (Brücker and Schröder, 2006).

In order to get an idea to what extent real convergence can affect migration, we focus here on the analysis by Alvarez-Plata *et al.* (2003), which is based on different convergence scenarios. The econometric model explains migration stocks by GDP per capita levels in the sending and the receiving countries, the employment rates, which are defined as one minus the unemployment rates, and a number of institutional variables which capture *inter alia* the free movement of workers in the EU, guestworker agreements, dictatorship and civil wars in the sending countries. The model is estimated in form of an error correction model, which can be derived from a rational expectations hypothesis (Hatton, 2004). For details see Alvarez-Plata *et al.* (2003), and for the theoretical foundations Brücker and Schröder (2006).

Thus, in the framework of this model, two types of real convergence affect the scale of migration stocks: first, the convergence of per capita GDP levels, and, second, the convergence of employment rates. Based on the observation that the convergence of per capita GDP levels between the EU-15 and the NMS resembles the famous 2 per cent rate found by Robert Barro and Xavier Sala-i-Martin (1991, 1995), the baseline scenario assumes that this convergence rate applies also in the future. In contrast, the low convergence scenario supposes that the convergence rate declines to 1 per cent per annum, while the high convergence scenario employs a convergence rate of 3 per cent per annum.

(Un)employment rates follow a random walk and are therefore hard to predict. In the scenarios presented here, three assumptions are applied. The baseline scenario assumes that unemployment rates in both the NMS and the EU-15 remain stable. The high convergence scenario relies on the assumption that unemployment rates converge in the NMS to the EU-15 level. Finally, the low convergence scenario supposes that unemployment rates increase by 50 per cent, that is, diverge in fact from the EU-15 levels.

The results of the simulations are displayed in Table 6.3. We observe that real convergence affects the scale of migration: the initial increase in the foreign population from the NMS-10 varies between 250,000 persons per annum in the fast convergence scenario and 350,000 persons

Table 6.3 The impact of real convergence on migration from the NMS

	2004	2005	2006	2007	2008	2009	2010	2015	2020
Net increase of foreign population p.a. (persons)									
Slow convergence									
NMS-10	346,186	432,613	428,460	386,075	330,228	273,808	222,745	75,862	34,889
NMS-8	256,000	341,366	343,038	309,457	263,003	215,525	172,508	51,209	21,164
NMS-2	90,186	91,247	85,422	76,618	67,226	58,282	50,238	24,653	13,725
Medium convergence (baseline)									
NMS-10	286,879	357,918	352,983	316,587	269,250	221,699	178,839	56,735	23,728
NMS-8	213,168	284,241	284,708	255,971	216,646	176,645	140,531	39,601	15,333
NMS-2	73,711	73,677	68,275	60,616	52,604	45,054	38,308	17,134	8,395
Fast convergence									
NMS-10	247,253	308,253	302,384	269,382	227,136	185,014	147,268	41,513	14,868
NMS-8	185,780	247,299	246,536	220,498	185,427	149,997	118,173	30,483	10,655
NMS-2	61,472	60,955	55,848	48,884	41,709	35,017	29,095	11,030	4,212
Foreign population (persons)									
Slow convergence									
NMS-10	1,301,585	1,734,193	2,162,657	2,548,732	2,878,961	3,152,768	3,375,514	3,983,158	4,216,739
NMS-8	1,009,955	1,351,322	1,694,359	2,003,816	2,266,819	2,482,344	2,654,852	3,096,588	3,243,563
NMS-2	291,630	382,876	468,298	544,916	612,142	670,424	720,661	886,570	973,176
Medium convergence (baseline)									
NMS-10	1,242,278	1,600,197	1,953,180	2,269,766	2,539,017	2,760,715	2,939,554	3,412,153	3,577,684
NMS-8	967,123	1,251,364	1,536,072	1,792,043	2,008,689	2,185,333	2,325,864	2,677,698	2,787,055
NMS-2	275,155	348,832	417,108	477,724	530,328	575,382	613,690	734,455	790,629
Fast convergence									
NMS-10	1,202,652	1,510,905	1,813,290	2,082,672	2,309,808	2,494,822	2,642,090	3,011,768	3,122,580
NMS-8	939,736	1,187,034	1,433,571	1,654,068	1,839,495	1,989,492	2,107,665	2,392,680	2,471,713
NMS-2	262,916	323,871	379,719	428,603	470,312	505,330	534,425	619,089	650,867

NMS-10: Bulgaria, Czech Republic, Estonia, Hungary, Latvia, Lithuania, Poland, Romania, Slovak Republic, Slovenia. NMS-8: CEEC-10 without Bulgaria and Romania. NMS-2: Bulgaria, Romania.

Sources: Calculations of the author. Based on Alvarez-Plata *et al* (2003).

per annum in the slow convergence scenario in the first year follow-ing enlargement, and from the NMS-8 who joined in 2004 at between 190,000 and 250,000 persons per annum. Moreover, real convergence has a long-lasting effect: the long-run migration stock from the NMS-10 varies between 3.8 million persons in the fast convergence scenario and 4.4 million persons in the slow convergence scenario (Table 6.3).

It is worthwhile to note that the baseline scenario from the Alvarez-Plata *et al.* (2003) study is fairly accurate in predicting migration flows and stocks from the NMS-8: it predicts an aggregate migration stock of 1.8 million persons from the NMS-8 in 2007, which almost exactly replicates the figure in Table 6.2. However, the Alvarez-Plata *et al.* (2003) projection supposes free movement in the EU-15, which holds true only for some of the member states. Moreover, migration stocks from the NMS-2, that is, Bulgaria and Romania, are underestimated.

Nevertheless, we can conclude that the convergence of per capita GDP levels as well as the convergence of labour market conditions affect the scale of migration. If these convergence scenarios grasp the realistic trajectories for GDP convergence and the development of unemploy-ment rates, we can conclude that potential migration is about one-third higher if convergence is slow compared with a situation when it is fast.

6.4   Outline of the simulation model

Building on Boeri and Brücker (2005) and Levine (1999), we employ here a simple general equilibrium model for the analysis of the impact of migra-tion on real convergence and labour markets. The simulation model which is used here relies on a number of stylised assumptions, but in particular it considers rigidities in the labour market. The labour market is modelled as follows: wages are agreed in a bilateral bargaining monopoly between employer federations and trade unions. Once wages are settled, employ-ers hire labour until the wage equals marginal productivity of workers. All parties in the wage negotiations are aware of this. As a consequence, the wage rate responds to an increase in the unemployment rate, albeit imperfectly. The elasticity between the wage and the unemployment rate has been taken from empirical estimates (e.g., Blanchflower and Oswald, 1995). This framework allows one to capture the wage and unemployment response to an increase in the labour supply through migration.

The other features of the model can be summarised as follows: there are three factors of production, skilled labour, unskilled labour and phys-ical capital. It is assumed that these three factors are imperfect comple-ments. However, migrants of the same skill type are perfect substitutes for native labour. Note that this assumption might result in an overestimation of the wage and employment effects of migration, if migrants are imperfect substitutes or even complements to native workers of the same skill category (Ottaviano and Peri, 2006). According to the overwhelming majority of the literature, it is assumed that production technologies are characterised by constant returns to scale. Allowing for increasing returns to scale would yield even larger economic gains from migration. The model considers only one sector in each economy and therefore rules out trade. Considering trade would mitigate the impact of migration on wages and employment, but also reduce its overall gains if trade and migration are substitutes. The converse holds true if trade and migration are complements. However, under realistic assumptions about the trade impact, the consideration of trade would not change the picture very much.

The general framework of the model is comparative–static, that is, the accumulation of physical and human capital is not considered. However, we employ two assumptions regarding the adjustment of the capital stock: in the first case we assume that the endowment of the economy with physical capital remains fixed; in the second, the physical capital stock adjusts to the increasing labour supply such that the interest rate remains constant, which would be the case if international capital mobility is perfect or if domestic capital accumulation holds the capital–output ratio constant. Indeed, the famous Kaldor (1961) suggests that the capital–output ratio is constant at least in the long run, which is also supported by recent evidence.[5] While the assumption of a fixed capital stock approximates the short-run response of an economy to a migration shock, the assumption of capital stock adjustment refers to the long-run impulse of migration.

Regarding the labour market, it is assumed that wage flexibility is higher for white-collar workers than for blue-collar workers. This is supported by estimates of the wage curve by skill levels (see, e.g., Brücker and Jahn, 2008). It is furthermore assumed that the unemployment risk of migrants is higher than that of natives, using actual unemployment rates of migrants and natives as a proxy. Moreover, unemployment benefits are considered. The replacement rate, that is, the share of unemployment benefits in the net income of workers, is allowed to vary across countries. The unemployment benefit is financed by a uniform tax or levy on labour income in such a way that revenues exactly match expenditures. Capital owners do not contribute.

The parameters of the model are calibrated in such a way that the differences in GDP per capita and wage levels of the model match the actual income gap between the EU-15 and the new member states (see the Appendix for details). Moreover, for the calculation of the marginal effects of migration we assume that the sending and the receiving countries have the same population size, that is, that the emigration of 1 per cent of the labour force equals the immigration of 1 per cent. In a later stage of the analysis, when we calculate the infra-marginal effects for the individual member states, we use the actual population size of the specific countries.

For analysing the effects of migration on real convergence we let the following parameters of the model vary:

- *Composition of the migrant workforce*: the proportion of white-collar and blue-collar workers in the migrant population is allowed to differ in all scenarios. As we will see below, it makes a substantial difference whether a country receives skilled or less skilled migrants.
- *Labour market flexibility*: We consider two cases: one with perfect labour market flexibility and no unemployment. This is the textbook case, which may not correspond to any country in the world, but may come close to conditions in destinations such as Ireland or the UK. We consider this case as a benchmark for the further analysis. The other case assumes that wages adjust imperfectly; the degree of wage rigidity roughly matches conditions in the continental European countries. The latter case is considered here as a realistic scenario for the migration impact.
- *Capital stock adjustment*: We distinguish two cases: in the short run, the physical capital stock remains fixed, while in the long run it adjusts in such a way that the interest rate remains unchanged (see above).
- *Homogeneous vs heterogeneous regions*: per capita income levels and unemployment rates in the regions of the recipient countries are allowed to differ. In the baseline scenario it is assumed that regions are homogeneous.

For a description of the technical details of the model and the choice of the parameter values see the Appendix.

6.5   A simulation of the migration impact on real convergence

This section starts with the simulation of the marginal impact of migration, that is, its effects at an immigration and emigration rate of

1 per cent of the population, in order to highlight the implications of different economic conditions. As a benchmark for the further analysis we start with the textbook case of completely flexible labour markets. These results are compared with the case of semi-rigid labour markets. The latter case is considered here as a realistic scenario of the short-run impact of migration under the conditions of European labour markets (Section 6.5.1). In the next step we compare these results with a scenario where the capital stock adjusts completely to the increasing labour supply. This can be interpreted as a reasonable scenario for the long-run impulse of migration (Section 6.5.2). Finally, we simulate the case of countries which are characterised by substantial differences in wage levels and employment opportunities across regions. This approximates the migration impact on large destination countries in the EU, such as France, Germany, Italy and the UK, where migrants cluster in prosperous regions (Section 6.5.3). On this basis we finally analyse the short- and long-run impact of east–west migration in the enlarged EU, employing actual and projected figures for the number of migrants from the new member states (Section 6.5.4).

6.5.1   The migration impact under flexible and rigid labour markets

The impacts of migration in the benchmark case of completely flexible markets are displayed in the first three columns, and the impact in the case of semi-rigid labour markets in the last three columns of Table 6.4. In both scenarios we vary the skill composition of the migrant workforce, that is, the share of white-collar workers among the migrant labour force, between 0.3 and 0.7. The results can be summarised as follows:

- *Substantial gains in the joint GDP*: the total GDP of the enlarged EU increases by approximately 0.2 per cent, which amounts to some €25 billion. The gains are higher if labour markets are flexible. Moreover, they tend to increase if the share of white-collar workers in the migrant labour force increases.
- *Income convergence*: not surprisingly, total GDP increases in the receiving area and declines in the sending countries. GDP per capita levels, however, increase in the sending country and decline in the receiving country (not reported here). More importantly, the income per capita of the native population increases in case of semi-rigid in the sending countries and declines slightly in the receiving countries. Thus, migration supports the convergence in the real income of natives.

- *Substantial gains for migrants*: the income of migrants increases by between 94 and 132 per cent. This may also have substantial effects on the welfare of the population in the sending countries, if we consider that on average more than 10 per cent of the migrant's income is transmitted to the home population as remittances.
- *Changing unemployment*: in the case of flexible labour markets there is of course no unemployment. In the case of semi-rigid labour markets, the unemployment rate increases slightly in the receiving countries by between 0.1 and 0.2 percentage points, depending on the skill composition of the migrant population. The higher the skill level of the migrant population, the lower is the increase in the unemployment rate in the receiving countries. Blue-collar workers suffer – at an increase in the unemployment rate by between 0.1 and 0.4 percentage points – more than white-collar workers (0.3–0.14 percentage points) from higher unemployment. Interestingly enough, the unemployment rate in the enlarged EU tends to fall. This can be traced back to the fact that migrants tend to leave regions or countries which are characterised by above average unemployment rates, and move into countries and regions which have unemployment rates below the average. Thus, migration contributes to the convergence of unemployment rates in the enlarged EU.
- *Winners and losers*: physical capital is, as expected, the winner from migration in the receiving countries, while it loses in the sending countries. Depending on the skill levels of the migrant workforce, the income of blue-collar workers net of all taxes and transfers to unemployed workers falls by between 0.15 and 0.7 per cent, while that of white-collar workers declines by between 0.1 and 0.4 per cent in the case of semi-rigid labour markets. Note that the losses of white-collar workers are substantially higher in the case of semi-rigid labour markets compared with the benchmark case of flexible labour markets as a result of transfer payments, while the impact on the earnings of blue-collar workers is similar in both scenarios.

6.5.2   The long-run impulse:
Considering the adjustment of capital

So far we have assumed that the capital stock is fixed. This may capture the short-run response of an economy which is affected by a migration shock. However, at least in the long run, it is reasonable that the stock of capital adjusts to the additional labour supply. This may be the consequence of either higher domestic investment or the influx of international capital. We make here the simplifying assumption that the interest rate remains

Table 6.4 The migration impact under flexible and semi-rigid labour markets

Share of white-collar workers in migrant population		Flexible labour markets			Semi-rigid labour markets		
		0.3	0.5	0.7	0.3	0.5	0.7
		Change in % at an immigration (emigration) rate of 1 % of the labour force					
Total GDP	West	0.53	0.56	0.59	0.43	0.47	0.51
	East	−0.58	−0.67	−0.77	−0.42	−0.52	−0.63
	Total EU	0.22	0.21	0.20	0.19	0.20	0.20
Total income	West	0.001	0.001	0.001	−0.077	−0.066	−0.054
natives	East	−0.001	−0.001	−0.001	0.140	0.133	0.126
	Total EU	0.001	0.000	0.000	−0.018	−0.012	−0.005
Of these:							
Blue-collar	West	−0.68	−0.39	−0.09	−0.70	−0.43	−0.15
workers	East	0.48	0.19	−0.10	0.68	0.36	0.05
	Total EU	−0.33	−0.21	−0.09	−0.30	−0.20	−0.10
White-collar	West	0.02	−0.15	−0.32	−0.12	−0.26	−0.40
workers	East	0.01	0.19	0.37	0.18	0.36	0.54
	Total EU	0.02	−0.04	−0.10	−0.03	−0.07	−0.11
Capital	West	0.30	0.32	0.34	0.24	0.27	0.29
owners	East	−0.33	−0.38	−0.44	−0.24	−0.30	−0.36
	Total EU	0.15	0.15	0.15	0.13	0.14	0.14
Income of migrants		132.25	110.38	93.62	136.84	115.24	98.68
		Change in % points at an immigration (emigration) rate of 1 % of the labour force					
Unemployment	West	–	–	–	0.19	0.15	0.12
rate	East	–	–	–	−0.25	−0.18	−0.11
	Total EU	–	–	–	−0.07	−0.05	−0.04
Blue-collar	West	–	–	–	0.40	0.24	0.09
workers	East	–	–	–	0.39	−0.20	−0.02
	Total EU	–	–	–	−0.11	−0.06	0.00
White-collar	West	–	–	–	0.03	0.09	0.14
workers	East	–	–	–	−0.07	−0.16	−0.25
	Total EU	–	–	–	−0.03	−0.05	−0.07

Source: Calculations of the author. See text for assumptions.

unchanged, that is, that the capital stock adjusts in such a way that the return on capital remains the same. Hence, there is an influx of capital into the receiving countries, and an outflow in the sending countries. We consider this as the long-run response of the economy to migration.

Another interpretation is that capital is likely to adjust to a persistent influx of migrants, such that these results would capture actual developments even in the short run. All simulations are based on the assumption of semi-rigid labour markets. The results are displayed in Table 6.5.

Table 6.5   The migration impact with capital stock adjustment

Share of white-collar workers in migrant population		Fixed capital stock			Adjustment of capital stock		
		0.3	0.5	0.7	0.3	0.5	0.7
		Change in % at an immigration (emigration) rate of 1 % of the labour force					
Total GDP	West	0.42	0.46	0.50	0.83	0.91	0.99
	East	−0.39	−0.48	−0.57	−0.73	−0.91	−1.08
	Total EU	0.17	0.18	0.18	0.40	0.41	0.42
Total income natives	West	−0.078	−0.067	−0.055	−0.030	−0.015	0.001
	East	0.112	0.109	0.105	0.083	0.062	0.041
	Total EU	−0.021	−0.014	−0.007	0.000	0.006	0.012
Of these: Blue-collar workers	West	−0.69	−0.42	−0.15	−0.44	−0.14	0.16
	East	0.68	0.38	0.08	0.46	0.09	−0.27
	Total EU	−0.29	−0.19	−0.08	−0.18	−0.08	0.03
White-collar workers	West	−0.13	−0.26	−0.40	0.15	0.03	−0.08
	East	0.19	0.38	0.57	−0.03	0.10	0.22
	Total EU	−0.03	−0.06	−0.10	0.09	0.05	0.01
Capital owners	West	0.24	0.26	0.29	0.00	0.00	0.00
	East	−0.22	−0.27	−0.32	0.00	0.00	0.00
	Total EU	0.10	0.11	0.11	0.00	0.00	0.00
Income of migrants		128.35	107.75	91.95	137.58	115.98	99.41
		Change in % points at an immigration (emigration) rate of 1 % of the labour force					
Unemployment rate	West	0.20	0.16	0.12	0.11	0.07	0.02
	East	−0.22	−0.17	−0.11	−0.17	−0.08	0.01
	Total EU	−0.04	−0.03	−0.03	−0.07	−0.05	−0.03
Blue-collar workers	West	0.41	0.25	0.09	0.29	0.13	−0.04
	East	−0.33	−0.19	−0.04	−0.29	−0.08	0.13
	Total EU	−0.06	−0.03	−0.01	−0.10	−0.04	0.02
White-collar workers	West	0.03	0.09	0.15	−0.03	0.02	0.07
	East	−0.07	−0.15	−0.23	−0.01	−0.09	−0.16
	Total EU	−0.03	−0.03	−0.04	−0.04	−0.05	−0.07

Source: Calculations of the author. See text for assumptions.

- *Higher GDP gains*: the GDP gains from a 1 per cent migration amount to 0.4 per cent of the enlarged EU's GDP. This is twice as high as under the assumption of a fixed capital stock.
- *Lower GDP convergence*: while the GDP in the receiving countries increases by between 0.8 and 1 per cent, it falls in the sending countries by the same amount. Thus, per capita GDP levels remain almost stable, that is, due to the adjustment of capital stocks to the labour supply shock the impact of migration on GDP convergence disappears. Accordingly, natives in the receiving countries lose less from immigration and gain less from emigration in the sending countries. Depending on the skill mix, natives may even gain in the receiving countries.
- *The gains for migrants remain unchanged*: the income gains of the migrant population remain almost unchanged under this scenario.
- *Smaller impact on the convergence of unemployment rates*: the unemployment rate increases less in the receiving countries, since the influx of capital generates a higher labour demand. If the migrant population is sufficiently skilled, migration is neutral for the unemployment rate in the receiving countries. Nevertheless, the unemployment rate of blue-collar workers can increase by up to 0.3 percentage points, if the migrant workforce contains largely blue-collar workers. In contrast, the unemployment rate of white-collar workers increases only slightly, even if the migrants are mainly white-collar workers. Accordingly, the unemployment rate in the sending countries falls less compared with the short-run scenario if capital stocks adjust.
- *Wage effects mitigated*: analogously, migration involves lower wage effects in the receiving and the sending countries, since the adjustment of capital generates a higher labour demand relative to the case with fixed capital stocks in the receiving countries and lower demand in the sending countries.

6.5.3 Regional disparities

Regional labour mobility in the EU-15 is low: only about one out of 200 workers changes residence every year compared with five in the United States (Barro and Sala-i-Martin, 1991, 1995; Boeri *et al.*, 2002; Decressin and Fatás, 1995; Puhani, 2000). According to George Borjas (2001), international migration can 'grease the wheels of the labour market' when domestic labour mobility is low. Suppose that in the host country – say, Germany – there are two regions: a low-wage region and a high-wage region. Regional migration equalises the costs and benefits of moving from the low-wage to the high-wage region for the marginal native migrant. Hence, there is no regional migration of natives. Moreover, let's assume that the incentives for domestic capital mobility have disappeared, that is, that the profits from investing in the low-wage region equal its costs. As interregional wage differentials in Germany are lower

Table 6.6 Impact of migration in economies with regional disparities

Share of white-collar workers in migrant population		Homogeneous regions			Heterogeneous regions		
		0.3	0.5	0.7	0.3	0.5	0.7
		Change in % at an immigration (emigration) rate of 1 % of the labour force					
Total GDP	West	0.42	0.46	0.50	0.66	0.70	0.73
	East	−0.39	−0.48	−0.57	−0.42	−0.52	−0.63
	Total EU	0.17	0.18	0.18	0.37	0.37	0.37
Total income natives	West	−0.078	−0.067	−0.055	−0.028	−0.032	−0.033
	East	0.112	0.109	0.105	0.140	0.133	0.126
	Total EU	−0.021	−0.014	−0.007	0.016	0.012	0.009
Of these: Blue-collar workers	West	−0.69	−0.42	−0.15	−0.90	−0.54	−0.18
	East	0.68	0.38	0.08	0.68	0.36	0.05
	Total EU	−0.29	−0.19	−0.08	−0.46	−0.29	−0.12
White-collar workers	West	−0.13	−0.26	−0.40	−0.05	−0.27	−0.49
	East	0.19	0.38	0.57	0.18	0.36	0.54
	Total EU	−0.03	−0.06	−0.10	0.02	−0.08	−0.18
Capital owners	West	0.24	0.26	0.29	0.39	0.41	0.43
	East	−0.22	−0.27	−0.32	−0.24	−0.30	−0.36
	Total EU	0.10	0.11	0.11	0.25	0.25	0.25
Income of migrants		128.35	107.75	91.95	227.58	197.31	173.68
		Change in % points at an immigration (emigration) rate of 1 % of the labour force					
Unemployment rate	West	0.20	0.16	0.12	0.02	0.02	0.01
	East	−0.22	−0.17	−0.11	−0.25	−0.18	−0.11
	Total EU	−0.04	−0.03	−0.03	−0.15	−0.12	−0.09
Blue-collar workers	West	0.41	0.25	0.09	0.02	0.00	−0.01
	East	−0.33	−0.19	−0.04	−0.39	−0.20	−0.02
	Total EU	−0.06	−0.03	−0.01	−0.28	−0.16	−0.05
White-collar workers	West	0.03	0.09	0.15	0.00	0.02	0.03
	East	−0.07	−0.15	−0.23	−0.07	−0.16	−0.25
	Total EU	−0.03	−0.03	−0.04	−0.05	−0.09	−0.13

Source: Calculations of the author. See text for assumptions.

than those between Germany and any NMS – say, Poland – incentives to migrate into the high-wage region are higher for Polish workers than for German workers. Hence, immigration from Poland reduces the regional wage differential in Germany. This increases the productivity of the remaining production factors, and the impact of international migration on GDP in Germany is higher than in the benchmark case with homogeneous labour markets.

In the calibration of this version of the model it is assumed that the receiving country consists of two regions, and that the proportion of white- and blue-collar workers is the same in each region. Total factor productivity and the physical capital stock are 25 per cent above the country average in the high-income region, and 25 per cent below in the low-income region, in line with regional income disparities in several European economies. We consider the long-run impulse of migration, that is, assume that the capital stock adjusts completely. It is assumed that all (foreign) migrants move to the high-income region.

As Table 6.6 shows, the economic benefits from migration increase substantially under regional disparities compared with the case of homogeneous regions:

- *GDP gains increase even further*: compared with the simulations with homogeneous regions, the gains in aggregate GDP increase from 0.4 to 0.7 per cent in the enlarged EU. This equals some €80 billion.
- *Almost no unemployment impact on receiving countries*: since migrants tend to move into regions with higher wage flexibility and lower unemployment, the unemployment rate in the receiving countries is almost negligible or can even fall if the share of white-collar workers is higher in the migrant labour force than in the native labour force.
- *Higher gains for migrants*: the income gains of the migrant population climb from between 100 and 140 per cent to between 175 and 230 per cent, since migrants tend to exploit the income opportunities in the receiving countries.
- *Larger income effects for native workers*: the income effects for native workers in the receiving countries tend to increase in both directions, since migrants move into regions where wages are higher and respond more smoothly to changes in labour supply. As a consequence, the earnings of blue-collar workers can fall up to 0.9 per cent if mainly blue-collar workers immigrate, and the wages of white-collar workers can decline up to 0.5 per cent if the migrant workforce consists mainly of white-collar workers. Note that immigration contributes to income convergence in the receiving countries.

6.5.4   The short- and long-run migration impact in the enlarged EU

So far the analysis has focused on the marginal effects of migration. This section analyses the infra-marginal effects of east–west migration in the enlarged EU, employing actual and projected migration figures. In the first three years since enlargement, that is, between 2004 and 2007, some 600,000 people moved from the NMS-8 into the EU-15. This corresponds to 0.15 per cent of the population of the EU-15, and to slightly below 1 per cent of the population of the NMS-8. We use this migration influx to calculate the economic impact on the individual member states. For assessing the long-run impact we employ the migration projections by Alvarez-Plata *et al.* (2003), which predict that some 4 per cent of the population of the NMS-8 will reside in the EU-15 in the long run (see Section 6.3). For the breakdown of this figure on the individual EU member states we use the regional distribution of migrants from the NMS-8 across the EU-15 in 2006. Note that this is a simplifying assumption, not a forecast – the

Table 6.7   The migration impact on the enlarged EU in the short- and long-run

	2004–2007 migration impact			Long-run impact		
	GDP	Native income	Unemployment rate	GDP	Native income	Unemployment rate
	Change in %		Change in % points	Change in %		Change in % points
Austria	0.10	−0.01	0.02	2.86	−0.02	0.13
Belgium	0.25	−0.03	0.06	1.71	−0.01	0.08
Denmark	0.05	−0.01	0.01	0.76	−0.01	0.04
Finland	0.05	−0.01	0.01	1.05	−0.01	0.05
France	0.00	0.00	0.00	0.19	0.00	0.01
Germany	0.05	−0.01	0.01	1.71	−0.01	0.08
Greece	0.03	−0.01	0.01	0.57	0.00	0.03
Ireland	0.61	−0.06	0.14	4.10	−0.02	0.18
Italy	0.05	−0.01	0.01	0.48	0.00	0.02
Luxembourg	−0.05	0.01	−0.01	0.48	0.00	0.02
Netherlands	0.05	−0.01	0.01	0.38	0.00	0.02
Portugal	na	na	na	na	na	na
Spain	0.10	−0.01	0.02	0.48	0.00	0.02
Sweden	0.00	0.00	0.00	0.86	−0.01	0.04
UK	0.25	−0.03	0.06	1.62	−0.01	0.07
EU-15	0.08	−0.01	0.02	1.05	−0.01	0.05
NMS-8	−0.38	0.08	−0.07	−3.87	0.23	−0.15
Enlarged EU	0.03	−0.01	−0.01	0.56	0.02	−0.01

Source: Calculations of the author. See text for assumptions.

regional distribution of foreign residents across the EU will certainly change in the future.

The short-run scenario is based on the baseline model as presented in Section 6.5.1, that is, we ignore any adjustment of capital stocks and assume that the receiving countries are homogeneous. In contrast, we assume for the long-run scenario that capital stocks adjust as in Section 6.5.2, but still rely on the conservative scenario which assumes that no regional disparities exist. The results are displayed in Table 6.7. For convenience, the analysis is here limited to the impact on GDP, native income and the aggregate unemployment rate.

- *Negligible short-run impact*: the 2000–06 migration from the NMS-8 into the EU-15 involved a mere increase of less than 0.03 per cent of the enlarged EU's GDP. This can be traced back to the rather small amount of migration (0.15 per cent of the population of the EU-15). Consequently, the impact on native income and the unemployment rate in the receiving countries is negligible on average. Even Ireland – which received immigration at the level of 1.2 per cent of its population, the highest per capita share of immigrants in the 2000–06 period – experienced a decline in native income of less than 0.1 per cent, and an increase in the unemployment rate of 0.14 percentage points, according to the simulation model.

- *Substantial GDP impact in the long run*: in the long run, it is assumed that the number of residents from the NMS-8 in the EU-15 reaches 4 million, which corresponds to an increase of 1.04 per cent of the population in the EU-15. This increases the GDP in the EU-15 by 1.1 per cent and in the enlarged EU by 0.6 per cent. However, the GDP per capita does not converge: the change in GDP almost equals the change in the population in both the sending and receiving countries. Unemployment is only slightly increasing in the EU-15, while it falls moderately in the enlarged EU. However, we observe some convergence in the unemployment rates. The impact on the aggregate income of natives is almost neutral as well. These results can be traced back to the adjustment of the capital stock in the long-run, that is, we find only very small labour market effects since the capital–labour ratio remains constant if the capital stock adjusts by either international capital mobility or domestic capital accumulation.

6.6 Conclusions

The main findings can be summarised as follows: first, we observe that real convergence has an impact on the scale of migration. At present, the real GDP growth rates of the NMS of the EU follow by and large the famous 2 per cent convergence rate found *inter alia* by Robert Barro and Xavier Sala-i-Martin (1991, 1995). This yields in the long run a migration of 3.7 per cent of the population from the NMS into the EU-15, if we follow the projections by Alvarez-Plata *et al.* (2003). This long-run migration stock increases to 4.4 per cent of the population in the NMS if we assume that the convergence rate declines to 1 per cent of GDP and if unemployment is increasing in the NMS, while it falls to 3.2 per cent if the convergence rate accelerates to 3 per cent and if the unemployment rate in the NMS converges to the EU-15 level. These figures should not be taken as exact forecasts. But our findings nevertheless demonstrate that the real GDP convergence and the convergence of unemployment rates may have a substantial impact on East–West migration in the enlarged EU.

Second, migration can affect real convergence by closing the GDP per capita gap and equilibrating unemployment rates across sending and receiving countries. In this context, it is useful to distinguish between the long-run and the short-run effects of migration. In the long run, the capital–output ratio is constant, as Kaldor (1961) has already observed. This implies that capital stocks adjust to labour supply shocks. As a consequence, the GDP per capita in the sending and the receiving countries remains largely stable. Small changes may result as a consequence of changes in the skill composition in the workforce. Thus, migration does not contribute much, if at all, to real GDP convergence in the long run. In the short run, however, migration may result in real GDP convergence if we assume that the capital stock is fixed. Altogether, the impact of migration on real GDP convergence is limited. Nevertheless, migration contributes to the convergence of unemployment rates across countries.

Third, our simulation results indicate that the effects of migration on the aggregate GDP in the enlarged EU are considerable. According to our simulations, a migration of 1 per cent of the population involves a 0.2 per cent increase in the joint GDP, which climbs to 0.4 per cent if we consider the adjustment of capital stocks. Moreover, if migrants move into the prosperous regions of the receiving countries, the GDP gains can increase to 0.7 per cent. These gains are certainly higher than those of a further integration of central and Eastern Europe into the goods markets of the EU.

Fourth, the native population in the recipient country can lose from migration, depending on the conditions in its labour markets and regional imbalances in income levels and job opportunities. Under the assumption of the short-run scenario, that is, assuming that the endowment with physical capital remains fixed, migration increases unemployment moderately and reduces native income slightly in the receiving countries. The long-run impact on natives in the receiving countries is likely to be neutral in the aggregate if the skill level of the migrant labour force matches that of the native labour force. In this case, the impact on labour markets is neutral as well. In principle, the gains of natives in the receiving countries tend to increase the lower the wage rigidities, the higher the skill level of the migrant labour force, and the larger the regional imbalances in income levels and employment opportunities in the receiving countries. Nevertheless, the gains or losses for the native population in both the recipient and the sending country are extremely small.

Fifth, labour loses in the recipient countries, while it wins in the sending countries. Blue-collar workers are particularly affected. Their earnings can fall by up to 0.7 per cent in the short run, and by slightly more than 0.4 per cent at an immigration rate of 1 per cent if the migrant workforce competes mainly in this segment of the labour market. Moreover, the unemployment risk of blue-collar workers can increase by up to 0.4 per cent in the short run and by up to 0.3 per cent in the long run if they are disproportionately affected by the competition of migrants. This has interesting implications for the assessment of the welfare effects of migration: while those at the bottom of the income distribution in the sending countries win from migration through lower unemployment and higher wages, those at the bottom of the income distribution in the recipient countries tend to lose through lower wages and higher unemployment. This tendency is even more pronounced if we consider that migrants tend to remit substantial parts of their income to their families at home. Thus, the inequality in the income distribution in the enlarged EU declines, since the poor in the low-income countries benefit from migration.

The impact of the migration following the EU's eastern enlargement is, however, surprisingly small. With an immigration level of 0.15 per cent of the population of the EU-15, migration was much too small to be felt in the receiving countries in the first years after enlargement. The aggregate GDP of the EU-15 has grown by less than 0.1 per cent through migration, and the unemployment impact is – at 0.02 percentage points – negligible. Even in countries which are disproportionately affected, such as Ireland, the UK and Belgium, the simulations yield only negligible results. Eastern enlargement may, however, involve more substantial effects in the long run, that is, when the transitional periods for the free movement expire and migration adjusts to the new economic opportunities in the enlarged EU. Indeed, at a GDP gain of more than 1 per cent in the EU-15 and 0.6 per cent in the enlarged EU, we can expect substantial income gains from further migration in the future. Moreover, if physical capital adjusts to the migration influx, there will not be much of an upheaval in the labour markets of receiving countries: the unemployment rate increases there by no more than 0.05 percentage points, according to our simulations.

6.7   Appendix

6.7.1   Description of the simulation model

The simulations of the migration impact are based on a highly stylised model of two economies, which produce one good and are – beyond migration and capital movements – closed. The model builds on Boeri and Brücker (2005) and Levine (1999). In contrast to the Levine model, the model employed here conceives that the labour market is split into an unskilled and a high-skilled segment and that the elasticity of wages with respect to the unemployment rate differs between the segments (see Bauer and Zimmermann (1997) for a similar assumption). The model also considers a number of other features like unemployment benefits and regional wage and employment differences. Moreover, in contrast to Boeri and Brücker (2005), the implications of an adjustment of the physical capital stock to migration are considered and a more flexible production function is employed. The model relies, of course, on a number of arbitrary assumptions, but it nevertheless allows analysis of some of the fundamental mechanisms by which migration affects the income, employment and welfare of parties in the host and source countries.

6.7.2   Outline of the basic model

The output of the economies in the host and the source country for migration is produced with unskilled labour, skilled labour and physical capital. Production technologies have constant returns to scale, such that

$$Y_i = F\left(\bar{A}_i, L_i^i, H_i^i, K_i^i\right), \quad i = f, h, \tag{A1}$$

where Y_i denotes output, $\bar{A}_i$ a productivity parameter, which reflects the level of technology and institutions, L_i unskilled labour, H_i skilled labour and K_i the physical capital stock. $i \in \{f, h\}$ is a country index where

f is the country of destination and h the country of origin, respectively. Let $\bar{N}_i$ be the initial, pre-migration, endowment of country i with unskilled labour, and let S_i be its initial endowment with skilled labour. The post-migration allocation of the unskilled labour force in the country of destination and the source country is given by

$$N_f = \bar{N}_f + \gamma M, \quad N_h = \bar{N}_h - \gamma M, \tag{A2}$$

where M denotes the number of migrants, and γ the proportion of unskilled labour in the migrant population. Analogously, the post-migration allocation of the skilled labour force can be written as

$$S_f = \bar{S}_f + (1-\gamma)M, \quad S_h = \bar{S}_h - (1-\gamma)M, \tag{A3}$$

where $1-\gamma$ denotes the proportion of skilled workers in the migrant population. In all simulations we assume that the total labour force, that is, the number of skilled and unskilled workers, is equal in the host and the home country in the pre-migration state. The model has a comparative static character in the sense that capital accumulation is not considered and that the productivity parameter is assumed to be fixed.

Wages and the demand for labour are determined sequentially. In the first stage, wages are fixed by a bilateral bargaining monopoly between trade unions and employer federations.[6] In the second stage, profit-maximising firms hire labour until the marginal product of labour equals the wage rate; the participants in the wage negotiations are aware of this. Given this wage-setting mechanism, wages respond – albeit imperfectly – to the unemployment rate in the economy as well as to other factors such as capital endowments which affect labour productivity. This allows us to express the wage rate for unskilled labour, w_i, and skilled labour, ω_i, respwectively, as functions of the unemployment rate and capital endowments in the economy, that is, as

$$w_i = f_i(u_{L,i}, K_i), \quad f_{u,i} < 0, \quad f_{K,i} > 0, \tag{A4}$$

and

$$\omega_i = g_i(u_{H,i}, K_i), \quad g_{u,i} < 0, \quad g_{K,i} > 0, \tag{A5}$$

where $f_{u,i}$ and $g_{u,i}$ denote the partial derivative of the wage rates with respect to the unemployment rate, and $f_{K,i}$ and $g_{K,i}$ the partial derivatives of the wage rates with respect to the capital stock in economy i.

The unemployment rates for unskilled and skilled labour are defined as $u_{L,i} = 1 - L_i/(N_i)$ and $u_{H,i} = 1 - H_i/(S_i)$, respectively. Thus, we allow the elasticity of wages with respect to the unemployment rate to differ for unskilled and skilled labour.

We consider two scenarios for the adjustment of the capital stock. In the first scenario, we treat migration as a shock for the economy and assume that physical capital is fixed. Clearly, this scenario captures only the short-term adjustment of the economy. In a second scenario, we make the converse assumption that the capital stock adjusts completely to the inflow of labour, that is, we assume that the interest rate remains constant. This can be justified by the assumption that either capital is internationally mobile or the domestic savings adjust to a persistent inflow of workers.

Let's start with the assumption of a fixed capital stock, that is, $K_i = \bar{K}_i$. The impact of migration on employment is then determined by the marginal product of skilled and unskilled labour and the flexibility of wages in the respective labour markets, that is, by

$$F_{L_i} = f_i\left(1 - \frac{L_i}{N_i}\right),\tag{A6}$$

and

$$F_{H_i} = g_i\left(1 - \frac{H_i}{S_i}\right),\tag{A7}$$

where F_{L_i} and F_{H_i}, respectively, denote the derivative of the production with respect to labour and human capital, respectively, and where we used the definitions for the unemployment rate on the right-hand side.

Equations (A6) and (A7) are a system of equations which determine, together with the production function in equation (A1) and the definitions in equations (A2)–(A5), the values for L_f, L_h, H_f and H_h. Write the *semi*-elasticity of the wage of unskilled labour with respect to unemployment as $\eta_i = - f_{u,i}\left(u_{L,i}\right)/w_i$, and, analogously, the *semi*-elasticity of the wage of skilled labour with respect to unemployment as $\mu_i = - g_{u,i}\left(u_{H,i}\right)/\omega_i$. Differentiating the system in equations (A6) and (A7) implicitly with respect to M and substituting from (A1)–(A5) yields then – after a good deal of algebra – the marginal response of employment of unskilled and skilled labour to migration in both economies:

$$\frac{dL_f}{dM} = \left(1 - u_{L,f}\right)$$

$$\times \frac{\gamma \eta_f \left(1 - u_{L,f}\right)\left[\mu_f/S_f - \omega_{H,f}/\omega_f\right]/N_f + (1-\gamma)\mu_f\left(1 - u_{H,f}\right)w_{H,f}/w_f/S_f}{\left[\eta_f/N_f - w_{L,f}/w_f\right]\left[\mu_f/S_f - \omega_{H,f}/\omega_f\right] - w_{H,f}/w_f\,\omega_{L,f}/\omega_f},$$

$$\tag{A8}$$

$$\frac{dL_h}{dM} = -\left(1 - u_{L,h}\right)$$

$$\times \frac{\gamma\eta_h\left(1 - u_{L,h}\right)\left[\mu_h/S_h - \omega_{H,h}/\omega_h\right]/N_h + (1-\gamma)\mu_h\left(1 - u_{H,h}\right)w_{H,h}/w_h/S_h}{\left[\eta_h/N_h - w_{L,h}/w_h\right]\left[\mu_h/S_h - \omega_{H,h}/\omega_h\right] - w_{H,h}/w_h\,\omega_{L,h}/\omega_h},$$

$$(A9)$$

$$\frac{dH_f}{dM} = \left(1 - u_{H,f}\right)$$

$$\times \frac{(1-\gamma)\mu_f\left(1 - u_{H,f}\right)\left[\eta_f/N_f - w_{L,f}/w_f\right]/S_f + \gamma\eta_f\left(1 - u_{L,f}\right)\omega_{L,f}/\omega_f/N_f}{\left[\eta_f/N_f - w_{L,f}/w_f\right]\left[\mu_f/S_f - \omega_{H,f}/\omega_f\right] - w_{H,f}/w_f\,\omega_{L,f}/\omega_f},$$

$$(A10)$$

$$\frac{dH_h}{dM} = -\left(1 - u_{H,h}\right)$$

$$\times \frac{(1-\gamma)\mu_h\left(1 - u_{H,h}\right)\left[\eta_h/N_h - w_{L,h}/w_h\right]/S_h + \gamma\eta_h\left(1 - u_{L,h}\right)\omega_{L,h}/\omega_h/N_h}{\left[\eta_h/N_h - w_{L,h}/w_h\right]\left[\mu_h/S_h - \omega_{H,h}/\omega_h\right] - w_{H,h}/w_h\,\omega_{L,h}/\omega_h},$$

$$(A11)$$

where $w_{L,i}$ and $w_{H,i}$ denote the partial derivatives of the wage for manual labour with respect to labour and human capital, respectively, and $\omega_{H,i}$ and $\omega_{L,i}$ the partial derivatives of the wage for non-manual labour with respect to human capital and manual labour, respectively.

Thus, the higher the flexibility of labour markets, that is, the higher the semi-elasticity between the wage and the unemployment rate, the higher is the marginal response of employment with respect to migration.

Consider two extreme cases: in the first case, the labour markets are completely flexible, that is $\eta_i \to \infty$, $\mu_i \to \infty$ and $L_i \to N_i$, $H_i \to S_i$. In this case, equations (A8) and (A10) converge to γ and $(1-\gamma)$, respectively, and equations (A9) and (A11) to $-\gamma$ and $-(1-\gamma)$, respectively. The labour force in the host country then increases exactly by the number of immigrant workers, and the labour force in the home country is exactly reduced by the number of migrant workers. This case corresponds to the textbook example of the impact of migration in an economy with clearing labour markets and an inelastic supply of native labour (e.g., Wong, 1995, pp. 628–32). In the other extreme case, wages for unskilled labour are perfectly inflexible, that is, $\eta_i \to 0$, while wages for skilled labour are perfectly flexible, that is, $\mu_i \to 0$. In this case, immigration of unskilled workers does not change employment of unskilled workers, such that it simply increases unemployment of unskilled workers in host countries. However, the immigration of skilled workers increases employment of unskilled workers in host countries, since skilled and unskilled workers are complements under the assumptions of our model. Thus, the impact of migration on (un)employment and income depends essentially on the composition of the migrant population with respect to their skill levels.

For the simulation, we have approximated production technologies with a standard *CES*-function, that is, as

$$F\left(\bar{A}_i, L_i, H_i, K_i\right) = \bar{A}_i\left(\alpha_i L_i^\rho + \beta_i H_i^\rho + \left(1 - \alpha_i - \beta_i\right)K_i^\rho\right)^{\frac{1}{\rho}}, \tag{A12}$$

where α_i and β_i are the income shares of manual and non-manual labour, respectively. The cases of flexible labour markets and wage rigidities are calibrated in Table 6.2 of Section 6.4.

6.7.3 Adjustment of physical capital

Our analysis has so far assumed that the capital stock is fixed. As a counterfactual, we assume in a second scenario that the capital is perfectly mobile and that the small-country assumption holds. Hence, capital adjusts in such a way that the interest rate remains constant in the sending and receiving countries, that is, that

$$\frac{dK_i}{dM} = -\frac{r_{L,i}}{r_{K,i}}\frac{dL_i}{dM} - \frac{r_{H,i}}{r_{K,i}}\frac{dH_i}{dM}, \tag{A13}$$

where $r_{L,i}$, $r_{H,i}$ and $r_{K,i}$ are the partial derivatives of the interest rates with respect to unskilled labour, skilled labour and physical capital in country i. Using this condition, we can solve together with equations (A6) and (A7) and the definitions in equations (A2)–(A5), for L_f, L_h, H_f and H_h:

$$\frac{dL_f}{dM} = \left(1 - u_{L,f}\right)$$

$$\times \frac{\gamma\eta_f\left(1 - u_{L,f}\right)\left[\frac{\mu_f}{S_f} - \frac{\omega_{H,f}}{\omega_f} - \frac{r_{H,f}}{r_{K,f}}\frac{\omega_{K,f}}{\omega_f}\right]/N_f + \left(1 - \gamma\right)\mu_f\left(1 - u_{H,f}\right)\left[\frac{w_{H,f}}{w_f} - \frac{r_{H,f}}{r_{K,f}}\frac{w_{K,f}}{w_f}\right]/S_f}{\left[\frac{\eta_f}{N_f} - \frac{w_{L,f}}{w_f} - \frac{r_{L,f}}{r_{K,f}}\frac{w_{K,f}}{w_f}\right]\left[\frac{\mu_f}{S_f} - \frac{\omega_{H,f}}{\omega_f} - \frac{r_{H,f}}{r_{K,f}}\frac{\omega_{K,f}}{\omega_f}\right] - \left[\frac{w_{H,f}}{w_f} - \frac{r_{H,f}}{r_{K,f}}\frac{w_{K,f}}{w_f}\right]\left[\frac{\omega_{L,f}}{\omega_f} - \frac{r_{L,f}}{r_{K,f}}\frac{\omega_{K,f}}{\omega_f}\right]},$$

$$\tag{A14}$$

$$\frac{dL_h}{dM} = -\left(1 - u_{L,h}\right)$$

$$\times \frac{\gamma \eta_h \left(1 - u_{L,h}\right) \left[\dfrac{\mu_h}{S_h} - \dfrac{\omega_{H,h}}{\omega_h} - \dfrac{r_{H,h}}{r_{K,h}} \dfrac{\omega_{K,h}}{\omega_h}\right] \Big/ N_h + (1-\gamma) \mu_h \left(1 - u_{H,h}\right) \left[\dfrac{w_{H,h}}{w_h} - \dfrac{r_{H,h}}{r_{K,h}} \dfrac{w_{K,h}}{w_h}\right] \Big/ S_h}{\left[\dfrac{\eta_h}{N_h} - \dfrac{w_{L,h}}{w_h} - \dfrac{r_{L,h}}{r_{K,h}} \dfrac{w_{K,h}}{w_h}\right]\left[\dfrac{\mu_h}{S_h} - \dfrac{\omega_{H,h}}{\omega_h} - \dfrac{r_{H,h}}{r_{K,h}} \dfrac{\omega_{K,h}}{\omega_h}\right] - \left[\dfrac{w_{H,h}}{w_h} - \dfrac{r_{H,h}}{r_{K,h}} \dfrac{w_{K,h}}{w_h}\right]\left[\dfrac{\omega_{L,h}}{\omega_h} - \dfrac{r_{L,h}}{r_{K,h}} \dfrac{\omega_{K,h}}{\omega_h}\right]},$$

(A15)

$$\frac{dH_f}{dM} = \left(1 - u_{L,f}\right)$$

$$\times \frac{\gamma \eta_f \left(1 - u_{L,f}\right) \left[\dfrac{\omega_{L,f}}{\omega_f} - \dfrac{r_{L,f}}{r_{K,f}} \dfrac{\omega_{K,f}}{\omega_f}\right] \Big/ N_f + (1-\gamma) \mu_f \left(1 - u_{H,f}\right) \left[\dfrac{\eta_f}{N_f} - \dfrac{w_{H,f}}{w_f} - \dfrac{r_{H,f}}{r_{K,f}} \dfrac{w_{K,f}}{w_f}\right] \Big/ S_f}{\left[\dfrac{\eta_f}{N_f} - \dfrac{w_{L,f}}{w_f} - \dfrac{r_{L,f}}{r_{K,f}} \dfrac{w_{K,f}}{w_f}\right]\left[\dfrac{\mu_f}{S_f} - \dfrac{\omega_{H,f}}{\omega_f} - \dfrac{r_{H,f}}{r_{K,f}} \dfrac{\omega_{K,f}}{\omega_f}\right] - \left[\dfrac{w_{H,f}}{w_f} - \dfrac{r_{H,f}}{r_{K,f}} \dfrac{w_{K,f}}{w_f}\right]\left[\dfrac{\omega_{L,f}}{\omega_f} - \dfrac{r_{L,f}}{r_{K,f}} \dfrac{\omega_{K,f}}{\omega_f}\right]},$$

(A16)

$$\frac{dH_h}{dM} = -\left(1 - u_{H,h}\right)$$

$$\times \frac{\gamma \eta_h \left(1 - u_{L,h}\right) \left[\dfrac{\omega_{L,h}}{\omega_h} - \dfrac{r_{L,h}}{r_{K,h}} \dfrac{\omega_{K,h}}{\omega_h}\right] \Big/ N_h + (1-\gamma) \mu_h \left(1 - u_{H,h}\right) \left[\dfrac{\eta_h}{N_h} - \dfrac{w_{L,h}}{w_h} - \dfrac{r_{L,h}}{r_{K,h}} \dfrac{w_{K,h}}{w_h}\right] \Big/ S_h}{\left[\dfrac{\eta_h}{N_h} - \dfrac{w_{L,h}}{w_h} - \dfrac{r_{L,h}}{r_{K,h}} \dfrac{w_{K,h}}{w_h}\right]\left[\dfrac{\mu_h}{S_h} - \dfrac{\omega_{H,h}}{\omega_h} - \dfrac{r_{H,h}}{r_{K,h}} \dfrac{\omega_{K,h}}{\omega_h}\right] - \left[\dfrac{w_{H,h}}{w_h} - \dfrac{r_{H,h}}{r_{K,h}} \dfrac{w_{K,h}}{w_h}\right]\left[\dfrac{\omega_{L,h}}{\omega_h} - \dfrac{r_{L,h}}{r_{K,h}} \dfrac{\omega_{K,h}}{\omega_h}\right]},$$

(A17)

6.7.4 The allocation of jobs among natives and migrants

For an analysis of the impact of migration on income of natives and migrants, it is necessary to make additional assumptions on the employment opportunities of natives and migrants. Following the traditional approach of Harris and Todaro (1970), we assume that in each period all jobs are randomly allocated among the total labour force, that is, among natives and migrants. However, we modify the selection process in allowing for the possibility that employment opportunities of migrants are below those of natives, that is,

$$p_{ML,f} = \lambda\left(1 - u_{L,f}\right), \qquad p_{NL,f} = \left(1 + (1-\lambda)\gamma M/N_f\right)\left(1 - u_{L,f}\right), \qquad \text{(A18)}$$

and

$$p_{HL,f} = \lambda\left(1 - u_{L,f}\right), \qquad p_{NH,f} = \left(1 + (1-\lambda)(1-\gamma) M/N_f\right)\left(1 - u_{H,f}\right), \qquad \text{(A19)}$$

where p_{Mj} and p_{Nj} denote the employment probability for migrants and natives in the host country, respectively ($j = L, H$), and the factor λ ($0 < \lambda \leq 1$) accounts for the possibility that the employment opportunities of migrants are below those of natives. Note that this implies that some of the employment risks of natives are shifted to migrants. For natives in the home country we assume that the employment probabilities are simply given by

$$p_{L,h} = 1 - u_{L,h}, \ p_{H,h} = 1 - u_{H,h}, \tag{A20}$$

6.7.5   The role of unemployment benefits

Migration does not only affect income by wages and employment, but also by welfare benefits. In order to consider the impact on welfare benefits, we assume that unemployment benefits are a fixed proportion of post-tax wages, that is, $b_i(1-t_i)w_{ij}$, where t_i denotes a uniform income tax rate, $i = f, h$, the respective country, and $j = L, H$, skilled and unskilled labour, respectively. Physical capital is not taxed. If we assume that the budget is balanced and if we ignore all other public expenditures, then taxes must equal unemployment costs, which gives for the tax rate

$$t_i = b_i \frac{w_{Li} \, u_{Li} \, N_i + w_{Hi} \, u_{Hi} \, S_i}{\left(1 - (1 - b_i) u_{Li}\right) w_{Li} N_i + \left(1 - (1 - b_i) u_{Hi}\right) w_{Hi} S_i}, \tag{A21}$$

where N_i and S_i are the post-migration endowments with unskilled and skilled labour.

Table 6.8   Assumptions of the simulation model

	EU-15	NMS-10
Proportion of less-skilled labour in workforce[a]	40	50
Proportion of skilled labour in workforce[a]	60	50
Physical capital stock in % of EU-15[b]	100	20
Income share of manual labour[a]	26	29
Income share of non-manual labour[a]	45	42
Income share of physical capital[a]	29	29
Productivity in % of EU-15[c]	100	80
Elasticity of substitution	0.6	0.6

Notes: [a] See Bauer and Zimmermann, 1997; [b] Corresponds to book value of physical capital stocks; [c] Assumption.

6.7.6 Choice of parameters

The parameters of the model have been chosen such that the differences in GDP and wages between the receiving country and the sending country match the actual differences between the EU-15 and the NMS-10. Some of the parameters on factor endowments and the parameters in the production function are based on empirical estimates; others are 'guesstimates'. A sensitivity analysis shows that the simulation results are relatively robust, that is, they do not depend on the arbitrary choice of parameter values.

Notes

This chapter draws on Brücker (2007) which has been published in the GMF discussion paper series. The author is grateful to Andreas Damelang for the collection of the migration data. The chapter benefited substantially from the comments and suggestions of Elke Jahn. The author also wishes also to thank Joe Guinan and Nicola Hardy and the participants of the ECB seminar on real convergence in Frankfurt (1–2 October 2007) for their valuable comments. The usual disclaimer applies.

1. Czech Republic, Estonia, Hungary, Latvia, Lithuania, Poland, Slovak Republic, Slovenia. These eight new member states from central and eastern Europe are labelled here as NMS-8, although ten countries joined the EU on 1 May 2004.
2. The NMS-10 comprise the NMS-8 plus Bulgaria and Romania.
3. Iceland, Liechtenstein and Norway. Switzerland rejected in a referendum to join EFTA, but participates also in the Common Market. It applies, however, safeguard clauses for the free movement of workers from the EU-15, and employs transitional periods for the free movement of citizens from the new member states.
4. For a detailed review of these studies and a test of the forecasting performance of different estimation techniques see Brücker and Siliverstovs (2006).
5. See Ottaviano and Peri (2006) for a similar assumption.
6. The argument elaborated here is consistent with different modes of wage setting, for example, models with a monopoly union or a bilateral bargaining monopoly (e.g., Layard *et al.*, 1992), efficiency wage theories (e.g., Salop, 1979) or shirking-models (Shapiro and Stiglitz, 1984). The analysis considers, however, only the long-run response of wages to a change in labour supply, that is, the impact of short-run fluctuations in (un)employment rates is ignored (Levine, 1999).

Bibliography

P. Alvarez-Plata, H. Brücker and B. Siliverstovs (2003) 'The Impact of Eastern Enlargement on Migration – An Update', Report for the European Commission, DG Employment, Social Affairs and Equal Opportunities, Brussels.

R.J. Barro and X. Sala-i-Martin (1991) 'Convergence Across States and Regions', Brookings Papers on Economic Activity, No. 1, 107–82.

R.J. Barro and X. Sala-i-Martin (1995) *Economic Growth*, New York: McGraw-Hill.

T. Bauer (1997) 'Do Immigrants Reduce Native Wages? Evidence from Germany', Münchner Wirtschaftswissenschaftliche Beiträge 97, University of Munich.

T. Bauer and K.F. Zimmermann (1997) 'Looking South and East: Labour Markets Implications of Migration in Europe and LDCs', in O. Memedovic, A. Kuyvenhoven, W.T.M. Molle (eds), *Globalisation of Labour Markets: Challenges, Adjustment and Policy Responses in the European Union and Less Developed Countries*, Dordrecht, Boston, MA and London, Kluwer, 75–103.

T. Bauer and K.F. Zimmermann (1999) 'Assessment of Possible Migration Pressure and Its Labour Market Impact Following EU Enlargement to Central and Eastern Europe', IZA Research Report 3, Bonn.

D.G. Blanchflower and A.J. Oswald (1995) 'An Introduction to the Wage Curve', *Journal of Economic Perspectives*, 9(3), 153–67.

T. Boeri and H. Brücker (2001) 'The Impact of Eastern Enlargement on Labour Markets in the EU Member States', Report for the European Commission, DG Employment, Social Affairs and Equal Opportunities, Brussels.

T. Boeri and H. Brücker (2005) 'Why are Europeans So Tough on Migrants?', *Economic Policy*, 20(44), 629–703.

T. Boeri, G. Hanson and B. McCormick (eds) (2002) 'Immigration Policy and the Welfare System', Oxford, Oxford University Press.

G.J. Borjas (2001) 'Does Immigration Grease the Wheels of the Labour Market?', *Brookings Papers on Economic Activity*, 1, 69–133.

H. Brücker (2002) 'Can International Migration Solve the Problems of European Labour Markets', UNECE Economic Survey of Europe No. 2, 109–42.

H. Brücker (2007) 'Labor Mobility after the European Union's Eastern Enlargement: Who Wins, Who Loses?', A Report to the German Marshall Fund of the United States, February 2007.

H. Brücker and E.J. Jahn (2008) 'Migration and the Wage Curve: A Structural Approach to Measure the Wage and Employment Effects of Migration', IZA DP No. 3423.

H. Brücker and P. Schröder (2006) International Migration with Heterogeneous Agents – Theory and Evidence, IZA Discussion Paper No. 2049, Bonn.

H. Brücker and B. Siliverstovs (2006) 'On the Estimation and Forecasting of International Migration: How Relevant Is Heterogeneity Across Countries?', *Empirical Economics*, 31(3), 735–54.

J. Decressin and A. Fatás (1995) 'Regional Labor Market Dynamics in Europe', *European Economic Review*, 39(9), 1627–57.

C. Dustmann, M. Casanova, M. Fertig, I. Preston and C.M. Schmidt (2003) 'The Impact of EU-enlargement on Migration Flows', Home Office Online Report 25/03, http://www.homeoffice.gov.uk/rds/pdfs2/rdsolr2503.pdf

M. Fertig (2001) 'The Economic Impact of EU Enlargement: Assessing the Migration Potential', *Empirical Economics*, 26(4), 707–20.

M. Fertig and C.M. Schmidt (2001) 'Aggregate-Level Migration Studies as a Tool for Forecasting Future Migration Streams', University of Heidelberg, Economic Department Discussion Paper No. 324.

J.R. Harris and M.P. Todaro (1970) 'Migration, Unemployment and Development: A Two-Sector Analysis', *American Economic Review*, 60(1), 126–42.

T.J. Hatton (2004) 'Seeking Asylum in Europe', *Economic Policy*, 19(38), April, 5–62.

N. Kaldor (1961) Capital Accumulation and Economic Growth, in F.A. Lutz and D.C. Hague (ed.), *The Theory of Capital*, London: Macmillan, 177–222.

H. Krieger (2003) 'Migration Trends in an Enlarged EU', European Foundation for the Improvement of Working and Living Conditions, Dublin.

R. Layard, O. Blanchard, R. Dornbusch and P. Krugman (1992) *East-West Migration: The Alternatives*, Boston, MA: MIT Press.

R. Layard, S. Nickell and R. Jackman (1991) *Unemployment – Macroeconomic Performance and the Labour Market*, New York, Oxford University Press.

P. Levine (1999) 'The Welfare Economics of Immigration Control', *Population Economics*, 12, 23–43.

G. Ottaviano and G. Peri (2006) 'Rethinking the Effects of Immigration on Wages', NBER Working Paper No. 12497, Cambridge, MA.

P.A. Puhani (2001) 'Labour Mobility: An Adjustment Mechanism in Euroland? Empirical Evidence for Western Germany, France, and Italy', *German Economic Review*, 2(2), 127–40.

D. Rodrik (2002) 'Final Remarks', in T. Boeri, G. Hanson and B. McCormick (eds), *Immigration Policy and the Welfare System*, Oxford University Press, Oxford, 314–17.

S.C. Salop (1979) 'A Model of the Natural Rate of Unemployment', *American Economic Review*, 69(1), 117–25.

C. Shapiro and J.E. Stiglitz (1984) 'Equilibrium Unemployment as a Worker Discipline Device', *American Economic Review*, 74(3), 433–44.

H.-W. Sinn, G. Flaig, M. Werding, S. Munz, N. Duell and H. Hoffmann (2001) 'EU-Erweiterung und Arbeitskräftemigration. Wege zu einer schrittweisen Annäherung der Arbeitsmärkte', Munich: Ifo-Institut für Wirtschaftsforschung.

K.-Y. Wong (1995) *International Trade in Goods and Factor Mobility*, Cambridge, MA: MIT Press.

World Bank (2007) 'World Development Indicators (WDI) 2006', CD-Rom, Washington DC.

Summary of discussion at 2007 ECB Economic Conference on Central, Eastern and South-Eastern Europe

Following up on Brücker, Cristian Popa (Banca Nationala a României) reviewed a number of indicators for real convergence in Romania relative to the euro area and other CEE countries. He argued that the real income gap vis-à-vis the euro area is mostly explained by the still sizeable labour productivity gap, even though labour productivity in Romania has considerably increased in recent years, both in absolute terms and relative to the euro area. Turning to the labour market situation in Romania, he showed that registered unemployment – more so than unemployment based on the labour force survey – has fallen sharply in recent years, from around 13 per cent in 2001 to around 4 per cent in 2007. This decline, which is *inter alia* due to the fast expansion of economic activity in the country (notably in construction, trade, hotels and restaurants, IT and pharmaceuticals) but also due to emigration, especially of skilled labour, has resulted in labour shortages in some sectors of the Romanian economy. These shortages are more severe than the headline unemployment figure would suggest due to the low regional mobility of the workforce, insufficient tailoring of education to labour market requirements and the lack of long-term human resource development strategies at the company level. At the same time Popa also pointed to the presence of informal unemployment, in particular in rural areas, where a relatively high share of the population is dependent upon subsistence agriculture.

Turning more specifically to the consequences of migration for Romania, Popa flagged the strong increase in remittances, which, at around 5 per cent of GDP, appear to have become a significant source of household income in certain regions. Remittances also help to alleviate foreign trade imbalances in the broader context of the Romanian economy, thus reducing the size of the current account deficit. In this context he flagged that efficient banking and payment systems are important to process remittances and that the central bank has played a role in supporting the emergence of the attendant financial infrastructure. Moreover, migration tends to lower unemployment rates in underdeveloped regions. On the downside, emigration implies drainage of skilled and highly skilled labour, which aggravates the above-mentioned labour market pressures in a number of sectors. These bottlenecks result in pressure for companies to increase wages beyond productivity gains, which in turn entails inflationary risks and competitiveness losses, especially in labour-intensive industries.

With regard to suitable labour-market policy responses, Popa emphasised the need for improvements of education and training by taking sectoral and regional labour market requirements into account. In this context he mentioned also the development of training programmes aimed at the rural sector, given that 50 per cent of job seekers aged below 34 years having poor educational skills come from rural areas. Furthermore, incentives to increase training participation of employed persons aged 45 and over, as well as incentives for regional mobility, should be improved and – more generally – labour contracts in Romania should be made more flexible.

Looking forward, Popa argued that future migration flows from Romania will crucially depend on the level of income as well as the income differences vis-à-vis possible recipient economies. At this point, however, he argued that most of the people who wanted to leave the country had ostensibly already done so. Against that background even easier access for Romanians to work permits abroad would be unlikely to result in a renewed increase in emigration.

Finally, Popa posed the question of how authorities should respond if domestic bargaining, coupled with international (and especially intra-EU) labour mobility, drives equilibrium wages upwards, thus also increasing equilibrium inflation rates. He suggested that a combination of prudent macroeconomic policies (including fiscal policy and, crucially, incomes policy for public sector employees) and structural reforms could restrict such shifts in wages and aggregate prices to a more limited time horizon, thus enhancing the macroeconomic sustainability of the catching-up process for a new EU member state such as Romania.

Altin Tanku (Bank of Albania) reviewed the Albanian experience with regard to the interaction of real convergence, labour market developments and migration. He started by stressing that more than 50 per cent of the Albanian population is below 30 years old, and that according to the World Bank a falling but still sizeable part of the population is defined as poor (18.5 per cent in 2005). Also the unemployment rate is still relatively high, at 14 per cent in 2006. Against that background, emigration from Albania has been very significant, with Greece and Italy being clearly the main recipient countries. The remittances transferred by the emigrants have become an important source of foreign financing and poverty reduction, contributing according to the Bank of Albania around 13 per cent of GDP at the end of 2006. More generally, emigration became a major driving force of real convergence in Albania with widespread positive impacts on labour markets and growth. The drop in the labour force contributed to reducing unemployment and improving the capital-to-labour ratio, which in turn increased labour productivity. In addition, the remittances impacted positively on consumption and savings and – to a smaller extent – on the capital stock, with mostly small family businesses benefiting from remittances. Finally, migration helped to increase both human and social capital in Albania.

Mr Tanku was rather sceptical with regard to the question of whether real convergence is likely to significantly reduce Albanian emigration trends in the near future. First, the UN predicts that until 2015 the working age population will grow 5 per cent annually. In addition, a significant part of the labour force is expected to exit the agricultural sector and to seek new employment, domestically or abroad. Moreover, at the moment not all potential migrants possess the necessary capital to migrate; a constraint that will be eased by the expected increase in income. More Albanians will be able to afford emigration while the income per capita gaps with the main recipient countries, a key determinant of emigration, is expected to remain large. Notwithstanding these migration-enhancing factors, the desire to migrate among Albanians has slowed down. In a recent survey 44 per cent of respondents stated that they would wish to emigrate, compared with 75 per cent back in 1998. The desire to leave the country remains particularly high among young and less educated people.

In sum, Mr Tanku argued that large-scale emigration has played a significant role in the Albanian economic growth process. Sustained growth and lower income have resulted in a slowdown in the desire to migrate. However, demographic factors, remaining structural labour market mismatches and other economic problems will continue to exert pressure on the Albanian labour market. In the absence of suitable structural reform measures and sufficient capital accumulation, these developments have the potential to result in further significant emigration flows.

Misa Tanaka (Bank of England) complemented the views from the two previous discussants by looking at migration from the perspective of a recipient country, namely the UK. She started her presentation by saying that, since May 2004, the date of EU accession by eight Central and Eastern European countries as well as Cyprus and Malta, citizens from the CEE countries have the right to work in the UK, subject to their successful application to the Worker Registration Scheme (WRS). By contrast, citizens from Bulgaria and Romania, the two countries that joined the EU in January 2007, face greater restrictions with regard to their right to work in the UK.

Between 1 May 2004 and 30 June 2007 a cumulative total of 683,000 citizens from CEE countries had applied to register on the WRS and 96 per cent of these applications were approved. But this number should not be interpreted as the estimated stock of CEE workers in the UK, as some of these migrants may have left the UK since. These are estimates that the number of workers from these countries residing in the UK was at most half a million in late 2006.

Looking at the nationality of approved WRS applications from 1 May 2004 to 30 June 2007, the highest proportion of approved applicants were Polish (66 per cent), followed by Lithuanian (10 per cent) and Slovak (10 per cent). With regard to migrants from Bulgaria and Romania, only a few have applied for accession worker cards; and the number of applications for registration certificates also remained low, with most applying as self-employed. Registered CEE workers in the UK were predominantly young: 82 per cent of workers registered by June 2007 were between the ages of 18 and 34. More than half of the approved applicants stated that they wanted to stay in the UK for less than three months and another quarter did not specify the intended length of their stay. The picture is rather diverse when it comes to the occupations of registered workers from CEE countries, but a large majority work in low-skilled and low-paid jobs.

Turning to the macroeconomic implications of immigration for the UK, Dr Tanaka argued that recent migrant inflows increased both aggregate supply and demand. The Bank of England believes that, in the short run, immigration probably had a slightly larger impact on aggregate supply than on aggregate demand, so it may have helped to moderate inflationary pressure. At the same time there is great uncertainty over the impact of immigration on the UK labour market: between May 2004 and June 2007, UK unemployment has risen from 4.8 per cent to 5.4 per cent, but this rise could reflect temporary structural factors which are unrelated to migration.

7
Real Convergence and the Balance of Payments

Angana Banerji and Juha Kähkönen

7.1 Introduction

Balance of payments pressures are building up in emerging Europe as it pursues real convergence with the EU-15.[1] Current account deficits have widened to record levels in many countries in the region. These deficits are being financed by massive capital inflows due to various push and pull factors. Rapid integration of, and ample liquidity in, global financial markets have abetted this process. Many of the standard indicators of macroeconomic vulnerability are flashing red, and policy makers have to decide how to deal with the balance of payments pressures.

Are emerging markets in Europe then headed for a crisis? There is a broad range of views on this issue. At one end of the spectrum is the view that takes comfort from the argument that emerging Europe is simply on a path of unconditional convergence with Western Europe and is unlikely to falter.[2] At the other end are those who balk at the rising current account deficits and possible balance sheet mismatches in the region, which have begun to look disturbingly similar to those seen in previous crises.

This chapter examines the challenges posed by the balance of payments developments in emerging Europe. What are the pressures that these countries are facing, and how do they manifest themselves? How concerned should we be about the balance of payments developments in these countries – are we seeing convergence at work or rising risks that may trigger a crisis? What should policy makers do to reduce vulnerabilities without impeding rapid convergence? These issues are being hotly debated in many fora. This chapter lays out the facts and the views across the spectrum, and concludes by outlining appropriate policy responses. However, it stops short of drawing definitive conclusions, not least because an assessment of vulnerability cannot be generalised across a region, especially one as diverse as emerging Europe.

7.2 What are the facts?

Emerging Europe is growing rapidly, but at divergent rates. The Baltic countries lead the pack with growth rates approaching 10 per cent in recent years, whereas South-Eastern and Central European countries have grown at a more sedate 4–6 per cent per year on average (Figure 7.1).

Growth is driven by private sector-led domestic demand, while net exports have languished (Table 7.1). The contribution of the public sector has been small as fiscal policies have generally been tight. As a result of strong growth, per capita incomes in emerging Europe are catching up with those in Western Europe. Central Europe, the more advanced among emerging European countries, passed the halfway mark a few years ago. While the Baltics are rapidly closing in to the halfway point, South-Eastern Europe still lags well behind (Figure 7.2). Despite the rapid growth and notwithstanding Balassa-Samuelson effects, inflation has remained subdued, reflecting generally prudent policies and a steady increase in potential output. More recently, though, inflation

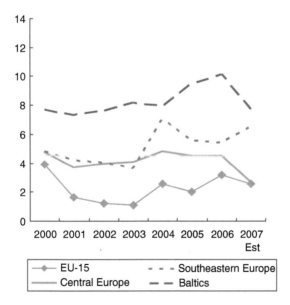

Figure 7.1 Real GDP growth

Sources: World Economic Outlook and IMF staff calculations.

Table 7.1   Average contributions to growth, 2000–2006

	Central Europe		Southeastern Europe		Baltics	
	Average	2006	Average	2006	Average	2006
GDP Growth	4.3	4.5	5.0	5.4	8.3	10.1
Consumption	3.1	1.7	4.5	3.7	5.5	8.4
Government	0.3	0.6	0.4	0.0	0.5	0.7
Investment	0.2	−0.8	2.4	2.5	4.3	6.1
Net exports	0.6	3.0	−2.3	−0.8	−2.2	−7.2

Sources: World Economic Outlook and IMF staff calculations.

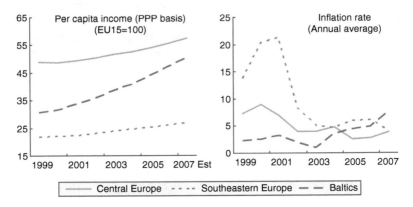

Figure 7.2   Income and inflation

Sources: World Economic Outlook and IMF staff calculations.

has started to creep up in the Baltics and South-Eastern Europe as those economies have faced overheating pressures.

Emerging Europe's convergence is manifesting itself in the current account balance, with some variation across the region. The Baltics and South-Eastern Europe are recording unprecedentedly high current account deficits, as exports have not kept pace with the strong growth in imports. Current account deficits in the more advanced Central Europe display a somewhat different dynamic. While import growth has also picked up in this region, the current account deficits have been contained by rapid growth in exports and export market shares due to competitiveness gains (Figure 7.3).

The large current account deficits have been accompanied by even larger capital inflows (Figure 7.4). The real exchange rate has appreciated steadily in response.

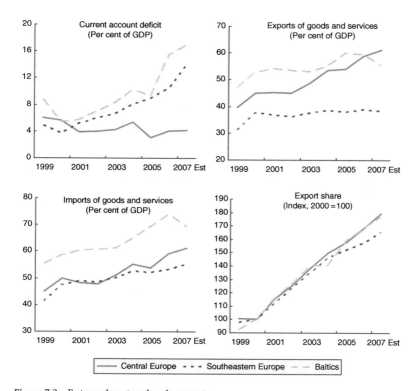

Figure 7.3 External sector developments

Sources: Direction of Trade Statistics, World Economic Outlook and IMF staff calculations.

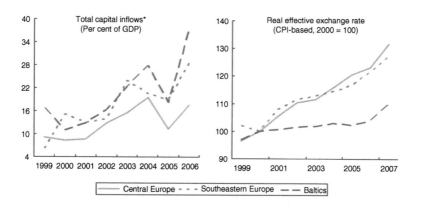

Figure 7.4 Capital inflows and real effective exchange rate

Note: (*) Capital inflows consist of Foreign Direct Investment (FDI), external debt flows, portfolio investment, remittances, and EU transfers.

Sources: Eurostat, International Financial Statistics, World Economic Outlook and IMF staff calculations.

These flows have taken place against the backdrop of a vastly more globally integrated financial market than in the mid-1990s. All around the world, home country bias has declined, and institutions and individuals are more willing and able to hold assets outside their own countries. The global trend toward increased cross-border asset trade has lowered the cost of capital for everyone. Emerging Europe has also benefited from exceptionally favourable external financing conditions in recent years, as the demand for financing has waned in other emerging markets, many of which are running large current account surpluses, and world interest rates and emerging market debt spreads have remained low. The capital inflows have more than compensated for the widening current account deficits in South-Eastern Europe and the Baltics, leading to a build-up in reserves, especially in countries where authorities have intervened to support fixed exchange rate regimes (Figure 7.5). The Central European countries have witnessed only a modest increase in capital inflows in recent years after a strong showing early in this decade. Here, the widening current account deficits have translated into a steady erosion in gross reserves.

Balance of payments pressures are especially marked in countries with fixed exchange rate regimes (Figure 7.6). In these countries, the current account deficits are larger and widening at a faster pace, as are

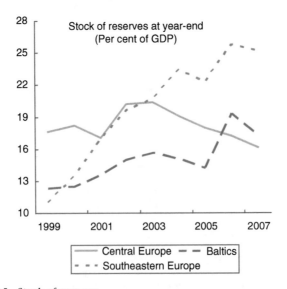

Figure 7.5 Stock of reserves

Sources: International Financial Statistics, World Economic Outlook and IMF staff calculations.

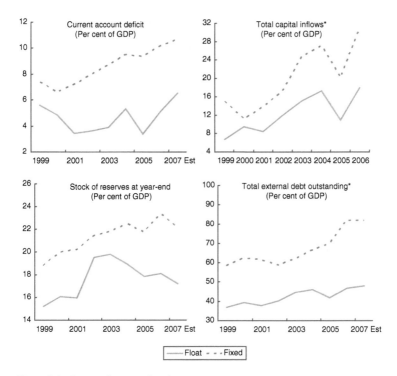

Figure 7.6 External sector developments

Note: (*) Capital inflows consist of FDI, external debt flows, portfolio investment, remittances, and EU transfers.

Sources: Eurostat, International Financial Statistics, World Economic Outlook and IMF staff calculations.

capital inflows, in particular external debt. This has led to a greater accumulation of reserves in contrast to countries with more flexible exchange rate regimes.

Emerging Europe is also becoming increasingly more financially integrated with the rest of the world, especially Western Europe (Figure 7.7). In recent years it has been a key destination for the vast flows of foreign capital looking for high returns, and emerging Europe has surpassed emerging Asia as the biggest recipient of debt flows (Figure 7.8). Among other things, this is due to capital account liberalisation and other measures which have increased financial integration, especially in Central Europe and the Baltics, but less so in South-Eastern Europe. Indeed, a study of capital controls in emerging markets suggests that emerging European countries have moved the furthest in relaxing controls on capital inflows

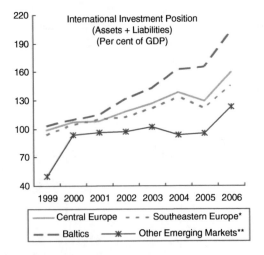

Figure 7.7   International investment position

Notes: (*) Data not available for Albania and Bosnia; and 1999-2002 for Macedonia.
(**) Comprises: Brazil, China, India, Indonesia, Korea, Malaysia, Russia, and Thailand.

Sources: International Financial Statistics and IMF staff calculations.

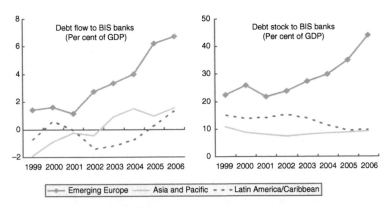

Figure 7.8   External debt to BIS banks

Sources: Bank of International Settlement, World Economic Outlook and IMF staff calculations.

since the late 1990s, with East Asian countries remaining quite restrictive (World Economic Outlook, International Monetary Fund (IMF), 2007).

Capital inflows into emerging Europe have taken many forms, but are predominantly in the form of remittances, foreign direct investment (FDI)

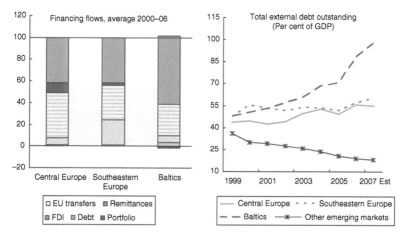

Figure 7.9   Financing flows and external debt

Sources: Eurostat, International Financial Statistics, World Economic Outlook and IMF staff calculations.

Table 7.2   Share of foreign direct investment in tradeables in emerging Europe*

	Central	Southeastern	Baltics
Tradeables **	42	31	20
Non-tradeables	58	69	80
Trade	14	15	14
Transport	7	14	9
Financial intermediation	18	24	27
Real estate	11	7	15

Notes: *Expressed in per cent of total stock in 2005 or the latest available date.
** includes manufacturing and mining sectors.

Source: Wiener Institut für Internationale Wirtschaftsvergleiche.

and debt flows (Figure 7.9). The bulk of FDI has gone to the non-tradeable sector (Table 7.2). While FDI initially made up the bulk of inflows, debt inflows, especially into domestic banking systems, have become important over time. As a result, Europe is the only emerging market region whose external indebtedness has increased during this decade, with gross external debt surpassing 50 per cent of GDP in 2006.

A significant portion of the large capital inflows has been intermediated by the financial system to the private sector. This has been

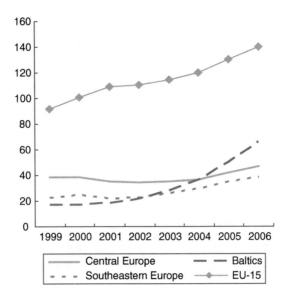

Figure 7.10   Bank credit to private sector
Source: Eueraert (2007).

Table 7.3   Vulnerability indicators, 1999–2006

	East Asia[*]	Central Europe		Southeastern Europe		Baltics	
	1996	2000–05	2006	2000–05	2006	2000–05	2006
Current account (per cent of GDP)	−4.5	−4.4	−4.0	−6.5	−10.5	−7.7	−15.5
External debt (per cent of GDP)	50.4	47.2	55.7	53.3	56.8	60.2	88.4
Fiscal balance (per cent of GDP)	1.1	−4.4	−4.1	−2.6	−0.6	−1.0	0.4
Reserves to short-term debt	29.9	183.7	139.7	363.6	181.3	60.2	68.7
Reserves/months of imports	3.4	4.4	3.5	4.5	5.7	2.8	3.1
GDP growth	7.3	4.3	4.5	4.9	5.4	8.1	10.1

Note: (*) Includes Indonesia, Korea, Malaysia, Philippines and Thailand.
Source: World Economic Outlook.

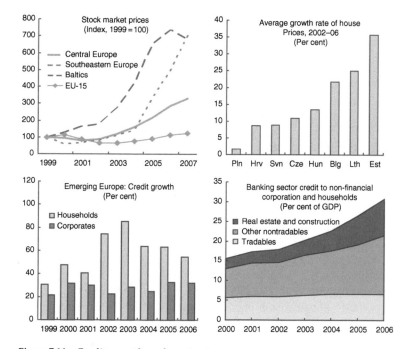

Figure 7.11 Credit growth and asset prices

Sources: Bank of International Settlement, Bems and Schellekens (2007), Bloomberg, Egert (2007), p. 54., International Financial Statistics, National Authorities and IMF staff calculations.

associated with buoyant credit growth (Figure 7.10) and a boom in asset prices (Figure 7.11). A large part of the lending has been directed at the non-tradeable sector – the household sector through mortgages – and domestic enterprises.

All this has made emerging Europe look a lot like pre-crisis Asia (Table 7.3). Indeed, in 2006 the current account deficits, external debt burdens and fiscal balances in emerging Europe were worse than those in East Asia ten years earlier. On the other hand, East Asia's reliance on short-term debt was markedly higher than is that of emerging Europe today.

7.3 Is Europe different? Yes, in several respects

Some observers dismiss the charge that emerging Europe is as vulnerable as pre-crisis Asia.[3] In the first place, they contend, a comparison of indicators in isolation is misleading. The initial conditions in emerging Europe today are not the same as those of pre-crisis Asia, and therefore the outcomes are unlikely to be the same. According to this view, the main differences between Asia then and emerging Europe now are that world capital markets are different, that emerging Europe's institutions are in better shape than those of Asia in the 1990s, and, more fundamentally, that the growth dynamics in emerging Europe reflects the convergence process.

According to this school of thought, emerging Europe's large current account deficits are a natural by-product of their consumption-smoothing behaviour in anticipation of eventual real convergence with Western Europe. Accession to the European Union – either completed or prospective – has generated confidence in the growth prospects of the region, due to deepening trade and financial market integration with the prosperous west. This process has bolstered investor confidence by signalling an irrevocable commitment to a set of well-known policies, thereby engendering policy stability and minimising discretion. Entering the orbit of the European Union has also raised prospects for increased political stability and security, which has improved the investment climate. The anticipation of a future increase in income is luring both domestic and foreign economic agents to participate in the convergence process, and is allowing emerging Europe to borrow against future savings to consume and invest now. This strategy is different from the export-led growth strategy of Asia, and has been an undeniable success for many emerging European economies so far.

Large current account deficits can also be seen as a normal part of the convergence process under capital mobility.[4] Capital inflows finance higher spending on all goods, both tradeable and non-tradeable. Whereas the demand for tradeables can be met through imports, the demand for non-tradeables has to be met through an increase in local production. In the presence of capacity constraints, the latter manifests in excess demand pressures and an increase in the relative price of non-tradeables, generating a real exchange rate appreciation. Over time, this shifts resources to the non-tradeable sector. In the process, relative prices and resources shift toward the tradeable sector, setting the stage for a gradual decline in the current account deficit. This adjustment process can be navigated more easily when markets are flexible and financial systems sound, and when there are adequate buffers to cushion the transition.

Those with a benign view also point to financial globalisation as a powerful force for good, especially in Europe. A secular shift in world financial markets is allowing capital-starved emerging Europe access to broader markets for savings, and, by so doing, is lowering the cost of capital. This is playing a catalytic role in developing domestic capital markets and financial sectors, improving the quality of institutions, promoting the adoption of strong macroeconomic frameworks and improving productivity by allowing the transfer of technology.

Indeed, one of the reasons Europe is considered special is because of the unique role of financial integration in its growth process (Abiad *et al.*, 2007). According to this view, Europe is different for two reasons. First, in Europe, unlike elsewhere, international capital has flowed downhill from advanced to poor countries, a process that has accelerated with increased financial integration and supported income convergence. Second, the extent of financial integration within Europe is greater than in any other region. This has allowed financial integration to play an important role in the convergence process by allowing productivity gains to accrue from efficiency gains in the financial sector. The large current account deficits are simply a manifestation of this process of financial integration, in the context of capital scarcity, relatively high levels of human capital, and the institutional anchor of actual or potential EU membership of emerging European countries. The current accounts in emerging Europe are predominantly influenced by the ability of these economies to engage in inter-temporal consumption smoothing by virtue of financial integration, unlike in less financially integrated regions where domestic growth and dependency rates are key factors in explaining the current account balance. Over time, as emerging Europe converges toward EU-15 income levels, the inter-temporal budget constraint suggests that the current account deficits can be expected to decline as resources shift to the tradeable sector.

Some contend that the nature of foreign financing used by emerging Europe serves to insulate it from the vagaries of global financial markets. While the large current account deficits imply a dependence on foreign capital, a significant proportion comprises remittances and transfers from the EU which are, arguably, not contingent on policies. Bilateral grants and transfers have the advantage of not increasing external liabilities, and they could also have a positive impact on the balance sheets of residents (e.g., remittances to the household sector). The amounts of volatile portfolio equity funding are equally low in most countries. The predominance of FDI is also reassuring. FDI flows are, by and large, considered to be less volatile than other forms of capital, despite a few examples to the contrary. Since the profitability of

FDI depends on the performance of the domestic economy, equity type flows allow the borrowing country to share risk with foreign investors more effectively than debt, and, to the extent that direct investors require an equity premium, provide a higher rate of return on external liabilities than the return on debt. Thus, FDI, by shifting the risk to the foreign investor, allows countries to run larger current account deficits than otherwise possible, accelerating the convergence process. Moreover, the nature of FDI is such that, were it to unwind due to a change in market sentiments, some of the impact of a change in the country's external position would be absorbed by changes in valuation (Lane *et al.*, 2006).

These observers take a benign view of the rapid increase in credit. They argue that, despite the spectacular growth in credit, financial systems in emerging Europe remain underdeveloped compared with Western Europe, and credit-to-GDP ratios remain lower than the euro area average. Thus, there is room for credit to increase even more rapidly to catch up with western levels. Indeed, since households are receiving a larger share of the increase in credit in countries where their share of finance has been the lowest, it could be argued that the financial sector is aiding the convergence process by allowing households to catch up. They also take comfort from the strong presence of foreign banks, which are seen to bring with them better risk assessment capabilities and experience (Figure 7.12), and, more importantly, are long-term

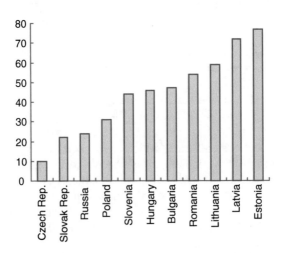

Figure 7.12   Share of foreign currency loans in total loans, 2006
Source: Financial Stability Forum.

investors controlling the disbursement of credits more directly than in Asia before the crisis.

Does the EU halo effect really exist, and how big is it? There is some evidence to support this. European emerging markets have long been enjoying lower external debt spreads (risk premia) in international capital markets than other emerging market economies. Although this difference has declined since 2004, it still remains positive and is estimated to be 50–100 bp, a difference that was preserved during the initial stages of global financial turbulence stemming from the US sub-prime crisis. An econometric analysis of the debt spreads (Luengnaruemitchai and Schadler, 2007) suggests that part of this bonus enjoyed by European emerging markets is not explained by economic fundamentals but reflects some non-quantifiable influence on markets' perception of risk. It therefore stands to reason that the key factor behind this influence is the prospect of EU membership and euro adoption. Moreover, Demekas *et al.* (2007) find that the EU factor is statistically significant in determining foreign direct investment flows.

There is also evidence that the capital inflows have led to gains in productivity. Clearly EU membership or joining the euro area alone does not ensure successful convergence; the increased capital flows need to be used productively. Fabrizio, *et al.* (2007) show that the new member states of the European Union, as substantial recipients of international capital, have achieved significant transformations of their production structures, raising the technology content and quality of their products. Moreover, according to Schadler *et al.* (2006), the growth experience of a group of new member states has been dominated by remarkable increases in total factor productivity (TFP) (Table 7.4), almost double

Table 7.4   Total factor productivity, 2000–2004

	Total factor productivity growth
Czech Republic	1.5
Estonia	5.2
Hungary	2.9
Latvia	5.8
Lithuania	5.2
Poland	1.8
Slovak Republic	3.0
Slovenia	1.7

Source: Schadler *et al.* (2006).

that in other emerging market country groups. This is not surprising in view of the large scope for managerial improvements, labour shedding and gains from inter-industry resource reallocation that existed in emerging European countries as a legacy of central planning. Looking ahead, though, the critical question is whether the significant TFP growth can be sustained, and, if not, what would replace it as the underpinning of a rapid catch up. On average, countries that recovered earliest from the transition shock – the central European countries – have seen a substantial slowing in TFP growth (although still higher than other emerging market country groups). By contrast, TFP growth in the Baltics, which recovered later, has continued to rise. Were the slowdown in TFP growth to spread to the Baltics, this region would become more vulnerable unless other sources of growth could sustain the push toward convergence.

Those seeing Europe as different from other emerging markets also point to the potential for large capital inflows to continue for a long time. Lipschitz, *et al.* (2002) look at the potential for capital inflows into emerging Europe in 1999 and conclude that capital inflows of about eight times the current flows would be required to equalise returns with Western Europe. Abiad *et al.* (2007) estimate that capital flows would need to continue for the next two decades before returns equalise; however, there is a wide variation between the low- and high-end countries. While financial integration in emerging Europe has increased sharply, it has not yet reached the levels observed in Western Europe, and could therefore be expected to increase further in the future, allowing current account deficits to remain large. Demekas *et al.* (2007) calculate the potential FDI for emerging European countries based on the actual values of gravity variables, which are exogenous to policy makers, and the 'best' values of the policy variables that are found to have a significant influence on foreign investment. While more successful emerging European economies are now close to their potential, they find that the gap between potential and actual non-privatisation-related FDI is

Table 7.5 Foreign direct investment flows, billions of US dollars, 2003

	Estimated potential FDI stock	Estimated actual FDI stock	Gap (per cent)
Central Europe	138	105	23
Baltics	17	15	13
Southeastern Europe	38	21	43

Source: Demekas *et al.* (2005).

still positive everywhere and in some cases, especially South-Eastern Europe, quite large. This suggests that capital inflows into emerging Europe could continue for several years (Table 7.5).

7.4 Is Europe different? Perhaps, but it is still vulnerable

Notwithstanding the factors that make emerging Europe more resilient than other emerging markets, the fact remains that current account deficits are uncomfortably high in many emerging European countries today. The current account deficit is one of the robust leading indicators of capital account crises, and, together with external indebtedness, indicates an important predictor of vulnerability (Chamon *et al.*, 2007). Large current account deficits indicate a greater reliance on foreign financing, which leaves countries more vulnerable to contagion and sudden stops. Historically, countries with high current account deficits have been vulnerable to a sharp reversal of capital inflows, as they have been particularly affected by the increase in aggregate demand and the real appreciation of their currencies (World Economic Outlook, IMF, 2007). Indeed, if the current phase of large capital inflows and an acceleration of GDP growth were to be followed by a significant tapering off of growth, accompanied by a sharp reversal in the current account deficit, as has been the case in previous crises, then this would stop the process of real convergence in its tracks.

Therefore, a happy ending is by no means inevitable.[5] The advantages of EU accession do not eliminate the vulnerabilities arising from inconsistent macroeconomic policies, excessive risk-taking and balance sheet mismatches. Moreover, while offering great rewards, financial integration also holds the threat of great punishment should market sentiments change.

There are a number of reasons why EU accession alone does not provide enough protection. First, given the considerable uncertainty in the conditionality and process of membership of the EU, countries are unlikely to be at similar stages of macroeconomic and financial stability at the point of entry into the EU. Thus, EU accession alone may not be able to prevent bad outcomes. Second, the considerable advantages of being a member of the EU materialise over the long run, leaving scope for risks in the short run. For example, while financial integration with the EU via capital account liberalisation is beneficial in the long run, in the short term it could provide a one-way bet for speculative investors while reducing the incentives for proper risk assessment, unless supported by sound macroeconomic policies and institutions. Third, while EU accession does improve the investment climate by signalling a commitment to market-friendly policies, not all EU policies can be considered equally investor-friendly (e.g., labour market policy). Finally, while it is true that institutions in emerging Europe compare favourably with other emerging markets, they are still far from Western European standards (Figure 7.13).

Despite the undisputable benefits of financial integration, it can also increase susceptibility to contagion. Access to financial markets may be severely disrupted because of adverse developments affecting another emerging market or a generalised shock affecting all emerging markets, regardless of where it originated. Global capital markets are huge relative to the size of the emerging European economies, and therefore shifts in market sentiments can exert an overwhelming influence on capital flows and domestic financial conditions. This was illustrated by the recent collapse in the sub-prime market and the subsequent global repricing of risk which affected emerging Europe as well, even if not overwhelmingly (Regional Economic Outlook, IMF, 2007). The risk of contagion is particularly pronounced in some emerging European markets because a large part of debt-creating flows into the region is intermediated by a small number of Western European banks.

These observers also note that emerging Europe's international financial liabilities have become increasingly more risky. Although FDI presently constitutes a significant share of capital inflows, it is clear that the trend increase in direct investment liabilities (relative to the size of the

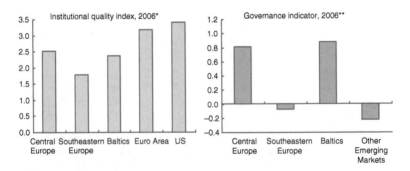

Figure 7.13   Quality of institutions

Notes: (*) Institutional quality index is the sum of property rights, control of corruption, bureaucracy quality, and rule of law indices. In ranges from 0 to 4. Higher index numbers indicate higher quality. (**) Simple average of Voice and Accountability, Political Stability, Rule of Law, and Regulatory Quality indices. Higher index numbers indicate better governance.

Sources: Freedom House, International Country Risk Guide, World Bank Governance Database and IMF staff calculations.

economy) cannot continue apace for political-economy reasons, once privatisation-related FDI is exhausted. This is particularly true in countries where the current FDI flows already imply a substantial foreign ownership of the domestic capital stock (Figure 7.14). Thus, countries will increasingly need to move away from FDI financing toward debt financing. Indeed, debt flows have been increasing steadily over time, and emerging Europe is more indebted than other emerging market economies. Debt flows tend to be more volatile and are susceptible to rollover risk, sudden stops, or reversals as a result of an abrupt shift in market sentiment. Moreover, they generate a build-up in external liabilities which have to be serviced down the road.

There is also a fear that banks' risk assessment capabilities have not kept up with the blistering pace of credit growth in emerging Europe, giving rise to vulnerabilities[6] (Sorsa *et al.*, 2007). While there is no disputing the benefits of greater intermediation, there is a risk that the financial sector, in competing for business and market share, may have relaxed lending standards by allowing borrowing against overly optimistic expectations. Although supervisory and regulatory standards have been modernised significantly in emerging Europe,

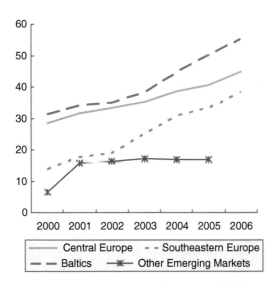

Figure 7.14 Foreign direct investment stock (Per cent of GDP)

Note: Data for Slovenia not available.

Sources: International Financial Statistics, National Authorities, World Economic Outlook, Wiener Institut für Internationale Wirtschaftsvergleiche and IMF staff calculations.

implementation capacity remains constrained by the availability of experienced supervisors and risk managers and the insufficient development of risk assessment tools that are compatible with local conditions. Moreover, credit quality is compromised by the lack of adequate credit history as the pool of prospective borrowers is enlarged to include first-time borrowers, and, despite high levels of collaterisation, loan recovery is hampered by weaknesses in the legal system and the ineffectiveness of bankruptcy procedures (Figure 7.15). Finally, the increasing euroisation[7] of credit also reduces the incentive to assess risks properly (Figure 7.16) by allowing creditors to take large claims on the country without a direct exchange rate risk.[8] Furthermore, natural hedges, high collateralisation and high exchange rate pass-through further shield banks from indirect exchange rate risks. The downside of insulating banks from nominal risk is that they have little incentive to scrutinise credit quality closely, thereby leading to a build-up of credit risk.

Despite the well-known benefits, the presence of foreign banks can give rise to some concerns. In many countries in emerging Europe, only a few banks dominate the field, providing a channel for contagion. The

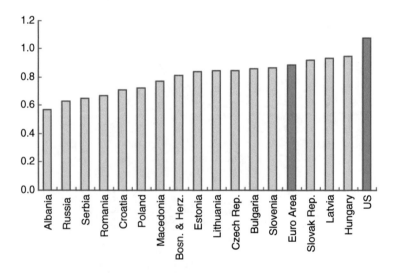

Figure 7.15   Financial sector developments, 2006

Note: Simple average of Capital Regulatory, Official Supervisory Power, Banking Reform and Interest Rate Liberalization, Securities Market Legislation, Corporate Governance, Credit Information, Legal Rights Indexes. Higher index numbers indicate better governance.

Sources: World Bank Governance Database and IMF staff calculations.

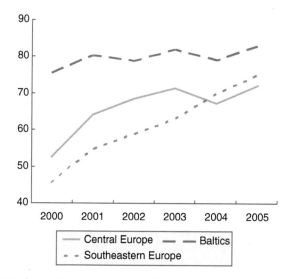

Figure 7.16 Asset share of foreign-owned banks
Sources: National authorities and IMF staff calculations.

scale and nature of involvement of foreign banks also raise questions. First, the branches of foreign banks are accepting higher risks to meet the high profit targets set by the parent bank (in some cases, the returns on equity for subsidiaries have been known to be set at double the levels of the parent banks). Such risky investments are not necessarily in the recipient country's best interest even though they may be optimal from the foreign banks' point of view (as part of the high risk–high return segment of the parent banks' portfolio). Second, there is considerable uncertainty about whether and how contagion from the mother banks will be transmitted to their branches in emerging Europe, and to what extent, if at all, the parent bank will provide liquidity support to its branches in the event of a crisis. While the parent bank is the lender of last resort, in practice the evidence has been mixed. Third, while the foreign banks may be more sheltered from domestic risk because of the support from the parent banks in the event of souring local financial conditions, they are vulnerable to strategic shifts in their parent companies. This could amplify the effect of the shocks of foreign origin on the host country. Fourth, to the extent that they are borrowed from the host country, risk management and supervision techniques may not be applicable to the domestic economy, and are therefore flawed. They are also compromised by the fact that foreign banks have no credit history or income data of their own creditors, and often do not make adjustments for the lack of hedging. All of this may affect credit quality. Finally, a large part of domestic credit is provided directly by the parent bank, a form of lending likely to be volatile in nature (European Bank of Reconstruction and Development, 2006).

Risks can also emerge on the funding side of the financial and corporate sectors. In several emerging European economies, banks are relying on the international bond market for funds (Table 7.6). These banks have needed additional funding as the pace of credit growth has exceeded the deposit base, and have been able to issue bonds in an environment of high global liquidity where international investors have readily lent even to countries with relatively high vulnerabilities. Bond financing has increasingly gone to banks where credit discipline is weaker, and which are unable to borrow from international banks in the inter-bank market, reflecting an adverse selection problem. Banking systems that rely on bond financing are likely to be more vulnerable because bondholders are less able to assess the risk than are international banks, increasing the potential for a sudden drop in demand for bonds once defaults start to rise, which could trigger bank funding difficulties. Emerging market corporations are also enjoying easy access to international markets, and credit discipline appears to be weakening as borrowers shift from banks to private markets. While such access, and at very low spreads, partly reflects low default rates and

Table 7.6 International bond issues, 2006

	International bonds in per cent of total external debt
Bulgaria	9.5
Croatia	13.3
Czech Republic	5.1
Estonia	10.9
Hungary	24.4
Latvia	5.9
Lithuania	14.2
Poland	11.8
Romania	3.6
Slovak Republic	7.3
Slovenia	5.2

Source: IMF staff calculations based on Bank of International Settlement data.

favourable fundamentals, laxer credit standards also seem to be playing a role, as evident in the growing importance of the private placement loan market in emerging Europe,[9] and the growing involvement of first-time issuers – some of which may be inadequately covered by analysts and rating agencies – in the high-yield debt market (Global Financial Stability Report, IMF, 2007).

The surge in lending, especially in foreign currency, may have left domestic balance sheets at risk. Large mismatches in the currency composition and maturity of financial assets and liabilities in the various sectors of the economy can either trigger or aggravate the effects of financial crises. While foreign banks have insulated themselves against bad loans (by providing highly collaterised foreign currency loans at variable interest rates), the risks have been passed on to the private sector, which may not fully understand the underlying risks and may not be fully hedged against those risks (especially the household sector). The boom in credit has also caused asset price rises and overheating in some countries, again leaving the creditors vulnerable to a burst of the bubble. While there is little information about whether households' assets and liabilities are well matched in the aggregate,[10] or this sector's short-term debt holdings in many emerging European countries, there is evidence that this sector is exposed to currency risk in some countries, such as Latvia and Hungary. The balance sheets of corporations also give cause for concern. The corporate sector – mostly in the non-tradeable sector – is exposed in foreign currency, often in countries with fixed exchange rates, but it is not clear whether these exposures have been hedged. The ability of the corporate sector, especially companies that are systemically important, to understand and manage risks – by taking into account cross-currency swap markets, transforming currency exposure, hedging the exposures to rate and currency derivatives that embed optionality to enhance yield – can be weak. Greater external borrowing by emerging market corporations is not subject to increased surveillance. In some emerging European countries, the absence of well-developed and liquid money markets could also pose a problem in the event of a deterioration in financial conditions.

7.5 Policy challenges

In recent years, emerging European countries have responded to the balance of payments pressures in a number of ways. They have allowed the nominal exchange rate to appreciate, accumulated reserves (with or without sterilisation) and tightened monetary and fiscal policies (Figure 7.17). Policy makers in most countries have taken measures to slow the rapid credit expansion, through fiscal tightening and increases in interest rates or reserve or liquidity requirements. Prudential and supervisory regulations have also been tightened and monitoring stepped up. In a few cases, marginal reserve requirements have been imposed on foreign borrowing. While these are steps in the right direction, they have not mitigated the balance of payments pressures in emerging Europe.

Going ahead, how should policy makers balance the contrasting views of those who see Europe as fundamentally different and those who worry about vulnerabilities? Clearly, policies will need to take into account arguments across the spectrum. Policy makers must remain mindful of vulnerabilities that can arise due to the private sector's expectations and risk assessment being off the mark, policy mistakes and weak implementation, and the insufficient development of institutions. At the same time, they need to bear in mind that large current account deficits are a natural part of the convergence dynamics. The policy dilemma, therefore, is how to reduce vulnerabilities without impeding the convergence process, and how to distinguish natural convergence from overheating. Complicating matters is the fact that

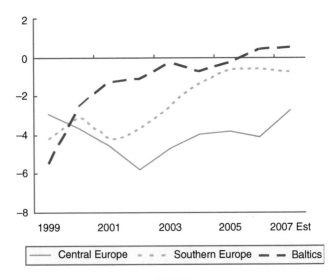

Figure 7.17   Fiscal deficits (Per cent of GDP)
Sources: World Economic Outlook and IMF staff calculations.

policy makers are navigating uncharted territory in the form of unprecedented levels of liquidity, investors' appetite for risk and globalisation of capital markets. Reversing financial integration is not an option as it would risk throwing the baby out with the bath water. Yet policy makers would need to find a way to manage the large capital inflows into their economy.

History can provide some guidance. While not identical, the present policy dilemma of dealing with balance of payments pressures is reminiscent of that in the 1990s. An important lesson from that period is that policy choices made in the wake of capital inflows matter and have an important bearing on outcomes, including the consequences of their abrupt reversal (Monteil and Reinhart, 1999). With the benefit of hindsight, a recent study revisits past crises to draw some general conclusions about the appropriate policy mix under similar circumstances (World Economic Outlook, IMF, 2007). It observes that countries with higher current account deficits and with stronger increases in both aggregate demand and the real value of the currency during the period of inflows experience more volatile macroeconomic fluctuations, including a sharp reversal of capital inflows. Second, countries where the decline in GDP growth was moderate after the reversal of inflows were those where the authorities exercised greater fiscal restraint during the inflow period, thereby successfully containing real appreciation and aggregate demand. Third, countries resisting nominal exchange rate appreciation through intervention were not able to moderate real appreciation and faced more adverse consequences when the surge in inflows stopped. The study concludes that the consequences of large capital inflows should be of particular concern to countries with substantial current account deficits or to countries with inflexible exchange rate regimes. In the latter case, the most effective policy instrument is likely to be counter-cyclical fiscal policy based on expenditure restraint; during episodes of large capital inflows, this policy has been associated with a smaller post-inflow decline in output growth, even after controlling for other factors that may have had a role in this decline.[11]

In the period ahead, policy makers should aim to mitigate risks and preserve solvency. Policies will need to continue to manage the macroeconomic pressures generated by the capital inflows and prevent forced excessive real appreciation and a loss of competitiveness through overheating in the goods, labour and asset markets. Policy makers will also need to look ahead to when the convergence process matures and capital inflows wind down, and when the current account deficit will need to turn around in order to stabilise the external position. Growth and investment will need to be rebalanced toward the tradeable sector, especially by exposing the non-tradeable sector to competition.

Specifically, the four main priorities for policies are as follows:

- Do no harm – sound macroeconomic policies: It is imperative that monetary and fiscal policies be sound and consistent, and that incomes policies preserve competitiveness. This will impart confidence and reduce the risk of a home-grown crisis. Fiscal tightening is the most effective means of controlling demand pressures from capital inflows, as monetary tightening can be counterproductive, resulting in greater inflows, and as the costs of intervention can be prohibitively high.[12] Fiscal restraint needs to go beyond cyclical stabilisation to offset exuberant private sector demand, while building up buffers to mitigate an increase in private sector dissavings in the event of a crisis and, in some countries, ageing-related costs over the medium term. Fiscal policy also needs to ensure that it does not create distortions for private sector behaviour. Greater exchange rate flexibility can help absorb some of the balance of payments pressures and reduce the need for buffers by allowing the nominal exchange rate to appreciate. However, in countries with pegs or currency boards, fiscal policy and structural reforms need to take on the predominant role in stabilisation, given the reduced effectiveness (or absence) of monetary policy in the presence of open access to global capital markets and euroisation. Finally, incomes policies need to be geared toward keeping wage increases in line with productivity growth.
- Trust, but verify – strong financial sector regulation and supervision: Strengthening the institutional and regulatory regime in the financial sector should proceed hand in hand with opening up market access. It would be important to develop the private sector's ability to assess and manage risks, and sensitise the private sector (especially the corporate sector) to currency risk, including through the availability of hedging instruments to mitigate exchange rate risk; tightening disclosure requirements of risk management and internal control policies and procedures. Financial markets must be deepened and supervision and regulation strengthened where needed by removing distortions in bank lending, identifying bank-specific capital requirements and raising them where necessary; establishing risk-based forward-looking supervision where necessary; improving enforcement capacity; and strengthening cross-border supervision. Well-developed capital markets can also help reduce systemic vulnerability by providing a richer array of investment options to financial institutions.

- Change, to grow – productivity-enhancing structural reforms: The prospects of countries in emerging Europe will depend on how well they establish macroeconomic and structural conditions needed to increase economic flexibility, productivity and competitiveness – conditions conducive to sustained rapid growth. As TFP growth begins to slow, other factors will be needed to shore up growth, such as higher labour force participation rates and higher investment rates. These can be fostered by reducing the real costs of investment by improving the quality of regulatory and economic institutions, reducing the size of the government, keeping inflation low and improving labour productivity by enhancing educational attainment. While emerging European economies generally do reasonably well in this regard relative to East Asia, they still have a long way to go before they catch up with Western European standards.
- Know thyself – better information: The dearth of timely information in some areas has undermined the policy maker's ability to assess risks and take pre-emptive measures. The information on private sector balance sheets, for example, would be crucial to determine whether or not the private sector is well placed to absorb changes in market conditions. It is also important to be able to monitor the sources and uses of capital flows, and have crisis preparedness plans ready in the event of a shock.

Notes

This chapter was originally prepared as a paper for an Economic Conference on Central, Eastern and South-Eastern Europe organised by the European Central Bank on 1–2 October 2007. The authors are staff members of the International Monetary Fund (IMF). They are grateful to Michael Deppler, Ashoka Mody, Dimitri Demekas, Christoph Rosenberg and Piritta Sorsa for their helpful comments, and to Cristina Cheptea and Haiyan Shi for their excellent research assistance. The views expressed in this chapter are those of the authors and should not be attributed to the IMF, its Executive Board or its management.

1. The following country groupings are used in this chapter: EU-15 (Austria, Belgium, Denmark, Finland, France, Germany, Greece, Ireland, Italy, Luxembourg, the Netherlands, Portugal, Spain, Sweden and the United Kingdom); the Baltics (Estonia, Latvia, Lithuania); Central Europe (Czech Republic, Hungary, Poland, Slovak Republic and Slovenia); and South-Eastern Europe (Albania, Bosnia and Herzegovina, Bulgaria, Croatia, Macedonia FYR, Romania and Serbia). The last three groups constitute emerging Europe for the purposes of this chapter, and Western Europe is used interchangeably with EU-15. All data for the country groups in this chapter represent unweighted averages.

2. Unconditional convergence has characterised Europe for the past 30 years, that is, poorer countries are seen to have grown faster even when no account is taken of other growth drivers.
3. Many of the arguments in this section can be found in Demekas *et al.* (2007) and Abiad *et al.* (2007).
4. Bems and Schellekens (2007).
5. Several of the arguments in this section draw on Sorsa *et al.* (2007).
6. Financial sector issues in Europe are discussed extensively in the Regional Economic Outlook for Europe (2007).
7. Financial euroisation refers to the denomination or indexation of credit to the euro.
8. For example, in Hungary almost all new household loans are in Swiss francs. Incentives to borrow in foreign currency are strong, with Swiss franc mortgage rates roughly ten points below those on forint mortgages. Roughly one-half of household and corporate debt is now denominated in foreign currency.
9. Private placements allow issuers to avoid the more extensive disclosures required by public listings. However, the rise in private placements brings with it the risk that loan covenants may be weak, as borrowers appear willing to accept minimal contractual protection.
10. Ideally this assessment would take into account the inflow of remittances, which is an indication of foreign exchange assets of the household sector held abroad.
11. The other factors include changes in the terms of trade, world output growth and the real US Federal funds rate.
12. In particular policy makers should remove tax-induced distortions that have contributed to the blistering pace of credit growth in some countries.

Bibliography

A. Abiad, D. Leigh and A. Mody (2007) 'International Finance and Income Convergence: Europe Is Different', IMF Working Paper No. 07/64.

R. Bems and P. Schellekens (2007) 'Finance and Convergence: What's Ahead for Emerging Europe?', IMF Working Paper No. 07/244.

M. Chamon, P. Manasse and A. Prati (2007) 'Can We Predict the Next Capital Account Crisis?', *IMF Staff Papers*, 54(2) 270–305.

D.G. Demekas (2007) 'Are European Emerging Markets Different?', 5th Emerging Market Workshop organised by European System of Central Banks and the Austrian National Bank, Vienna.

D.G. Demekas, B. Horvath, E. Ribakova and Y. Wu (2005) 'Foreign Direct Investment in South-Eastern Europe: How (and How Much) Can Policies Help?, IMF Working Paper No. 05/110.

European Bank of Reconstruction and Development (2006) Transition Report.

B. Egert and D. Mihaljek (2007) 'Determinants of House Prices in Central and Eastern Europe', BIS Working Paper No. 236.

L. Everaert (2007) 'Financial Sector in Emerging Europe – Recent Developments and Issues', IMF Seminar, JVI, Vienna.

S. Fabrizio, D. Igan and A. Mody (2007) 'The Dynamics of Product Quality and International Competitiveness', IMF Working Paper No. 07/97, Revised: 10/2/02.

International Monetary Fund (2007) 'Making Financial Systems More Efficient', Regional Economic Outlook for Europe, November, Washington.

International Monetary Fund (2007) 'Weakening Credit and Market Discipline Warrants Increased Surveillance in Emerging Markets', Global Financial Stability Report, September, Washington.

International Monetary Fund (2007) *World Economic Outlook*, October, Washington.

P. Lane and G. Milesi-Ferretti (2006) 'Capital Flows to Central and Eastern Europe', IMF Working Paper No. 06/188.

L. Lipschitz, T. Lane and A. Mourmouras (2002) 'Capital Flows to Transition Economies: Master or Servant?', IMF Working Paper No. 02/11, Revised: 10/2/02.

P. Luengnaruemitchai and S. Schadler (2007) 'Do Economists' and Financial Markets' Perspectives on the New Members of the EU Differ?', IMF Working Paper No. 07/65.

P. Montiel and C.M. Reinhart (1999) 'Do Capital Controls and Macroeconomic Policies Influence the Volume and Composition of Capital Flows? Evidence from the 1990s', *Journal of International Money and Finance*, 18(4), 619–35.

I. Ötker-Robe, Z. Polanski, B. Topf and D. Vavra (2007) 'Coping with Capital Inflows: Experiences of Selected European Countries', IMF Working Paper No. 07/190.

C. Rosenberg (2007) 'Economic Trends and Challenges in Central and Eastern Europe', IMF Seminar, Vienna.

S. Schadler, A. Mody, A. Abiad and D. Leigh (2006) 'Growth in the Central and Eastern European Countries of the European Union', IMF Occasional Paper No. 252.

P. Sorsa, B. Bakker, C. Duenwald, A. Maechler and A. Tiffin (2007) 'Vulnerabilities in Emerging Southeastern Europe – How Much Cause for Concern?', IMF Working Paper No. 07/236.

Summary of discussion at 2007 ECB Economic Conference on Central, Eastern and South-Eastern Europe

Ševčovic (Národná banka Slovenska) opened the discussion on the chapter by Banerji and Kähkönen (IMF) by focusing on links between real convergence and the balance of payments for the Slovakian case. In Slovakia, real convergence gained momentum over the last decade, as GDP per capita (in purchasing power parity terms) rose from about 50 per cent of the EU-25 average in 1997 to more than 60 per cent in 2006. It is expected to reach 70 per cent by 2009. Slovakia is a very open economy, with an openness ratio (the sum of exports and imports divided by GDP) exceeding 170 per cent in 2006. Thus, the external sector plays a crucial role for growth and convergence.

Until recently stronger GDP growth has been associated with a deteriorating current account balance. In line with standard economic theory, investments, financed to a significant extent by foreign savings, fostered real convergence. Moreover, since 2002, when the reform process accelerated, the large current account deficit largely reflected imports of machinery, mainly related to FDI inflows. Accordingly, the structure of the current account financing changed, as FDI became the dominant component in the capital account.

As FDI inflows were mainly directed to export-generating industries, Slovakia has been enjoying a healthy growth in exports. In 2006, export growth was so strong that the acceleration of growth was accompanied by a slight improvement in the current account, pointing to a sustainable process of real convergence. However, current account deficits remain large due to the worsening income balance, reflecting dividend payments to foreign investors, as well as reinvested earnings.

Ševčovic closed by referring to the challenge of climbing up the higher value-added ladder in terms of production and exports. This will be a key precondition for a sustainable convergence process as labour costs are on the rise. To this end, policies need to foster investment in education as well as research and development, while reducing the administrative burden on the business environment and increasing flexibility and mobility of the labour force. This should attract further FDI inflows and sustain growth for the longer term.

Financial aspects were the focus of the presentation by Faulend (Croatian National Bank) on the link between convergence and the current account. As in Slovakia, real convergence in Croatia has been advancing at a rapid pace. Large current account deficits have been a permanent feature of recent Croatian economic development, increasingly reflecting strong investment and consumption by the private sector, particularly households. The rise in private expenditures has been financed by a largely foreign-owned banking sector, the backbone of a financial sector that compares well in terms of financial depth with other countries of the region. The related high credit growth, not starting from a low base, has been mainly financed by parent banks abroad, hence the link with increasing external debt (which is among the highest in the region).

Given a high degree of unofficial euroisation in the Croatian economy, the Croatian National Bank (CNB) has been conducting a so-called quasi currency board monetary policy, keeping the nominal exchange rate broadly stable, without explicitly committing itself to a peg. With this approach, the CNB has credibly anchored inflation expectations via the exchange rate anchor, while discouraging speculative capital flows. Therefore, there are few degrees of freedom for an independent monetary policy. In particular, the CNB is not in a position to use the interest rate as an instrument to contain rapid credit growth.

Against this background, and being concerned with high (and rising) external imbalances, the CNB has been resorting to both prudential (e.g., reassessing the risk weights for unhedged borrowers) and unconventional measures to slow down credit expansion and to fight against strong capital inflows. Such unconventional measures include the compulsory purchase of CNB bills (credit control), a marginal reserve requirement, special reserve requirement and minimum liquid asset ratios. However, there are limits to the effectiveness of these measures, as banks react by aggressive marketing of savings instruments and raising capital, while companies are switching to financing through retained profits and direct borrowing from abroad. Thus, over the longer term, to contain external imbalances and the associated risks, an important contribution should come from fiscal consolidation and wide-ranging structural reforms. In the end, the sustainability of external imbalances will mainly depend on the unwinding of credit growth, future patterns of FDI flows, international interest rates and the sentiment of foreign investors.

Herrmann (Deutsche Bundesbank) put developments in the region's balance of payments in a global context. In particular, she highlighted the diverging pattern of real convergence and current account in emerging Europe and emerging Asia. Central, Eastern and South-Eastern European countries have seen the standard textbook case of capital flowing from rich to poor countries, recording substantial current account deficits in their convergence process. By contrast, emerging Asia has been observing growing current account surpluses, supporting the Lucas paradox as capital has been flowing uphill, from relatively poor to richer countries.

Focusing on the role of financial market characteristics as determinants of current account developments in the European and Asian emerging market economies, Herrmann presented results from an econometric panel analysis, suggesting that – in line with the literature – catching-up countries with more developed and more integrated financial markets are able to engage in borrowing abroad, thus raising domestic investment relative to domestic savings. However, several standard indicators of financial development and financial integration fail to account for the divergent patterns of the current account in emerging Europe and emerging Asia. Instead it is the degree and institutional pattern of financial integration with the euro area (for Central, Eastern and South-Eastern Europe) and with the US (for countries in emerging Asia) that significantly help to explain divergent current account developments in the two regions. In Europe this intra-regional integration is *inter alia* based on the presence of foreign (euro area-based) banks and the associated substantial rise of cross-border claims by euro area banks on the region. As this pattern of financial integration is strongly linked to the overall integration approach in Europe, the European experience might not be generalised for other emerging market economies that aim at engaging in consumption-smoothing activities in an increasingly globalised financial system.

Backé (Oesterreichische Nationalbank) closed the session by highlighting some of the peculiar features shaping the pattern of real convergence and balance of payments in Central, Eastern and South-Eastern Europe, namely the role of European integration and financial integration coupled with a low initial level of financial intermediation. This resulted in a reshaping of balance sheets, especially for households, strong consumption-smoothing effects and a shift towards investment in real assets, such as housing. Therefore, many Central, Eastern and South-Eastern European countries have witnessed a fairly persistent demand impulse, on top of the supply-driven catching-up process. While the adjustment of balance sheets is an equilibrium phenomenon, it carries risks if it takes place rapidly. Moreover, it can overshoot, if expectations on future income developments prove to be overly optimistic, leading to undue risk taking.

Notwithstanding this common setting, there are important cross-country differences in terms of the dynamics of the sectoral balance sheet changes as well as the speed of macroeconomic developments. Therefore, in terms of actual vulnerabilities, countries are heterogeneous. Focusing on five Central and Eastern European countries (the Czech Republic, Hungary, Poland, Slovakia and Slovenia) and three South-Eastern European countries (Bulgaria, Croatia and Romania), the analysis shows that the income balance drives current account deficits in Central and Eastern Europe, while the trade balance still dominates current account developments in the South-Eastern European countries. The competitive position of the eight countries seems to be broadly intact and in some cases it is even comparatively strong. Real exchange rates, based on manufacturing unit labour costs, appreciated strongly only in Romania in recent years, while output-to-labour-cost ratios tend to be favourable relative to EU-15 countries and export market shares have tended to rise, especially in Central and Eastern European countries. In general, a technological upgrading of exports is evident in all countries, with Romania and especially Bulgaria lagging somewhat behind. A high share of incoming FDI went to manufacturing, other services and finance. At the same time, net foreign debt in per cent of GDP increased in all economies except for Poland and Romania, and some countries have witnessed rising shares of debt in gross foreign liabilities, and in Romania increasing short-term indebtedness to foreign banks. From a macroprudential perspective, the concentration of creditor risks and the high share of foreign currency loans in most countries are noteworthy as well.

In concluding, Backé drew attention to the lack of a sufficiently ambitious policy response in some of the countries with major imbalances. In particular there is room for a further strengthening of prudential measures, in particular borrower-based measures, and added efforts to raise debtors' risk awareness and risk-management skills. In addition, ensuring transparency and the availability of reliable up to date data are crucial requirements. Finally, in most countries fiscal and incomes policies, including public sector wage policies, could do more to counter vulnerabilities in emerging Europe.

Index